WEST OF THE MOUNTAINS

James Sinclair and the Hudson's Bay Company

WEST OF THE MOUNTAINS

James Sinclair and the Hudson's Bay Company

by D. GENEVA LENT

University of Washington Press Seattle 1963

Library of Congress Catalog Card Number 62-9802
Printed in the United States of America

This book is published with the assistance
of a grant from the Ford Foundation.

To my beloved mother, the late Carrie Belyea Lent, without whose consistent faith and help the writing of this book would not have been possible.

NOTE

At this time of unprecedented interest in western melodrama, an explanation of the title of this book, *West of the Mountains*, is in order. It is not used as a romantic phrase, but has a special implication relative to the period of this narrative. "West of the Mountains" was a colloquialism in general use throughout Rupert's Land and in the Oregon a century ago, and was employed in correspondence and conversation to convey the idea of banishment from one part of the territory under Hudson's Bay Company jurisdiction to another. When the presence of a company employee became untenable in Red River, he was often removed "west of the mountains" to the Oregon. If, on the other hand, the presence of someone was felt to be against company interests in the Oregon—as in the case of Alexander Ross—he was sent "east of the mountains" to Red River. Thus, when James Sinclair incurred the displeasure of Sir George Simpson, the company's powerful governor, he was banished "west of the mountains" from Fort Garry to Fort Walla Walla. This banishment led to his most significant explorations and ultimately to his death at the hands of Indians on the Columbia River.

PREFACE

This is a life of James Sinclair, a notorious free trader from Rupert's Land who in 1856 gave his life in an attempt to save a party of American settlers besieged by Indians. The story of this man has never been fully and factually told. The century since his death has remained silent concerning his somewhat unusual exploits. Regional problems and the delicate political issues in which he was undoubtedly involved remained tender long after he was killed.

James Sinclair did not live long enough to vindicate himself in much that appears to be questionable concerning him. Since his death he has often been unfairly blamed for unorthodox behavior and seeming insubordination to the legally constituted authority of the land to which he belonged by birth. This book is written with the belief that Sinclair's activities and affiliations should be revealed as part of the true story of western North America. In the light of serious investigation his exploits appear to have been more loyal to the country and company that he served than has been believed. But his efforts to seek liberty in the free trade for the Red River *Métis* have brought about considerable controversy and may long continue to do so.

The troubled period of North American westward expansion in the crucial years from 1818 to 1846 presented many difficulties; the boundary dispute between the United States and Great Britain had not yet been settled, and final disposition of the rich Columbia River country was undecided. During this uneasy period Sinclair undoubtedly acted for a time as the personal agent of Sir George Simpson, Governor-in-Chief of the Hudson's Bay Company, and on behalf of the British cause he served. Many of his activities constituted an effort to compete with the Americans in their aggressive free trade north of the border in "Red River"—the area near the junction of the Red and Assiniboine rivers where the present city of Winnipeg is situated—and to further the interests of Great Britain in "the Oregon"—the term used to convey the general idea of the region "west of the mountains," specifically including the area of the states of Washington and Oregon.

James Sinclair was one of those characters who seem drawn at crucial moments to a vortex of history: he participated in a number of colorful incidents of his day, such as the California gold rush, and he knew many of the unusual and influential figures of his time, both in Rupert's Land and in the United States. In Red River he counted among his intimate friends the witty, experienced Oregon trader and historian, Alexander Ross, and the rich, eccentric Irish merchant, Andrew McDermot. Both of these men acted as mentors in many of Sinclair's important undertakings, and they were kept fully advised as to the extent and danger of his exploits. More than mere casual acquaintances were some of the fur tycoons of St. Louis, including General Henry Ashley, William Sublette, and Pierre Chouteau, Jr., as well as the great John Jacob Astor himself. Even the fabulous Ulysses S. Grant was a close friend of Sinclair's from the time he had befriended Grant in his youth.

Something of a cosmopolite, Sinclair knew the sophisticated life of Edinburgh, London, Paris, and Havana—all this in striking contrast to the life he led on the rugged American frontier and in the rigorous fur trade of Rupert's Land. He was, moreover, no mere spectator of life, but a participant in most exhilarating events. He experienced, for instance, almost unrivaled adventure in the dangerous country of the Sioux and Blackfeet, at a time when none but the boldest dared venture through their hotly contested territories. He knew firsthand the life of the rowdy Mountain Men of St. Louis during the most zestful period of their "rendezvous" in the Rockies during the 1830's. He shared the stern labors and independent spirit and the song and laughter of the French-Canadian *voyageurs* engaged in transporting goods over the dangerous northern waterways between Fort Garry, York Factory, and Fort Edmonton. Indeed, Sinclair's travels took him far beyond—even in the company's bateaux down the treacherous Columbia River from "the Boat Encampment" to Fort Vancouver. For many years he went with the *Métis* hunters annually to the buffalo plains south and west of Fort Garry. But the phase of his life that holds perhaps the most unusual interest is the period of his Rocky Mountain exploration.

Between the years 1841 and 1854, Sinclair made some daring trips across the Rockies for which he has never been given full credit or justifiable recognition. He traveled by passes never before negotiated by other than wandering Indians, including the pass that bears his name in the Rocky Mountains and the passes now known as the Whiteman Pass and Kananaskis Pass. These discoveries came about largely through Britain's need to establish, within British territory, new overland routes to the Oregon, for trade and for the protection of her valuable possessions west of the mountains.

In 1841 Sinclair was appointed by Governor George Simpson to lead a large party of British subjects—mostly *Métis*—from Red River to settle in the Oregon, in an effort to fortify by occupation British claims to that important region and to secure the company's interests along the Columbia, as well as to relieve the pressure of dissenting elements in Assiniboia. In 1854, Sinclair was asked to conduct another such migration, which he undertook with the added intent of settling in the Oregon. This decision led to his involvement in the vicious Indian wars then being waged, and so to his untimely death.

Thus, Sinclair's perilous journeys carried him as pathfinder across the sparsely traveled Canadian plains, then vigilantly guarded by the fierce Blackfoot Confederacy, as well as across some of the most difficult mountain terrain in North America. That he succeeded in conducting several large parties of men, women, and children safely to Oregon via routes largely previously untrodden is little less than miraculous and is surely unequaled in the pioneer history of this continent.

Sinclair's only memorial for such exploits is the pass through the Canadian Rockies that today bears his name. But few who travel along the scenic Banff-Windermere highway know of the man whom the spectacular Red Rock Canyon on that road immortalizes.

This study of Sinclair's life had its inception in some investigations made by my late father, W. F. W. Lent, K.C., when considering certain developments in western Canadian law relative to his legal practice. A few references to James Sinclair were observed pertaining to the fur trade, but these were scarce and often vague or distorted. I inherited my father's interest in Canadiana, and it has led me in pursuit of original sources as far afield as Great Britain, and in Canadian national and provincial archives.

In this particular piece of research my special thanks go to the Hudson's Bay Company for their invaluable aid—especially to Miss A. M. Johnson, the company's archivist, and other members of the staff in London, England, where I was privileged to consult the Old Company's rich resources in 1950. Valuable aid has been afforded me for many years by the company's officers in Winnipeg, and particularly grateful thanks are given to the late Mr. Douglas MacKay and to Mr. Clifford Wilson. It is from such authoritative sources as these that much of Sinclair's correspondence with Sir George Simpson has come to light, revealing the real nature of Sinclair's services to the Hudson's Bay Company and the British cause behind the scenes.

Sincere appreciation is expressed to Dr. W. Kaye Lamb, National Archivist in Ottawa, and to Mr. Willard E. Ireland, Provincial Archivist in Victoria, B.C. The introduction to the interesting letters written by Sinclair to his son-in-law, Dr. William Cowan, and the more recent discovery of other important documents relative to Sinclair in the priceless Donald Ross Collection came through the kindness and courtesy of the British Columbia Provincial Archives. My thanks also go to Miss Inez Mitchell and to Miss Madge Wolfenden for their valuable assistance in the pursuit of these studies.

Grateful acknowledgment for much help throughout the years of research goes to my friend and counselor, the late Dr. J. L. Johnston, Provincial Archivist and Librarian in Winnipeg, Manitoba. Dr. Johnston made available to me some most important documents relating to Sinclair and provided invaluable background material on Red River history.

My sincere thanks are also due to Dr. D. C. Appelt, Librarian of the University of Saskatchewan, and to Mr. Bruce Peel, formerly of the Shortt and Morton Libraries in Saskatoon, and now associated with the Rutherford Library in Edmonton, Alberta, who so ably assisted me in unraveling the old trails across the prairies traveled by Sinclair and his parties.

I am most grateful to Mrs. Edith Gostick, Provincial Librarian, Edmonton, Alberta, and to Miss Edith Hilton of the same library, not only for enabling me to find much valuable material relative to Alberta history, but for introducing me to two most important and little-known journals—one kept by Sinclair's father, and the other by his father-in-law, Chief Trader Colin Campbell of Fort Dunvegan. My sincere thanks are also expressed to Miss Georgina Thompson and her associates in the reference department of the Calgary Public Library for their kind assistance in helping to meet the problems that inevitably arise in the preparation of an historic manuscript.

Special tribute is also paid to the authorities of the British Museum in London, England, where I was granted permission to use the resources of that incomparable treasure house of history, and introduced to its various departments for research through the kindness of a great scholar and personal friend, Dr. L. A. Sheppard.

To all the above and to many others I am deeply indebted for generous help in providing me with historical data, invaluable advice, patient encouragement, and aid of various kinds necessary to the preparation of a work such as this through many long years of endeavor.

Finally, my very special expression of thanks goes to Professor W. L. Morton, Chairman of the Department of History at the University of Manitoba. Professor Morton, an authority on western Canadian history, gave me valuable critical advice in the final preparation of this work. I am deeply indebted to him for seeing that the manuscript has been properly completed, references authenticated, and for his consideration and kindness at all times during the involved processes of assembling the work.

While these acknowledgments are most sincerely and gratefully made, the responsibility for the text as it stands and for the opinions expressed therein must remain my own.

This narrative, then, strives to remain close to fact and as consistently as possible to actual events, places, dates, and contemporary personalities. These findings, therefore, may have some historical value to other students, for only those portions have been added or surmised as have been felt requisite to establishing a genuine sense of background and atmosphere, and to lend substantial fabric to the story for the general reader.

This study of James Sinclair is thus presented, with the hope that a sympathetic interest may be created in this fascinating and disputable period of western North American history, as well as in the life of an unusual and in some respects truly great man.

D. Geneva Lent

September, 1962
Victoria, British Columbia

CONTENTS

ILLUSTRATIONS

Maps

Photographs

WEST OF THE MOUNTAINS

James Sinclair and the Hudson's Bay Company

PROLOGUE: WILLIAM SINCLAIR, THE FATHER

I

About the year 1806 a boy was born in the northern wilderness of Canada,[1] then known as Rupert's Land. He was born at the Hudson's Bay Company trading post of Oxford House, situated half-way between the northern end of Lake Winnipeg and the western shore of Hudson Bay. The child's father was William Sinclair, master of the post, and his mother was a native of the country, half-Cree, half-white, known as Nahovway. The boy was given the family name of James by his father, for there was as yet no clergy of any denomination in Rupert's Land to marry or baptize.

The advent of a boy in William Sinclair's family was welcome, for the first-born son and namesake had arrived ten years before to be followed by five daughters, and James had now come to break the sequence of girls. William Sinclair felt renewed hope that, while his eldest son should become a fur trader like himself, the second son should one day return to his father's people in the Orkney Islands and ultimately receive a university education such as he had received at Edinburgh. William Sinclair, however, was not spared to see these plans for his sons fulfilled. His untimely death not only ended his own unhappy career but long jeopardized those of his sons'. Therefore, a little of his story must be considered as an integral part of the colorful life of James Sinclair.

II

William Sinclair, known as "the elder," the father of James, was born in the Orkney Islands in 1766 on the family freehold croft, called East-on-quay.[2] It was situated on the island of Pomona, close to the ancient port of Stromness from which the Hudson's Bay Company ships sailed annually, laden with goods to be traded for furs with the Indians of the New World. The Orkney Sinclairs claimed that they were descended from Norsemen, one of whom as early as A.D. 888 had been named a *jarl* or earl of the Orkneys by King Harold the Fair of Norway. The most notorious of the Sinclair ancestors had been known as Rognavold or Rollo, who as a wandering viking gave the Sinclairs their name. About A.D. 912 he landed with his band of followers near St. Lô in France and there claimed a site for himself near a holy well, where an English monk named Clare wrought miracles in healing the eyes. At that spot, Rollo built a castle known as "the hive of the Sinclairs," which became recognized as the family's ancestral home. They adopted the name "St. Clair," which eventually took on the useful paronym of "Sinclair."

Close blood ties existed through marriage and descent with the family of William the Conqueror. Five Sinclairs fought at his side at the Battle of Hastings, and for this service they received handsome rewards in English lands and titles. But one Sinclair, more independent than the rest and the first to bear the name of William, dared defy the Conqueror and—it is said—defeated him in a joust. For this bold feat the first William Sinclair was compelled to flee for his life, taking refuge at the court of King Malcolm III of Scotland, where he found favor and gained both wealth and power. He was thus enabled to establish another proud line of Sinclairs in Midlothian, known as the Sinclairs of Roslin; it was from this strain of inveterate rovers—some of whom returned to the Orkneys to knit the kinship closer—that fur trader William Sinclair of Rupert's Land claimed his descent. These Orkney Sinclairs were less rich but no less proud than the Sinclairs of Roslin, for they had adopted the lonely Outer Isles as their family home and had come to love them well.

William Sinclair's people on Pomona dwelt close to the sea. They worked at fishing and crofting, eking out a Spartan existence with their boats and coaxing spare crops of oats and bere from the stubborn soil. Scant as was their living, the Orkney Sinclairs lived proudly as men who had never served a feudal lord: they owned their own land and cottages.

With all their simple, rugged existence, the Orkney Sinclairs were instilled with a genuine love of learning that demanded great sacrifice in a family to have one son receive a higher education. William Sinclair was the fortunate one in his family. After completing his schooling at Edinburgh, he joined the Hudson's Bay Company at the age of twenty-six. In those days, the Old Company was eagerly seeking for likely young Orkneymen to enter the fur trade in Rupert's Land. They had proved themselves to be good laborers, boatmen, builders of forts, and traders inland. They possessed by inheritance and experience the skills necessary for survival and success in the life of the trade and the harsh land in which it was carried on. William Sinclair, the elder, was no exception.

III

Sinclair set sail from Stromness in the summer of 1792; he reached the Hudson's Bay Company headquarters at York Factory on Hudson Bay in August of that year. His superior officers soon realized that here was a company "servant" more promising than most, for Sinclair possessed not only a sound education but an intelligent, trustworthy nature and gave evidence of some breeding. He had, however, little liking for the task to which he was assigned at the company's great depot. With other young clerks he was set at the tedious task of transcribing in the company's voluminous ledgers an exact record of every fur received at York Factory from all parts of Rupert's Land in return for the quantities of shot, gunpowder, tea, beads, sugar, tobacco, guns, beaver traps, axes, pots, kettles, and other trade articles that arrived each year from Britain to do business with the Indians. Sinclair continued at this work for the entire season of 1792–93.[3] It had to be endured if he were to receive advancement in the company's ranks, but he was deeply grateful when in 1794 the commanding officer at York released him from his desk and sent him out as a "trader inland from York" to establish new trading posts. He was instructed to secure as many "made beaver"—the term used for good, well-preserved beaver skins—as the country was capable of yielding and to thwart wherever possible the serious inroads of the North West Company, which since 1766 had been encroaching upon the chartered territories of the Hudson's Bay Company.

At the matter of post-building, as in dealing with the Indians, Sinclair proved himself exceptionally successful. In a few years he managed to establish and become master of several good trading posts in the region between the Churchill and the Nelson rivers, at Nestoowyan, Setting Lake, and Hulse House.[4] In his endeavors to carry out orders Sinclair also found himself engaged in a fierce struggle with the rival Nor'Westers—North West Company men—for which he was later to pay dearly. Nevertheless, there were some happier aspects to his life at this earlier stage in Rupert's Land.

IV

Shortly after he established his first outpost at Nestoowyan, Sinclair took to wife the half-Cree girl, Nahovway. He had married this young native woman "in accordance with the custom of the country." Nahovway was beautiful; she was skilled in the crafts of her mother's people; and she had been brought up in the camp of her grandfather, a Swampy Cree chief, with whom Sinclair traded advantageously. She was the daughter of a British ex-soldier, known only to records as "Holden," [5] who had been stationed for a time at Fort Prince of Wales during the last quarter of the eighteenth century. The name of Nahovway's Cree mother is unknown.

William Sinclair seems to have regarded his "marriage of the country" as a sacred and binding obligation for the remainder of his life. Nahovway, in turn, performed her wifely duties faithfully to Sinclair for the twenty-five years they were together, bearing him some eleven children and remaining with him through all of his vicissitudes.

Six years after he reached Rupert's Land Sinclair was rewarded for his services to the company. He was ordered to build a good permanent trading post and home for his growing family at a desirable site on an island in Oxford Lake where he was to remain as master for some time. The official record of this assignment reads:

> On July 5th, 1798, Sinclair was sent with four or five canoes and provisions to build a substantial house. Three men were to reside with Sinclair until five more came from the ship. Double trip money was to be paid to the men and to Sinclair for his work. Explicit instructions were given to build a good house, a stone house for trade goods and for a dwelling. Timber was to be prepared and care taken against fire. "Stockadoes" were to be built as a prevention from attack by the Indians. Work was retarded through the uneven cutting of timber lengths. Oxford House was 42 feet by 24 feet in size, and the height of the upper storey was 9 feet under the ridge poles. Considering that "most of the sticks nearer to the house than a mile distant was not fit to be roofing sticks," good work was done by August 9th, 1798. . . . From that date William Sinclair was continually in charge at Oxford House until 1814.[6]

It was for greater safety that Sinclair had built his post on the island in the middle of Oxford Lake. He had set it back a little distance from the water's edge on the brow of a grassy hill. The Indians spoke of the island as "Pathepow Nippi," meaning in Cree "Bottomless Water." To the white men it was "Holey Island," so called from an Indian legend that a deep cavern leading to the nether world was hidden somewhere on the island.

The company had reasons other than as a reward for a good service for having Sinclair construct Oxford House. It had been found necessary to build a strong defense at this particular point; Oxford House lay at the very center of an important labyrinth of rivers, lakes, and rapids. It was at the heart of what was known to the fur trade as the "Hayes River route." This useful waterway traversing Oxford Lake had been discovered earlier by some of the company's most capable explorers—Matthew Cocking, Samuel Hearne, and William Tomison. As the tempo of the fur war between the Hudson's Bay Company and the North West Company increased at the close of the eighteenth century, it was realized that this waterway provided the best route to the interior from Hudson Bay and must be carefully safeguarded. When Sinclair built Oxford House in 1798, the fur war was reaching a peak of violence and would continue until union brought peace to the combatants some twenty-three years later.

V

Sinclair made his post at Oxford Lake something more than a mere frontier establishment. Outwardly, it appeared little different from other trading houses of the day, with its high log palisade and its large main gate fronting the lake, protected by a particularly strong bastion. Inside the stockade there was the usual collection of low wooden buildings spaced around three sides of an open square, but these were decidedly more commodious than at most outposts. At his own expense, Sinclair sought to make his post not only exceptionally efficient and well defended but a comfortable homesite for himself as well.

Oxford House, placed on a slight rise of land, some hundred miles inland from Hudson Bay, had a more equable and pleasant climate than York Factory. There the bone-chilling fogs off the Bay and the sterile surrounding bogs that remained semifrozen even in midsummer discouraged the growth of even the simplest kitchen garden. But at Oxford House it was different.

William Sinclair found that his island had patches of fairly fertile soil worth cultivating. He therefore ordered seeds to be sent to him from Britain on the next company ship-of-the-year in order that he might plant a garden and a field of grain at his post as soon as possible. When he had raised sufficient fodder he imported some cattle from the Orkney Islands at his own expense. The stock survived the long ocean voyage to York Factory, and Sinclair accomplished the all-but-impossible feat of transporting a bull and several cows, while they were yet calves, up the difficult Hayes River route to Oxford House in York boats. The poor animals were herded in and out of the boats and forced to cross the dangerous portages on the way inland, but they arrived unharmed. Sinclair thus established a small dairy at his post—surely the first of its kind in all Rupert's Land—in order that he might have fresh milk and butter for his family.

The innovations that Sinclair introduced to his outpost, at his own expense and initiative, were to lead eventually to his downfall, for such novel amenities were not even enjoyed by his superior officers at York Factory. Such was the nature of the company's service in that day—stiff with tradition, routine, and careful regard for rank—that jealousies were bound to arise from such divergencies to regular life at an outpost as Sinclair had dared to institute. Nevertheless, through his own efforts Oxford House was made a pleasanter place than most for his family.

This, then, was the environment into which James Sinclair was born. At his father's post there was enough to eat: the garden, herd of cattle, and small fields prospered for a while; the surrounding forests abounded with game, and the rivers and lakes provided plenty of fish. However, the abundance and comfort were not to be enjoyed for long. Serious trouble was brewing in this remote wilderness outpost at the height of the fur war, which even the momentarily fortunate Sinclair family could not long escape.

VI

After his establishment of Oxford House in 1798, William Sinclair was continually in charge there until 1814, prosecuting the fur trade for the Hudson's Bay Company with the friendly

Indians related to his wife's people, the Swampy Crees. Sinclair managed to hold these natives' loyalty, when many other bands turned their trade to the aggressive Nor'Westers who were now steadily gaining a foothold near the company's long-established posts on Hudson Bay.

During the years of fort-building, Sinclair had gained some favor with the company officials through his own capabilities and the good offices of his close friend, William Auld, then officer in charge of company affairs at York Factory. Auld had come to Rupert's Land as an apprentice clerk and surgeon about the same time as Sinclair, and it was then that their friendship had become established. Auld had advanced more quickly than Sinclair in the company's ranks through family prestige in the Old Land as well as through his own medical qualifications. He was thus in a position to bring Sinclair to the attention of the company's governor and committee in London when he attended their annual meetings to make reports. As a result of this relationship, in the year 1810 when drastic reorganization of company affairs was undertaken, William Sinclair was made a governor and chief factor of an important part of Rupert's Land.

This new appointment designated Sinclair as "Chief Factor of the West Winnipeg Factory and its dependencies, including Cumberland House, Swan River, Fort Dauphin and Brandon House." [7] He was thereby given supervision of an enormous and important territory extending from his home base at Oxford House to the west and south of Lake Winnipeg. This region included some of the most violently contested country near the North West Company's stronghold at the forks of the Red and Assiniboine rivers. It was provision country for the securing of pemmican, to supply food for the fur brigades and winter outposts, as well as being the chief point of entry to the rich Indian country beyond.

Despite the personal success that William Sinclair had achieved in securing from his immediate region a considerable amount of valuable fur from friendly Indians who had resisted the blandishments of the Nor'Westers, the prolonged fur war had seriously depleted the general reserves of the Hudson's Bay Company and had deflected much of the fur usually secured by the Old Company from Indians farther to the west. The fur was now finding its way to the merchants in Montreal instead of to the company's old posts on Hudson Bay where it had formerly been annually received. This naturally reduced the amount of traffic and business that had previously passed through Oxford House with the brigades of York boats that traveled each year to and from York Factory.

The Old Company was also feeling sorely the pinch of reduced profits through the destruction of much of its lucrative European trade in furs as a result of the Napoleonic War. This had left the great London warehouses glutted with unsold, spoiling fur, which placed the company in serious financial straits. Certainly, in the year 1809, the Hudson's Bay Company seemed to have reached the darkest hour in its history, and no dividends could be paid the irate shareholders. Besides all this, within the company itself a private war was being waged between powerful rival interests eager to gain control of the company's stock, not only for financial advantage, but to secure large grants of land in North America. Fantastic colonization schemes were afoot and great pawns were at stake, with powerful protagonists pitted against each other—Thomas Douglas, the fifth Earl of Selkirk, and his influential brothers-in-law, Andrew Wedderburn and John Halkett, who stood high in the company's councils, versus Sir Alexander Mackenzie, the great North West Company explorer and financier, and his associates.

At the same time, those seeking advantage in the Hudson's Bay Company circles in London were stubbornly ignorant of the actual conditions on the fur frontiers in the distant continent of North America. Little sympathy was shown by the company shareholders toward William Auld and the officers and men serving under him, who were endeavoring against great odds to secure fur and carry on trade as usual in the field, at the same time as they were safeguarding company property and preserving valuable territory for the British crown—often at the risk of their own lives, with insufficient arms for defense and insufficient goods to carry on satisfactory trade with the Indians. William Auld, at the company's annual meetings in London, vigorously defended the interests of the men actually engaged in the fur trade, for he was knowledgeable and capable, if a somewhat tactless and misunderstood officer, who defeated his own ends in the cause he served.

Auld had vociferously opposed the grandiose plans of the astute if idealistic Lord Selkirk to place a colony of evicted Highland crofters at the forks of the Red and Assiniboine rivers, which chanced to be within William Sinclair's new sphere of administration.[8] Auld realized that such a settlement of farmers would further jeopardize the already declining returns in furs and drive the Nor'Westers to greater violence. He regarded the matter entirely from the standpoint of a practical fur trader who disliked Lord Selkirk personally and who felt that he and his friends were exploiting the Old Company solely for their own interests. Evidently Auld had not been informed of the fact that the purpose behind the formation of such a colony, placed in the most strategic position in all Rupert's Land, was to secure British territory, not only against the rival North West Company, but from an even more serious and long-term threat in the possible advance of the lusty new American Republic to the south of the forks of the Red and Assiniboine rivers.

Auld's opposition to Lord Selkirk and his faction surely brought about his downfall and was a factor in the demotion of his friend William Sinclair as well. The latter was actually in sympathy with, and did all in his power to aid, the unhappy Selkirk people after their arrival in his territory. Nevertheless, he was to suffer for his convictions and was permitted to enjoy only briefly the emoluments and grandeur of his rank as chief factor. All this brought into being a curious sequence of events, which was to involve many persons in a relentless struggle for almost half a century to come.

While the Hudson's Bay Company was reft with dissension

in its ranks, the rival North West Company was experiencing grave threats to its own existence through the plans set afoot by Lord Selkirk and his associates. The powerful partners of the North West Company in Montreal were becoming desperate, through the drain upon their financial resources of the prolonged conflict with the Hudson's Bay Company. Its stakes in the rich Athabaska fur region were threatened by the Old Company's determination to secure fur there at all costs, and the prospect of the Hudson's Bay Company placing a colony of agriculturalists at the forks of the Red and Assiniboine rivers was a grave threat to the Nor'Westers' life line of supplies and furs between their depot at Fort William and the Indian country beyond to the northwest.

Sir Alexander Mackenzie—still actively representing the North West Company and his associates—determined to make one last attempt to defeat the Hudson's Bay Company. It was realized that Selkirk's plan was intended to offset the North West Company's line of outposts, but, worst of all, a colony of settlers at the forks would command the buffalo herds that were hunted annually along the Red and Assiniboine valleys. The Nor'Westers had long taken from these herds large quantities of pemmican for their *voyageurs* and trading posts. In view of the serious threat to the North West Company's economy, it determined to put a stop to Selkirk's plan at the outset. Mackenzie and his men would try to bring the long and wasting contest to an early close in their favor. They would endeavor to hamper recruitment for Selkirk's settlement. They would seek to discourage those colonists who came. They would hope the settlement might fail and perhaps aid the failure. Certainly they would increase the tempo of the conflict by harassing the Hudson's Bay Company traders at their outposts and on the trail. They would take all the fur they could get from the Indians for their partners in Montreal. They would even carry the contest to the London stock market in their effort to gain control over the Old Company. Sir Alexander had found a focus for his attack upon the company in Lord Selkirk and his project for settlement, and Mackenzie's chief aim henceforth was to bring down Selkirk, no matter who suffered in the process.

Such, then, were the chief considerations that drove both the Hudson's Bay Company and the North West Company to precipitate action in the crucial season of 1809–10. At the same time, as chief factor of the most strategic area in Rupert's Land, William Sinclair was to be held responsible should members of Selkirk's new colony, planted within the bounds of his administration, suffer from attack by the Nor'Westers. Sinclair, therefore, enjoyed his exalted factorship only until these insurmountable difficulties confronted him shortly after his appointment to his high office. The company officials and shareholders in London, while they accepted William Auld's recommendation of Sinclair's capabilities as justification for his advancement, did not support him with either adequate means of defense or sufficient trade goods to carry on satisfactory dealing with the Indians in his vast and troublesome domain. The country had been stripped of beaver and required a severe regime of conservation to restore it to its former productivity, and the methods necessary for this were impossible under the existing conditions created by the prolonged fur war. Sinclair, however, was expected to carry out his duties expeditiously, to bring in good returns in fur, and be mindful of the prestige his position warranted.

> He had a freedom of action and control within his own charge which brought him the obedience of the servants and the reverence of the natives. This was greatly enhanced by the ceremonial in which a Chief Factor's position was exalted. Even in the old days when the Indians arrived at the post in a band it was marked by a volley from the visitors. A return from the fort was made with a salvo from guns in the bastion more dangerous to those who served them than they could ever be to any who might attempt an assault. Then came the procession through the gates and a solemn council with the Chief Factor about the happenings of the trade and the hunt for furs and provisions.[9]

Sinclair was aware of the obligations placed upon him, and he did his utmost to uphold the dignity of his rank. With his promotion, life for William Sinclair and his family had been markedly changed at Oxford House. Although the company's new rulings of 1810 prohibited the importation of luxuries for officers in Rupert's Land at the company's expense, one of Sinclair's position was expected to indent for certain amenities befitting his station. A chief factor's personal requisition was sent to Britain every year from York Factory. Orders were placed with merchants in Edinburgh and London, and the goods were sent out to Rupert's Land on the next company's ship-of-the-year bound for York Factory. After his appointment, Sinclair's orders show such items charged to his personal account as fine household linens, silver, crockery, good clothing for himself, Scotch shawls, and bolts of cloth or suitable cotton prints to be made into apparel for his wife and children. Books for himself—both current and classical—were also ordered for his personal library at Oxford House.

James Sinclair was too young at the time to remember much of his father's brief moment of glory and grandeur, but there was instilled in him throughout his youth by hearsay and tradition a pride of rank and family that was to remain with him throughout his days despite vicissitudes and changes of fortune. All his life he was to be reminded that his father had been a chief factor and governor of an important "factory" in Rupert's Land, and this fact colored vividly his entire career and influenced his course of action. His father's name and prestige—especially among the Selkirk people—became a byword of entry, and wherever James Sinclair went throughout his life it always seemed there were those ready and willing to help him and open advantageous doors for him. Most of those eager to aid him were associated in some way or another with his father in his earlier days, such as Jean-Baptiste Lagimonière, the renowned French-Canadian guide and hunter; Andrew McDermot, the notorious Red River merchant and free trader; and James Curtis Bird, retired chief factor and leader of the company's colony, to name but a few. William Sinclair, at the height of his power, had cast his bread upon the waters, although he was not spared to see it returned in any measure to his sons. This was particularly the case as a result of what he had done to help the Selkirk people in the dark hour of their greatest peril and distress.

William Sinclair's association with the Selkirk settlers came about in the following way: in August, 1813, a party—the third since 1812—of ragged, weary Highlanders had passed through Oxford House, on their way to their new settlement at the forks of the Red and Assiniboine rivers. They had come upstream from Hudson Bay with a brigade of York boats, having received little sympathy and none too hospitable a welcome from Superintendent William Auld at York Factory.[10] However, feeling close kinship with these unhappy people, William Sinclair had extended to them every courtesy and benefit his establishment at Oxford House could afford. He replenished their limited stocks of food and presented the leader of the expedition with a fine bull and heifer from his own small herd in order that the women and children, expected to reach the settlement later, might have milk and butter on their scanty board.[11]

With the second party of Selkirk settlers to reach Oxford House in 1813 was a jovial, fiery-tempered, very clever young Irishman named Andrew McDermot. Sinclair little guessed he would one day influence the career of his son James as would no other man. It had so happened that Sinclair had taken an instant liking to McDermot and felt impelled to give him a chest of his own China tea.[12] Agreeably surprised at Sinclair's impulsive show of generosity, McDermot left Oxford House with his prize tied in a calfskin and slung triumphantly over his shoulder—this prize, he later said, became the basis of his free trading with the Indians. However that may have been, he never forgot Sinclair's kindness or failed to return it later to his son.

Once these unhappy strangers had left his outpost Sinclair felt deep concern for their safety. He well knew what hardships and dangers were bound to confront them, for they were almost certain to suffer attack in the territory that the Nor'Westers claimed as theirs by occupation at Red River. So troubled was Sinclair for the settlers' welfare that he set out in the dead of winter to visit them at their proposed headquarters, Fort Douglas, at the forks of the Red and Assiniboine rivers. When Sinclair reached Red River he did not find the settlers at their new fort, but at a pathetically inadequate encampment farther to the south, near Pembina. There the Selkirk people had set up a group of hastily constructed shelters, which they called Fort Daer, close by the buffalo plains. Hunger had forced them to join a band of friendly half-breed hunters and Indians in order to secure sufficient meat to sustain them through the winter.

William Sinclair carried on his person certain important papers for the settlers' leader, Captain Miles Macdonell, from Lord Selkirk, to prevent them from falling into the hands of the Nor'-Westers. These papers had reached Sinclair from York Factory, where they had been brought on the company's annual ship after this party of settlers had departed for Red River. To commemorate Sinclair's visit to the Selkirk people at Fort Daer in the winter of 1813–14, Captain Macdonell wrote in his journal: "Assembled our people. Mr. Sinclair asks for a holiday for them, and also liquor for them to drink. The people enjoyed themselves much and kept it up for the greater part of the night. The gentlemen did the same." [13] Certainly thereafter the Selkirk people had little cause for such simple rejoicing as Sinclair had afforded them on this occasion, and his kindness was not soon or easily forgotten.

Sinclair was not permitted to do much more for the Selkirk people. The ship that brought the papers in the autumn of 1813 for delivery to Captain Miles Macdonell also carried a dispatch ordering Sinclair to London by the next company ship bound for Britain. He was commanded to give a personal account of himself to the company's governor and committee, with good and sufficient reason for his failure to produce the expected returns in beaver from his factory that had warranted his appointment as head of it four years before. In obedience to the order, "in the autumn of 1814, Mr. Sinclair returned to England by the Company's ship-of-the-year," [14] which also carried Superintendent William Auld to receive his own dismissal.

The rebuff Sinclair was given was somewhat less final than Auld's, for he was instructed to "return to Hudson Bay as a Chief Trader," but his post would be "determined upon by the Governor of the Country." [15] This provided a poor prospect for Sinclair, since he did not stand in the same favor with Auld's successor at York Factory, Governor Thomas Thomas. Nevertheless, the sting of personal indignity that Sinclair suffered in his reduction in rank was somewhat alleviated when he learned that he was not alone in demotion. A company ruling of retrenchment had been passed at the annual meeting in London, signifying that there would be a general reduction of commissioned officers to the status of ordinary company servants under a new system of unified control that would henceforth be in effect throughout Rupert's Land.

Furthermore, as if to somewhat soften the company's action toward Sinclair, Andrew Wedderburn—now known as "Colvile," and a man of growing influence in company affairs—in recognition of Sinclair's kindness to the Selkirk people, signed a document appointing him "one of the Councillors of Governor Robert Semple," [16] who had replaced Captain Miles Macdonell as leader of the Selkirk settlement. But Sinclair was not permitted to enjoy this belated honor. He returned to York Factory in August, 1815, to be assigned by Governor Thomas to an inferior post at Knee Lake, with the title of "Chief of the Island Lake Trading District," which permitted him to retain the status of a commissioned officer in the company, although of lower rank than he had previously held.

Sinclair's post at Knee Lake was an old establishment on an almost abandoned waterway between Oxford House and Hudson Bay. In earlier days the post had been used extensively, but since the building of Sinclair's good establishment at Oxford House it had fallen largely into disuse. He was, therefore, assigned to a most difficult country with poor prospect of bringing in much beaver. His dilapidated post was situated on an irregular body of water some forty miles in length, not actually a lake but a natural widening in the Hayes River. The only compensation the place afforded was that it was comparatively near his old post at Oxford Lake. There his wife and children had remained during Sinclair's absence in Britain, in the care of his oldest son, William, whom he had trained to be an efficient assistant trader. Two of Sinclair's daughters had also married resident traders at his old home post.

Despite the poor prospects Knee Lake presented, Sinclair put every effort into rebuilding the old post. He strove to revive the trade with the Indians of the region, but they had grown accustomed to doing business at Oxford House, and now largely by-passed him at Knee Lake. In desperation Sinclair traversed, throughout the winter and summer, the difficult surrounding country of swampland, lakes, rivers, and bush in an effort to find trade and fur, but to little avail. The harsh demands now made upon him with advancing age, seriously impaired health, and the frustrating conditions experienced in his demotion took their toll, and he determined to return to Britain. He was evidently anxious not only to seek competent medical aid but to once more place his case before Colvile and the company's London committee in the hope of securing a more promising post. He succeeded in reaching York Factory in the autumn of 1816,[17] accompanied by his eldest son William, in time to board the company's annual ship bound for Gravesend.

Among the company officers also taking passage on the same ship, the *Prince of Wales*, setting forth from York Factory on October 6, 1816, was Chief Factor Colin Robertson, a man in a position to enlighten Sinclair concerning many important company matters. Robertson had been at the Selkirk Settlement as recently as June, 1816, and it had not been long after he left it that word reached him on the way to York Factory of the startling "Seven Oaks Massacre," in which Governor Semple and twenty-one of his officers and men had lost their lives at the hands of the French half-breeds who had once been in the North West Company service and were inspired by their former masters. "Robertson, hearing that a party of settlers, terrified by the Massacre of Seven Oaks, and the murder of Semple, were fleeing to

York Factory, met them, rallied them and led them back once more to Lake Winnipeg where he handed them over to James Bird," [18] in an effort to have them try to rebuild their settlement.

Robertson was also able to give Sinclair a firsthand account of conditions in the Athabaska region, where he had been sent as leader of an expedition in opposition to the Nor'Westers. Robertson was enthusiastic about the country, and what the future held for the Hudson's Bay Company in that region, as well as in New Caledonia and the Columbia River country west of the Rocky Mountains, if the conflict with the North West Company could be brought to a speedy end. While Colin Robertson was not popular in some company circles, his statements were known to be usually well founded in fact, and it seems certain that if circumstances on the voyage to Britain had not gone against them, this meeting between Sinclair and Robertson might have been propitious for both of them when they reached London.[19] As it proved, fate was against them.

The ship bearing them to Britain had been unusually late that year in setting out from York Factory. September 23 had long been considered the latest possible date of sailing in order to avoid being trapped for the winter in the ice of Hudson Bay. For some reason, in the year 1816 the ship did not leave port until October 6; she was out of York Factory but seven days and racing against time when she was overtaken by a severe storm near Mansell Island. The entrance to Hudson Bay was already closed by floe ice, which had formed over an old, unthawed ice ridge that had remained from the year before. No means of escape from the Bay was left for the ship. A fierce northeast gale suddenly drove the ship back the full length of Hudson Bay. Having his bearings accurately, the experienced captain wisely sought shelter at Charlton Island, near Moose Factory in James Bay, the headquarters of the Hudson's Bay Company's southern department. The ship remained there, frozen in for the winter, with its valuable cargo of fur kept under close guard until the journey to Britain was resumed the following year.

At Charlton, the ship's company was removed across the narrow channel from the island to the mainland in small boats, for the water there was still free of ice. The party from the ship arrived at Moose Factory on October 28, 1816.[20] Winter set in quickly, and the disappointed passengers were forced to remain in the region until spring or risk a dangerous overland trip to York Factory in the dead of winter.

William Sinclair, the elder, was immediately placed in the company's service at Moose Factory. That post found itself in a difficult situation, with insufficient food to support the unexpected ship's company thrust upon it as well as its own usual complement of servants. Sinclair knew this part of the country well from former trading expeditions through it. He was at once set carrying dispatches and escorting parties between posts despite his failing health. The Moose Factory journal of November 6, 1816, states: "despatched to Severn William Sinclair with news of this unfortunate event," [21] meaning the detention of the ship at Charlton and the holding of the passengers, crew, and furs in and near Moose Factory for the duration of the winter.

Severn House was another old company post halfway between Moose and York Factories on the western shore of Hudson Bay. The officer commanding Moose Factory decided to send Sinclair's son, William, with other of the ship's passengers including one woman and twenty men, to a nearby goose camp at Capusco for the duration of the winter.[22] This decision was reached after careful consideration, when it was realized that without sufficient food it was the part of wisdom to send the ship's company to the goose camps. These had been established for some years at Capusco for the hunting and salting down of wild geese, which migrated over this area each spring and fall.

William Sinclair, the elder, was kept busy transporting goods and carrying dispatches from Moose as far as Albany Post—another outpost halfway between Moose and Severn House—from the end of October to December 10, 1816. It was a severe and ignominious assignment for a man who had once been a chief factor and who still held the rank of chief trader, quite apart from the serious condition of his health. Nevertheless, on December 12, 1816, Jack Corrigal—the master of Albany Post—wrote the following instructions for Sinclair:

> Having received instructions to despatch you to the N'ward Department as soon as possible with news of the unfortunate event of the ship's wintering in the country, I have, therefore, engaged an Indian, (Nequal), to guide you to Severn, and being much disturbed for want of provisions, I am under the necessity to send the following returned passengers along with you. They are able men, and I hope you will make a quick journey.[23]

Sinclair made this trip to Severn House and on to York Factory in the dead of winter to bear the news of the ship's misfortune to the company's northern headquarters. For the remainder of the winter he appears to have resumed his trading between York and his post at Knee Lake. There is proof of this in his somewhat remarkable "Journal, York Factory to Oxford House, 1816–1817," [24] which gives striking evidence of the difficulties and suffering he experienced at this time with increasingly poor health. His ailment seems to have been an advanced form of dropsy in the legs. The harrowing experiences he endured when caught in a blizzard that winter further strained his already seriously impaired heart. Somehow he was able to cover the long distance to the post at Brandon House beyond the forks of the Red and Assiniboine rivers to see once more his old friend, the famous trader, Peter Fidler. On December 30, 1817, Fidler wrote in his journal, "Sinclair's dropsy very bad. Twice tapped for it." [25]

It was evidently Fidler who saw that Sinclair, now gravely ill, was transported by sled with a party of company men, traveling with a winter packet to York Factory up the ice of Lake Winnipeg and along the Hayes River route, for Sinclair died at York Factory on April 20, 1818. He was buried "across Schooner Creek where the Company's small trading ship was laid up for the winter outside of the old Indian graveyard upon which the Hayes River was encroaching and eating away the banks." [26]

This simple tribute was paid Sinclair by the company's officers at York: "He was a good trader, a steady man, and beloved by the natives." [27]

VII

During the period of Sinclair's misfortunes and wanderings, his native wife, Nahovway, had remained mostly at Oxford House to care for their children as best she could. Time and again Sinclair seems to have returned for a short visit with his family and to add another child to the brood—the last son, Colin, being born several months after the death of his father.

James Sinclair was nearly twelve years of age when his father died. The oldest son, William, was now twenty-four and doing well in the company's service at a post near Lesser Slave Lake. Between William and the infant Colin ranked the other nine children of the Sinclair family—most of them girls—with James at the center of the group. To all of these children William Sinclair, the elder, left bequests in his peculiarly involved will, except to one, his daughter Elizabeth, known familiarly in the records as "Betsy" Sinclair.

Surprisingly enough, Sinclair's assets at the time of his death were not inconsiderable for one in the fur trade of his day. His estate had accumulated largely from hard earnings saved during his more prosperous years, and for the most part in the form of company securities deposited with an agent in London. As was the custom of the day in many instances, Sinclair left his wife to the mercies of their children, with but a small annual interest accruing to her from a block of shares.

Sinclair remembered to provide for his sons' education, in accordance with the long-established family tradition, stating explicitly that "two of my younger sons shall go to Britain to be educated before the age of fourteen years." To meet this provision—if permission were granted by the company's governor at York Factory, and if the oldest son, William, could be released from service long enough to accompany his young brothers, James and John, to Britain—the lads were to be sent in the autumn of 1818 on the company's ship-of-the-year bound for London.

Throughout his will,[28] Sinclair displayed a rare if humorless discretion that was quite in keeping with the company's edict that personal matters should be concisely recorded. He ordered that "all my papers of every description be immediately destroyed . . . all that is not relative to monies." He disposed of his personal possessions with labored forethought. Strangely incongruous items for a fur trader on a remote frontier were mentioned as specific bequests to friends and relations—items such as sterling-silver knives, forks, and spoons and candlesticks; a "fine dressing case with instruments"; jewelry; books; crockery; "suits of superfine cloth, shirts of finest lawn, and linen pocket handkerchiefs" —all purchased in his better days. He bestowed these items upon his sons, sons-in-law, and Thomas Bunn, his closest friend and confidant, who was then chief accountant at York Factory. To the latter he also left a fine watch and chain, and "monies for a ring that he shall purchase in remembrance of me." The freehold property in the Orkneys that Sinclair had inherited on his native island of Pomona, and which endowed him with a kind of lesser nobility, he bequeathed to his brother, Thomas, with the instructions that he should care for his two unmarried sisters for the remainder of their lives.

William Sinclair had not lived to see the union of the North West and Hudson's Bay Companies, but their conflict had cost him dear. Only when the two leaders in the contest had died, three years after Sinclair's death, did the merciless feud cease. With the charming, inconsistent, indubitably brave Earl of Selkirk and the more brilliant, ruthlessly stubborn Sir Alexander Mackenzie removed from the scene, more constructive, conciliatory forces could come into play, and some measure of peace was brought to Rupert's Land. The sequence of events that had clouded William Sinclair's life with disappointment had spun itself to exhaustion; but another equally complicated web was about to be woven for Sinclair's young son, James.

PART I: THE LIFE OF JAMES SINCLAIR (1806–56)

I. A CHIEF FACTOR'S SON

I

Despite his father's misfortunes, Oxford House in Rupert's Land proved an excellent training ground for the adventurous free trader and explorer James Sinclair was to become. As an intelligent, observant lad, he early learned the skills of hunting and trapping mink, marten, fox, and beaver and how to prepare the pelts to meet the company's requirements, as well as how to press and bale the fur in the customary "pieces" of ninety pounds that had been found to be the most convenient weight and size for efficient handling at the portages. He learned to paddle the tricky birch-bark canoes on the northern rivers and lakes, and to race, portage, or meet any other exigency of the rapids near Oxford Lake. In winter he learned to run behind and drive the sled or cariole, drawn by six or eight well-trained sleigh dogs, and could soon keep up with the older men at the usual rate of thirty to forty miles a day. He was taught by the friendly Cree relations of his mother to make such useful equipment as birch-bark utensils, the bows and arrows still used by Indian boys for play, and the long, pointed snowshoes characteristic of the Wood Cree. On these he learned to travel easily over long distances, with a quick and apparently tireless tread. In short, James Sinclair was trained to become a self-confident, self-reliant frontiersman, and nothing he learned was lost on him in later life.

In addition to all this, James Sinclair was initiated into many of the tribal ways of his mother's people before he reached the age of twelve; and he learned to speak fluently her native tongue. The discipline and knowledge gained as a lad served Sinclair well in many an emergency, especially what was required for self-defense and survival, learned from experienced traders, *voyageurs*, and Indians who frequented his father's post. From them the precept was thoroughly instilled that caution should precede action, and that little should be left to chance. At a later date, he often had to depend upon such precaution when leading parties of settlers with exceptional surety and safety across the untrodden plains and mountain passes of the North American wilderness.

At an early age, Nahovway taught James the use and vagaries of the thoroughly unreliable, long-barreled, muzzle-loading trade gun in general use in those days. The badly mutilated hands of Indians and traders, with thumbs and fingers blown away by exploding guns, attested to the serious consequences that might result from carelessness or accident when handling the fractious weapons; and caution served as the best protection.

Many of James Sinclair's earliest recollections were naturally colored by the normal routine of the northern fur post, and he held many subtle memories of its peculiar atmosphere. The sounds of the normal day's work, which combined in a curious harmony, were only too familiar—the constant screech of the fur press; the clang of workmen's hammers; the rasp of whipsaws as men built sheds, crude furniture, and York boats. All of these merged with the continuous barking, whining, and snarling of hungry sleigh dogs, fighting and begging for scraps of meat and whitefish.

Occasionally at Oxford House a peculiar solo would emerge

from the ensemble, as the guttural grunts of Indians, traveling by canoe, announced their approach at the landing stage. If satisfied that the visitors were on legitimate business, James Kirkness and Josiah Cook [1]—the post's traders and brothers-in-law of young James Sinclair—would let the natives come inside the stockade to barter their furs for trade goods at the "Indian shop." Sometimes the sharp crack of a gun would rend the air. This could mean the approach of friendly strangers, the warning of someone lost in the woods, an accident, or the shot of an Indian hunter after game.

There was always the fear of fire at Oxford House—whether set by unfriendly Indians or the result of human negligence. Such ever present danger had impelled the elder Sinclair to build his stronghold on the island in the center of the lake. Bitter experience had taught him to exercise caution during his lifetime, and it was not to be lost on his son. The warnings of flood and blizzard were no less ominous and taught their own exacting lessons.

Certainly, throughout his lifetime, James Sinclair had reason to call often upon the wisdom instilled in him at an early age by his father. The elder Sinclair had exerted a strong and lasting influence upon his family in the comparatively few years allotted to him. Even after his death Nahovway carefully observed her husband's instructions for their children. While William Sinclair had permitted no show of undue intimacy to break the barrier of his Scottish reserve, he had nevertheless demanded a proper respect and admiration from his family. He had seen to it that the explicitly written instructions, issued each year from company headquarters at York Factory,[2] were strictly obeyed. The master of a company post was expected to teach his children a somewhat rigid code of ethics. He was instructed to give them some elementary education in the "three R's." Children were expected to converse in the language of the father, be taught the catechism and short bedtime prayers, and to be thoroughly inculcated with the fundamental rules of good behavior, decency, cleanliness, and moral propriety. Such virtues were firmly implanted in James Sinclair's youthful mind and were never completely forgotten throughout his life.

In addition to this, a master of a post was expected to hold simple religious services regularly for the benefit of his family and the servants under his command. He was to follow the English "Book of Common Prayer" for matins and evensong when possible. William Sinclair had tried to obey such rulings punctiliously each Sabbath, and an honest effort was made by his son to do likewise, whether at fur post or when encamped on the trail.

William Sinclair had further instilled in his son the value of hard work. Especially after his father's death, James discovered that there was no lack of essential labor for any of the Sinclair family at Oxford House, whether male or female, young or old. Everyone about the fort had to earn his keep, and James was no exception. Each person was allotted his task when old enough to bear it. For a child this meant mostly fetching and carrying, and James had often to take the added burdens of his ailing younger brother, John, who could not keep up with the others in work or play. James also had a genuine affection for his sisters. They too were kept busy with the never ending woman's work about the post. They had been taught by the native mother to sew useful garments of cloth and buckskin, to make Indian shoes or moccasins, to cook and clean from morning to night. Several of these sisters had married young. Ann, the eldest, was wedded to a man named Spencer, who had taken her to Upper Canada to live before James could remember much about her. The next younger sisters, Jane and Catherine, were wives of Kirkness and Cook,[3] traders at Oxford House. Each of these girls had their own small dwellings, which kept them occupied with the arduous duties of their households.

Of all the Sinclair family, James may well have found his carefree sister, Betsy, the most companionable. She was exceedingly kindhearted, generous, and of happy disposition. She was capable and hard-working, but somewhat too amiable and off-hand with the visiting boatmen and traders at her father's post, apparently without guile or any intent of wrong. Nevertheless, it was Betsy Sinclair's careless ways that led to her father's keen displeasure and his complete ignoring of her in his will.

In contrast to Betsy with her willful ways, the next younger sister, Phoebe, was discreet and shy. She was already betrothed to Sinclair's close friend, Thomas Bunn,[4] a widower more than twice her age. This was an agreeable arrangement to the girl's family for Bunn was a man of fine character. He had come to Rupert's Land about the same time as the elder Sinclair, and his education was somewhat better than that of most company servants of his day. Bunn had risen gradually in the company's ranks to the responsible position of chief accountant and storekeeper at York Factory; but he managed to come often to Oxford House, and the entire family was devoted to him.

There was also James's youngest sister, Mary—a pretty, chubby child of seven at the time he left for Scotland to secure his education—and a little brother, Thomas—a serious wee chap, obedient and well mannered. Of all these brothers and sisters, perhaps the one he remembered with the warmest affection was the infant Colin, born posthumously to William Sinclair and Nahovway, who was but a few months old when James last saw him. Nor was he ever privileged to see this brother again, although their paths nearly crossed in a curious way during middle age.

II

With the death of the father, the tenor of James Sinclair's life suddenly changed. As was the custom of the Hudson's Bay Company in that day, if an officer left a will, it was immediately read by the authorities at York Factory, and its terms promptly carried into effect. Therefore, in this instance, Governor Thomas Thomas, then in charge at York, sent an express canoe to bring back Sinclair's oldest son, William, from the company's post at Lesser Slave Lake,[5] in order that he might accompany his younger brothers, James and John, to school in Scotland.

Early in September, 1818, one of the annual York boat brigades, manned by Orkneymen and English half-breeds, reached Oxford House from the Saskatchewan River country, bringing with it young William Sinclair. William picked up his brothers and continued on the rest of the way to York Factory, in order that they might reach that great depot in time to catch the company's ship-of-the-year before it sailed for Britain at the end of the month.

After the sad farewells with their mother and the rest of the family, the trip downstream from Oxford Lake to York Factory was filled with excitement for the Sinclair lads. They were placed in the middle of one of the York boats, with their pathetically few personal belongings and the "pieces" of company fur piled around them. From this point of vantage they could watch the *boutés*, or endmen, serving as steersman and bowman in each craft, and the middlemen pull the great oars, toiling from daylight till dark in the swift waters of the northern river route, pulling through the shallows or dozing for a short spell in the quieter stretches, as the fur brigade progressed down the two hundred miles from Oxford House to Hudson Bay.

The routine of making camp each night proved a source of interest also, with meals consisting largely of *rouchou* or pemmican soup and strong tea, and entertainment provided by the songs and stories of the men as they lounged about the camp. There was a moment of particular excitement when about fifty miles east of Oxford House they entered the Hill River and soon reached one of the most famous portages in the north country, known as the Rock. Here a large ridge of stone in the river bed forced the stream to race through a narrow gorge, creating a dangerous rapids. All the pieces of fur and trade goods had to be carried around this on the men's backs. So intense was the activity and so occupied was every man with essential work that young James and John had to carry their own bags over the portage; when this was done they could stand aside to watch the trotting, sweating boatmen bearing the burdens of fur across.

The sight was not easy to forget; and it never lost its fascination for James Sinclair throughout the years he was compelled to come this way in the course of his later free trading. The *voyageurs* scrambled over the rocky path, worn dangerously smooth in places by the many moccasined feet that had traversed this portage since its first use by fur traders many years before, as there was no other way to cross this important region. Once the portage was completed, larger boats awaited to transport the fur the rest of the way to Hudson Bay.

At this point, there was always an appraisal of the wear and tear on human flesh. However, injuries seemed soon and easily repaired when the men were rewarded for their arduous labor with a welcome day of rest, and some rum and jollity at Rock House. This post had been established in 1813—just five years before young James first saw it—by Thomas Bunn, who now awaited the boys at York Factory.

Once the barrier of the Rock was passed, traveling downstream became easier, although the Steel River had yet to be negotiated —with its treacherous current and shoals that exacted the best skill of the brigade's steersmen to avoid grounding their crafts on hidden sandbars. As the waterway approached the Bay it widened to some three hundred yards, flowing sluggishly between low clay banks. As far as the eye could see there was nothing but a monotonous expanse of wasteland. Where the Steel and Hayes rivers joined, the tamarack, spruce, and willow thinned noticeably. The pleasant variety of scene that young James remembered at Oxford House vanished into uninteresting flatness. The Hayes River took the brigade straight to York Factory, running swift enough for fair progress until they reached Ten Shilling Creek, where the water became sluggish again in the midst of marshland, and only a scattered growth of dwarfed, distorted brush interspersed with a few scrub spruce relieved the landscape.

As the brigade approached the company's great northern depot, the boatmen labored harder than ever to reach their goal. James experienced the same excited expectancy the crew displayed, for he had heard much of this wonderful place from Thomas Bunn whenever he visited Oxford House. York Factory stood on the northern bank of the Hayes River, just six miles inland from the western shore of Hudson Bay. The river here was almost a mile wide—one bank barely discernible from the other through the almost perpetual mist that hung over the land. James's first glimpse of the place was most disappointing; it seemed as drab as Thomas Bunn, in his homesickness for England, had often painted it. Seen from a distance and against the bleak swampland that surrounded it, the fort's large white buildings within its strong stockade looked small as a toy village. But as the boats drew closer it became more impressive.

Just before they reached the quay, a place of poignant interest was pointed out to the two Sinclair lads by their older brother who had been this way before: it was the graveyard where their father had been buried near the mouth of Schooner Creek. Here the company's small fleet of boats was put up for the winter, and not far beyond was the powder magazine, which for safety was placed outside the fort's stockade.

Before the main gate of the fort a ramp ran up from the water's edge. The landing stage was a crowded scene of feverish activity when the brigade arrived. A throng of men worked with urgency and dexterity to bring in the trade goods from the ship that now lay at anchor out in the Bay, the men returning to it as quickly as possible by the little schooners with the precious bales of fur to be shipped to Britain. On each trip the small boats were laden to the gunwales to get this urgent business over as quickly as possible, so the company's ship-of-the-year could get away to sea.

As he had promised, Thomas Bunn was at hand to greet the Sinclair boys when they arrived; as an executor of their father's will, he had been advised of their coming well in advance. Bunn was indeed a remarkable man for the fur trade; his background and bearing were decidedly different from most of those with whom he worked. But he had proved himself one of the most trusted and efficient men in the service. Born at Hendon in Middlesex, England,[6] Bunn had been a "Grey Coat Boy," and had once belonged to a "Liveried Company" in London before joining the Hudson's Bay Company in 1797. After the usual apprenticeship served at York Factory, he had been sent inland at the same time as William Sinclair and William Auld to establish outposts to check the inroads of the advancing North West Company—a task for which Bunn was less well fitted than for his present services as accountant and storekeeper.

A mutual affection existed between Bunn and young James Sinclair, for the aging man appreciated the lad's innate ability, and the boy was impressed with Bunn's unusual fund of interesting tales. So it was with genuine pleasure that the accountant set about to show the lads the sights of York Factory in the limited time at his disposal, for with the ship in, this was Bunn's busiest season of the year.

As they entered the fort, Bunn pointed out the twelve-pounder cannon and four smaller brass fieldpieces, which stood impressively near the gate and for which there had been no urgent use since the French had come in 1782, although they still answered the salute of an incoming ship while she was still well beyond sight of land.

Young James saw that the factory buildings stood in orderly array about three sides of a large open square. In the center stood a tall flagstaff bearing the company's red ensign. As Bunn escorted the lads along the boardwalks, which alone made walking possible over the boggy soil, he pointed out the governor's residence, the single men's quarters, and the small dwellings for married servants and their families. Bunn was permitted to retain one of the cottages for himself although he had been widowed and his family was gone; he now led the boys to be billeted there with him during their stay at York. Some of the large buildings, such as the warehouses for the storing of fur and trade goods, were two or more stories high. All were constructed of square-adzed logs in true company style—mortized, clapboard faced, and scrupulously whitewashed.

Once at Bunn's simple dwelling, a hearty meal was ready for them, prepared from the accountant's own rations of a pound of wheaten flour and other supplies. He was granted a regular apportionment of dried peas, oatmeal, salt pork, goose, pemmican, fish, venison, caribou meat, and so forth, which he was glad to share with the lads along with the supplies of tea, sugar, and fats, which he paid for himself. It was hoped that a generous share of these provisions might warm the bleak confines of York for the boys, who Bunn well knew would be soon setting out for a world that would seem strangely remote and alien to them from the even now distant Oxford House.

While Bunn set out to make the lads' visit to York a memorable one, he also sought to enlighten young James concerning the intricacies of the fur trade from his long experience at this greatest-of-all fur depots of his day. He took pains, for instance, to explain to him that now the ship was in he and his staff of apprentice clerks must work far into the night by the light of whale-oil lamps in the company's countinghouse to clear away the past year's business before the ship could get away again to Britain. It was necessary that every item passing through the depot should be recorded—not only check lists of the incoming bundles of trade goods from the ship and outgoing bales of fur, but detailed and accurate inventories must be made, in patient, precise handscript and in several copies for the company's governor and committee in London. From such reports, the actual profit and loss of the entire fur trade in Rupert's Land was estimated and presented for the approval or disapproval of the critical company shareholders at the next annual meeting when the future policy of the organization would be framed.

As company storekeeper at York, in addition to his arduous duties as chief accountant, Bunn was in a position to show young James the workings of the interesting "Indian shop." This information was one day to stand James in good stead in his own trading. York Factory's Indian shop held a peculiarly diversified assortment of trade goods, much of which was not usually included in the ordinary stock-in-trade of smaller posts such as Oxford House. At York, the shop had the character of a "sample room," maintained for the convenience and information of visiting company officers who sought peculiarly tempting articles to stimulate trade in their respective districts. It also served as a supply base for the "Home Indians"—those Indians who, during the troubled days of the fur war, remained loyal to the Old Company—who came along the coast of Hudson Bay to trade as they had for many years.

At this Indian shop James was shown the carefully arranged shelves that lined the walls and were piled high with assorted bolts of cloth, "bath" coating, bright cotton yardage, stacks of white, dark blue, and red capotes, as well as various grades of trade blankets, ranging from the cheaper quality to the specially fine "point blankets" in different sizes, weights, and colors. In carefully separated divisions were stored quantities of steel files, skinning and hunting knives, axes, canoe awls, gun flints, fire steels, various sizes of nails and screws, balls of twine for fish nets, and other essential needs of the trader, trapper, and hunter—different weights of rope and quantities of porcelain and glass beads to induce trade with the squaws. As an added incentive to draw business, in the shops' drawers were kept a number of important small items that brought good returns, such as pins, needles, thimbles, and scissors; retaining the good will of the squaws was an important factor in holding the loyalty of the various tribes to the Old Company. There were also small containers of vermilion powder—then in great demand at good profit—used by the natives to paint faces as well as carioles, canoes, parfleches, tobacco bags, and even the warriors' horses on the plains.

On the floor of the shop, arranged around in equally tidy array, were piles of tin and copper kettles, along with iron pots, ranging in size from small mugs to vessels of gallon size. In the corners stood long-barreled trade guns, with their accompanying powder horns and bags of shot; bear and beaver traps; ice chisels; and other such items requisite to securing the maximum of fur—all of these but a few of the useful commodities displayed to advantage in York Factory's somewhat unique Indian shop, to make possible the most successful trade with the Indians from the shores of Hudson Bay to the Arctic Circle, and as far afield as the distant regions of the Oregon and New Caledonia, west of the Rocky Mountains.

Such important details of the fur trade were not lost on the unusually observant young James Sinclair, who often in later years had reason to thank Thomas Bunn for much that he patiently taught him during that visit to York Factory in August of 1818. James also learned from Bunn the important truth that York was definitely more than an indispensable depot for receiving trade goods and exporting vast quantities of fur in return. He was shown the actual workshops that made York Factory a factory in every sense of the word. Here were constructed as many articles for the trade as was practicable, to avoid the necessity of bringing them across the Atlantic in the limited space of the company's annual ship. For example, tin cups and "porringers," then in general use throughout the country for the consumption of tea and pemmican soup, were all constructed in York's tin shop from imported sheets of metal; they were made without handles so they might be conveniently packed or nested one inside the other for easier transportation over the numerous portages on their way inland.

At York Factory, also, many kinds of well-finished iron equipment—from trapping and fishing gear to door hinges and latches—were fashioned in the blacksmith's shop. Even good, sound wooden kegs were manufactured in the cooper's shop for carrying such things as spirituous liquors and the limited amounts of such luxuries as currants and raisins for which officers indented at their own expense. Some good furniture was also constructed in York's cabinetmaker's shop, such as chairs, tables, and cupboards in somewhat ludicrous conformity with prevailing British styles for gentlemen's residences at their outposts.

James had wondered when he arrived at York what the revolting smell might be that seemed to envelop the place; it was a rancid reek that added an unpleasant stench to an atmosphere already redolent with the pungent odors of smoked hides and musty fur and the subtle scent of dwarf spruce. Bunn explained that large numbers of oiled sheets and tarpaulins were prepared at York for use throughout the country for divers purposes, such as ground sheets and as protective coverings for fine furs. For such articles, large quantities of sail cloth were imported annually from Britain. It was soaked in oil distilled in huge vats from the considerable number of arctic whale caught each year in Hudson Bay by the company's schooner master and his able crew with the little fleet of ships maintained at the factory.

Of all the activities carried on at York perhaps none proved more interesting to young James than the final preparation of furs for shipment to Britain. This was something he could readily understand and seemed to bring him nearer his home in the natural moments of nostalgia experienced by a twelve-year-old lad. Here at York the constant creaking, squalling fur presses made evident the fact that tens of thousands of pelts were gone over and finished, for the long voyage to Gravesend and placement in the great London warehouses, where they were sold at the company's famous "candle auctions"—truly enormous numbers of beaver, muskrat, marten, fox, lynx, and even bear skins, brought to York Factory by the inland brigades each summer.

III

After their brief but enlightening visit with Thomas Bunn, the time arrived when James Sinclair and his brothers must depart with the company's ship-of-the-year for Britain. She rode at anchor at Five Fathom Hole, surrounded by treacherous shallows, some miles out in Hudson Bay beyond the mouth of the Hayes River. Here it was that the company's schooner master must see to the swift unloading and reloading of the ship, best utilizing every available man to accomplish a heavy task in a limited space of time, and avoid possible serious loss of life and property in the precarious business of not only handling large quantities of valuable trade goods coming in and furs going out, but transferring gunpowder from the ship to the small boats waiting to carry it to the company's magazine outside the walls of the fort.

When the ship was in, the company servants labored ceaselessly from dawn till dark, clambering over the ship with the bales of trade goods, placing them hurriedly in the little schooners drawn up alongside in order to get them back as quickly as possible to the factory. With equal urgency the schooners had to be unloaded, refilled with precious bundles of fur to be placed in the emptying hold of the ship without delay; she would have to put out to sea not later than the last week of September, if she were to escape the hazard of the thickening ice floes that had compelled the ship to turn back the year before, in 1817. The company could not afford to run such a risk again, for if the ship failed to make the voyage this year, the entire fur trade would be thrown completely out of gear on both sides of the Atlantic.

For days on end the little fleet plied back and forth over the dangerous, shifting mud banks of the Bay—the schooner master ever fearful lest a craft be swamped in the sudden squalls that could whip up in a matter of minutes. Always he prayed for a high tide and continuing fine weather, with wind in a fair quarter to hasten the work. Luck was with him the autumn of 1818, for the ship was emptied, refilled, and ready to sail before the deadline, and young James Sinclair and his brothers departed with it.

The company's ship-of-the-year, the *Prince of Wales*, was a barque-rigged vessel of some five hundred tons burden—as rugged a craft as they came in that day, but puny enough to face the gales of the North Atlantic and the ice floes of Hudson Strait and Bay. Such ships were manned by hardy crews and captained by skilled men who for over a century had sailed their ships between the Old World and the New with surprisingly little loss to the company.

The *Prince of Wales* weighed anchor in Five Fathom Hole and set sail for Britain on September 21, 1818.[7] The captain of the ship was John Davison—a strict but able master. He soon gave his young passengers to understand that there would be no nonsense aboard. They were not to go forward or mingle with the ordinary seamen, nor were they to make a nuisance of themselves in any way; it was a motley crew that manned the ship, gathered from the roustabouts of the London docks who feared neither shipwreck in the North Atlantic nor other perils. They were hardened men, among whom the Sinclair lads might easily learn mischief and rough ways, and the ship's captain was held responsible for them.

Of an inquiring mind, young James soon learned many of the ways of the sea. He was old enough to feel the tension that oppressed the ship's company when the weather was uncertain and to share the anxiety of captain and crew when it was downright bad. A strong sou'wester at the outset of the voyage swept them quickly across and out of Hudson Bay. As they approached Mansell Island, the captain had to sound the lead continuously to avoid piling on a hidden reef; the entire region was engulfed in a blanket of thick fog. Calm and storm seemed to threaten the safety of the ship by turn, with little to relieve the tension and monotony of the long voyage save the expected encounter with Eskimos near Prince of Wales Land. They brought seal-skin bladders filled with fish oil, finely wrought walrus ivory ornaments, and toggle hooks, to exchange for small saws, files, needles, pins, and scissors with which to carry on their handcrafts during the long winters in their lonely igloos.

At Upper Savage Island the ship would be about a month's full sailing time from Gravesend if all went well, and once around Cape Farewell they would be in open sea, headed on the shortest course for Land's End. When they approached this place the captain informed young James that it had been as good a voyage as one could expect, which set him wondering what a "bad" voyage might be like. When they finally reached Gravesend, at the end of November, 1818, James was convinced that the life of a sailor was not for him. He preferred the life of the fur trade and an eventual return to Rupert's Land, even against his father's dying wishes for him.

IV

James was not permitted to see much of the famous sights of London on this first visit to the great city, beyond the environs of the Hudson's Bay Company's headquarters near Bishopsgate. He and his brothers were taken at once to Fenchurch Street by a ship's officer and turned over to Alexander Lean,[8] Secretary of the Honourable Company's Committee, who sometimes served as administrator in the settlement of company officers' estates.

Sometime before his death, William Sinclair, the elder, had appointed Lean to see to the distribution of his assets among his heirs. Because they were mostly in the form of company securities they had lost considerable value during the period of the company's distress in recent years. Lean was also authorized to see that Sinclair's oldest son, William, was placed at once in useful employment at the company's London warehouses, until such time as he could embark on the next company ship for Rupert's Land and return to his work in the fur trade the following year.[9] The two younger Sinclair lads, James and the ailing John, were packed off on the first little ship bound for the Orkneys to start their schooling under the care of their uncle and aunts, and as wards of their father's friend and executor, Adam Isbister,[10] a prosperous merchant of Stromness.

John does not appear to have survived the hardships of the strenuous voyage from Rupert's Land for any length of time, for no further record of him can be found after his arrival in the Orkneys. But young James lived to receive his schooling in the village school near East-on-quay in Pomona, where he lived with his uncle Thomas and his aging maiden aunts, Ann and Mary Sinclair,[11] until he was ready to enter Edinburgh University.

Life in the Orkneys early in the nineteenth century was strikingly different from what he had known at his father's fur post at Oxford House. His uncle's drystone dwelling was of utmost simplicity—the floor rough-paved with blue flagstones; the furniture crude, consisting mostly of handmade chairs, tables, and open cupboards fashioned from the sea-wrack of driftwood.[12] Yet all was as neat and clean as possible in the Sinclair homestead, despite the clutter of tools and materials essential to sustain life in this harsh region. The one big living room was hung with nets, skeins of knitting yarn, lobster pots, and cooking vessels fastened to the smoke-blackened rafters. In the farthest corner was the store of winter's food—dried fish and sea fowl—as well as bladders of whale oil for burning in the little lamps fastened to pegs in the wall to lighten the darkness of the long winter evenings.

With all its inadequacies the Sinclair's Orkney cottage was homelike and friendly—and better than most of the ordinary crofters' dwellings in Pomona, for this was the home of a "peerie laird"—a kind of lesser nobility who inherited freehold land, thereby enjoying certain privileges. As time passed, James was to feel a peculiar fondness for the place, although he had no desire to stay in this bleak land of his forefathers for the remainder of his life.

James labored on his uncle's farmstead after school hours, and he soon learned what was expected of a lad of thirteen in the Orkneys. Tilling the poor soil to get the little it would yield was work for the strongest man. There was hard toil for everyone, indoors and out, although the Sinclair household was considered more fortunate in every way than most on the Isle. All the men —outside of the few comparatively rich merchants like Adam Isbister in Stromness, with his good shop and fine house—were half-crofter, half-fisherman. James soon found that his uncle Thomas risked his life every day in order to supply sufficient food for the family. He learned that all Orkneymen must help to share the burden of their kinfolk, and that he, too, must become "farmer with a boat," as the Orkneymen called themselves, and take the rough with the smooth and the bitter with the sweet in the normal round of existence in the Outer Isles.

It was also obvious that life at the port of Stromness was strikingly different from the simple, lonely existence of the Sinclair homestead. James was grateful that he was required to go daily to the town for his schooling. Stromness was a snug, interesting, and busy little town, with but a few fine houses like those of Adam Isbister and his associates, John Clouston and William Inkster. For the most part, the old Orkney port had simple stone dwellings and humble little businesses. The sea rippled familiarly up the shore lanes of the town between the rows of plain structures built to the water's brink. The bows of anchored ships stretched across the second-story windows of houses and shops built so close to the harbor's edge a mariner could easily step from ship to shore.

Stromness stood on the slope of a little hill overlooking a beautiful sheltering arm of the sea. The port had afforded safe refuge and fine anchorage for whaling ships and sealers since olden times, and the Hudson's Bay Company had used the port for more than a century for the departure of its ships to the New World. Each succeeding year, the company's ship bound for Rupert's Land made it the final stopping place before setting out across the Atlantic. Here it replenished its stores and enlisted hardy young Orkneymen for the fur trade. The lucrative business of chandlering had enriched a few folk like Adam Isbister, and it was here that James began thinking of prospects for a future in trade.

The shops at Stromness held all manner of tempting incongruities in their windows. Tackle for fishermen and gear for whalers mingled indiscriminately with Scottish hard "sweeties," hand-knitted stockings, bright woolen scarves and caps, reels of cotton thread, and a few glittering baubles for sailors' wives and sweethearts. There were things to tempt all manner of customers, and why should it not be the same in the New World if a man found out how to go about it?

However, it was the very oldness of everything in and around Stromness that charmed James most. It conjured up strange broodings in the boy's mind, and he particularly wondered about the queer prehistoric monuments of mysterious ancient peoples and the peculiar pinnacle of rock beyond the harbor's mouth, which was called "the Old Man of Hoy." There were also curious "barrows," and a cavern with a small stone bed that had once belonged to the "wee folk." James longed to know more about such things, but who was there to tell him? Most Orkneymen's tales were fey and full of legend; this young part-Indian boy from beyond the sea to the west had a literal mind. He wished to hear not so much the myths of the Isles as the plain facts of the matter.

School was somewhat difficult for the boy to endure after the freedom he had enjoyed at a fur post in North America, but James applied himself well, was a good scholar, and learned easily. He progressed better than might have been expected in his four years at the Stromness school, although he was not all earnestness and study. More than once he tasted the sting of the "tawse" as reward for mischief or truancy. The temptation was great for him to explore, and his wandering feet often led him to the historic, rival town of Kirkwall, without first seeking permission from his schoolmaster. There he would search for the curious tombs of his Norse ancestors, buried beneath the strange paving stones in the floor of the great St. Magnus Cathedral, for his father had planted a deep sense of family pride in him, typical of most Sinclairs.

As a son of a local burgess—through his father's inheritance of the freehold croft of East-on-quay—James was entitled to the advantages a liberal education afforded at the Stromness school. Clever lads often entered the university in Scotland in those days at the age of sixteen, and James was not far behind. He was ready to go into Edinburgh at seventeen, in the autumn of 1822.[13] The years spent there, until 1826, were difficult for him in many ways: it was a time of struggle, loneliness, frustration, and hard work. His father's reduced dividends left James little silver for anything beyond the bare necessities of books, food, and lodgings.

Nevertheless he enjoyed his course in arts, to which he added some study of law. Then too, the mellow environment of the old university had its attractions, for when James attended Edinburgh it was already nearly two hundred and forty years old from the date of its founding in 1583. He secured his books mostly by canny bargaining at quaint shops or stalls along Leith Walk. He found simple diversion in watching the colorful crowds that milled about in the older, shockingly overcrowded parts of the city. At this time Edinburgh had quite outgrown itself. The new was arrogantly overlapping the old, and appalling contrasts of poverty and wealth presented themselves everywhere. Many aspects of life witnessed during James's four years' sojourn in Edinburgh indelibly stamped his eager, imaginative mind with doubts and provocations; he saw the ancient battling the new, not only for survival but for supremacy. High Street and Cannongate were still lined by tall, uncomfortable old tenements, as unsanitary as they were unsafe. Broods of squalid, ragged children played in the gutters. Slattern women jostled grand ladies and gentlemen in their fine clothes but a stone's throw from the affluence and grandeur of Princes Street, and it was hard for a youth of James's temperament to judge the just from the unjust.

Indeed, life as James Sinclair saw it in Edinburgh taught him many things, for it seemed to manifest much that he wanted to avoid, and it determined his course of action for the future. He found that he had no desire to enter the mercantile trade in Britain as his father had wished. He was also intelligent enough to observe social contrasts and exclusions, recognizing that he had little chance to succeed in Britain, at this dawn of what appeared to be a great industrial revolution, without ample backing and some social prestige—neither of which he possessed, despite his paternal pride of birth. Under such circumstances, there was but one thing left for him to do—return as quickly as possible to the wilderness he had known as a child and try to carve out some sort of future for himself, even in the face of his father's disappointment, sickness, and defeat in the difficult New World.

2. RETURN TO RUPERT'S LAND

I

Having reached his majority in 1826, James Sinclair signed on with the Hudson's Bay Company as an apprentice in order to return to Rupert's Land. He put his name to a carefully worded contract, or indenture, that bound him to a year's service with the Old Company. The contract further required him to work his way across the Atlantic as a seaman on the company's annual ship, as was demanded of all persons who engaged for service with the company in the New World.

Sinclair took passage on the *Camden*, sailing from Stromness for Hudson Bay on June 25, 1826,[1] commanded by Benjamin Bell.[2] On September 3 of that year the ship reached its destination at Moose Factory—the point at which his father and brother had been weatherbound in 1817.[3] It was a Hudson's Bay Company fort similar to York Factory but on a less impressive scale, and was administrative headquarters for the southern department of the Old Company. Sinclair and his companions of the voyage spent four days at Moose Factory, where they were outfitted, before being set at winter work and dispatched to Albany Post.[4]

At this time, posts in this vicinity were largely provisioned from the goose hunts held each autumn at the Chicknee and Capusco camps,[5] situated on the usual migratory routes of the flocks of water fowl. Trader Corrigal, then in charge of Albany, at once sent Sinclair to the Chicknee goose tents, where he was to work until December of that year in transporting barrels of salted wild goose and other supplies back and forth by dog sled between this camp and Albany Post.

Sinclair was thus occupied in various kinds of work for Corrigal until April 28, 1827, when he was sent on his last trip to the goose tents. However, he had yet to complete the final three months of his contract, at the end of which time he was entitled to, and did, demand his release from the district officer at Moose Factory. This being granted, he was permitted to accompany a party of men setting out with a small brigade of canoes for Red River,[6] where he intended to find some means of livelihood outside the service of the company.

The expedition that Sinclair had joined was headed by Thomas Corcoran; it followed a route by the Albany and English rivers, over which Hudson's Bay Company traders had first traveled to reach the Red River. Such a trip normally required some forty-six days of travel over rough terrain of rock, forest, lakes, and rivers lying between James Bay and Lake Winnipeg. An intelligent and widely experienced trader named David Sanderson was also a member of the party. Sinclair found him congenial and heard much from him of the prospects in the Red River free trade, as well as the changes wrought generally in Rupert's Land since he had left for Britain nine years before. Sanderson also gave Sinclair a bit of the background of the country through which they traveled, and which was familiar to him from his trading. So the time passed as they were carried up the gentle Albany and made the portages at the upper reaches of the river.

Corcoran remained at Martin Falls, leaving the others to proceed past Fort Osnaburgh and over the height-of-land by way of Lake Seul to the English and Winnipeg rivers. Most of the party stayed here, leaving Sinclair and Sanderson to continue the rest of the trip alone by light canoe.[7] Nicol Finlayson, who was then master at Osnaburgh, on August 19, 1827, issued them with seven days' European provisions to see them on their way.

Sinclair was grateful to Sanderson for his skill and experience. He knew the route well and could cope expertly with the numerous whirlpools and rapids they were required to run in their light canoe. As the Winnipeg river broadened toward Traverse Bay, Sanderson pointed out the sites of some old fur posts—La Vérendrye's Maurepas, the Nor'Westers' Otter Point, and Bas de la Rivière, the latter standing some forty rods from the Hudson's Bay Company provisioning base at Fort Alexander. Here Sanderson's friend, Roderick Mackenzie, Jr., made them heartily welcome. Sinclair and Sanderson spent a night at this post before setting out again with their canoe to cross the southern lobe of Lake Winnipeg. Fortunately, it was a fair August day, with little risk of one of the storms that could lash the shallow waters of this great and treacherous inland sea into a fury that easily swamped any light craft. They had now to reach the marshy delta of the Red River, and after some brisk paddling across the open water of the lake, they reached the six deceptive openings of the Red's estuary, hidden in the confusing labyrinth of sand banks and reeds. Sanderson seemed to choose the correct middle channel easily enough to reach the main stream of the Red. They would continue up the Red River some forty miles to their destination at the junction of the Red and the Assiniboine rivers, where thirteen years earlier Lord Selkirk had placed his settlement, and where, since the union of the Hudson's Bay Company and North West Company, a number of retired company officers and servants had come to swell the numbers of Selkirk's people.

It did not take too long for Sinclair and Sanderson to reach the rapids of the Red—Old Pelican Ripple, Sanderson called them, but known more recently as the Grand Rapids. A group of buildings had sprung up around the Anglican church here, built but three years before by the bluff, good-natured William Cockran, as good a farmer as he was a cleric.

Sinclair was interested in all Sanderson had to tell him of the country and the growing Red River Settlement, for he had learned prior to leaving the Orkneys that his mother and sister Mary had moved there with his young brother Thomas the year before. He had also learned that five years before, his old friend Thomas Bunn had moved to Red River on a good pension, and had been given a large grant of land to which he had brought Sinclair's sister Phoebe as his wife.

Sinclair had felt deep concern for the well-being of his family and friends in Red River, since a great flood had all but destroyed the settlement in the previous year, but fortunately with little loss of life. Sinclair had heard the details of this from traders at Moose Factory who had seen for themselves the ravages of the flood. Apparently it had been little less than a miracle that anything had been saved from the disaster; but Sanderson had assured Sinclair that the settlement had recovered remarkably in little more than twelve months. Only the Swiss and De Meuron soldier-settlers had given up and left. The remainder, regardless of race and creed, had worked together feverishly, aided by the Old Company and the clergy, to save life and property and to reconstruct their homes and lives as quickly as possible. So successful was the effort, that a recent census of Red River disclosed that now some one thousand settlers were scattered along the Red, from the rapids to the forks and south toward Pembina some seventy miles away. The census did not include numerous half-breeds living throughout Assiniboia.

As Sinclair and Sanderson continued up the river, they saw on the west bank men rebuilding houses and constructing new ones beside fields of ripening grain. They passed the Scottish settlement of Kildonan; and, as they neared Fort Garry, Sanderson pointed out a large stone windmill belonging to the prosperous miller, Robert Logan, and the fine house of Andrew McDermot, the Red River merchant and free trader, with the new dwelling of Alexander Ross, the Red River schoolmaster, close by.

On their way upstream Sinclair had glimpsed the broad expanse of plains beyond the fringe of trees along the west bank of the Red, realizing that these actually reached as far as the foot of the Rocky Mountains thousands of miles away. There were, Sanderson said, little so-called bluffs of aspen poplar scattered here and there across the plains, but mostly it was one wide expanse of grasslands. However, in the vicinity of Red River, the little aspen groves provided ideal spots for the secretion of packs of contraband fur by those engaged in the illicit free trade, since vigilant company men could not search all likely hiding places in the bluffs or in the groves along the river banks. This was a bit of information Sinclair was to find useful some time later.

They at last reached Fort Garry at the forks of the Red and Assiniboine rivers, where their ways would part for the time being. They beached their canoe at the company's boat landing just two hundred yards above the junction of the rivers. Then they began the ascent to the fort by a path that led up from the river's edge. At the top of the bank Sinclair stopped to survey the scene and saw that the recent flood had done much damage that was still unrepaired. Indeed, from all Sanderson had said, an entirely new establishment was sorely needed to cope with the company's business that had come to Fort Garry since Governor George Simpson had given it the importance formerly enjoyed by York Factory as company headquarters for Rupert's Land.

With astonishment Sinclair noted that at this time Fort Garry's only apparent defenses against possible attack by hostile Sioux Indians were a few cannon and several large, well-placed bastions with numerous loopholes for musket fire to the fort's approaches. A portion of what must have once been a massive log palisade had been washed away by the flood and had not yet been replaced, evidently through the greater urgency to construct settlers' dwellings.

Ranging three sides of the fort's large square were several

whitewashed administrative buildings, warehouses, trade shops, and quarters for officers and men, constructed in the style Sinclair remembered having seen at York Factory. The governor's residence faced impressively across the open square toward the main gate, which opened to the road leading north through the settlement on the west side of the Red River for some miles.

When Sinclair passed through the fort it seemed busy with Salteaux Indians, half-breeds, and settlers going about their business at the various company shops and offices. He obtained directions to his mother's house at Seven Oaks [8] from a trader in one of the shops where goods were supplied to retired company people. Following these instructions he walked across the fort's square toward the main gate, then struck across the open space to the company's reserve with its few scattered Indian tepees. Immediately beyond this he passed Andrew McDermot's residence, which Sanderson had pointed out from the river, with some dilapidated trade sheds near by that served to do the Irishman's lucrative business.

Sinclair hesitated beside the large windmill beyond, noticing how solidly it was built; it had withstood the onslaught of the recent flood, serving as a place of refuge for some settlers, and had come through comparatively unscathed. It presented an astonishing sight, with its huge whirling sails reminiscent of Holland or Spain, and somehow completely incongruous here on the fringe of the North American wilderness.

As he strode along the road leading north from Fort Garry, no carts seemed to be traveling his direction to give him a lift. Everywhere he looked as he passed he saw people busily at work in the fields. They toiled steadily without allowing their attention to be diverted. Whites, half-breeds, and Indians; men, women, and children—all labored together with scythes, sickles, and wooden rakes as if their very lives depended on it. And no doubt they did, for surely, so soon after the devastating flood and the poor buffalo hunt, nothing in all Red River could be more precious than this year's yield of grain. In this land grain must be garnered in early if it were to escape the first frost. Sinclair also noted that other folk were bringing in crops of good vegetables, and he recalled how his father had secured seeds for his first garden at Oxford House.

Some cattle and a few sheep were to be seen now in Red River, either in their little "parks" with protective slab fences or farther out on the plain tended by boys and dogs. Some of the cattle, Sinclair realized, were likely descended from those his father had given the Selkirk folk when they passed through Oxford House fourteen years before, but Sanderson had also said that recently two smart American traders, Alexis Bailey and Hercules Dousman, had been bringing in stock at great profit to themselves, from the American outpost of Prairie du Chien to the south of Red River.

Sinclair also noticed how the women and girls toiling in the fields were clad—their garb not unlike the clothes of the women in the Orkneys—with their simple, tight-bodiced frocks made from heavy dark cloth, the full skirts reaching to their feet, their shoulders draped with somber shawls; and most with dark kerchiefs tied over their heads. He concluded from their drab appearance that here was an opportunity for an enterprising trader if he encouraged these people to procure brighter garb—that is, if the smart Irishman, McDermot, had not already struck upon the idea. Sinclair knew the natural tendency of human beings to buy "finery" when they could afford it, and the women of Red River should prove no exception. Before long, they would be demanding bright ribbons, laces, and kerchiefs of dainty lawn, once there was sufficient prosperity in the land to permit them to barter for such luxuries. He also knew such trade would not be allowed through the ordinary channels of business as conducted by the Old Company through its stores within the fort.

Considering the matter all round, Sinclair could see there were many things the people of Red River would soon wish to purchase, which would make their lives more pleasant and comfortable and which would surely yield good profit to a canny trader. The clever Irishman, McDermot, had evidently discovered this, but surely in such a vast land there was room for others in private trade, and Sinclair meant to look into it for himself as soon as opportunity offered.

It did not prove too difficult for Sinclair to find the little house where his mother, Nahovway, lived. It was a poor enough place, built hastily since the flood. The aging woman was living with her daughter, Mary, now grown to pretty young womanhood. Mary was betrothed to the son of the highly respected, well-to-do Inkster family who lived close by, and Sinclair was relieved to learn that his sister would soon know greater comfort. His young brother, Thomas, was away with one of Andrew McDermot's York boat brigades, bringing back the Irishman's trade goods that arrived on the latest company's ship-of-the-year at York Factory. But word of Sinclair's youngest brother brought misgivings. The child had been spirited away on the ship that had set sail the previous autumn from York Factory. Only after the ship had left was Nahovway told that little Colin was being sent to London to be educated in accordance with the terms of the late William Sinclair's will, as James and John had been.[9] Sinclair only hoped that this were true.

Recognizing the fact that his mother and sister had suffered much hardship since the father's death, Sinclair also questioned them concerning the whereabouts of the sister Betsy, forgotten in their father's will. They seemed reluctant to speak of her, and all he could learn from them was that Betsy was married to a company officer named "Miles," and was living at York Factory. He determined to learn more concerning her at the earliest possible moment from his old friend Thomas Bunn, whom he discovered was living not far from his mother's house.

Most obvious to Sinclair on this first meeting with his family in Red River was that he must seek employment at once to make the lot of his mother more tolerable; his best prospect seemed to be to find employment with Andrew McDermot in the free trade.

II

The day after his arrival in Red River Sinclair sought his old friend Thomas Bunn. He discovered he had grown quite old, but was still the same genial, capable self he had known as a lad. The old accountant was unrestrained in his delight at finding James returned from Britain a fine-looking youth, well mannered and possessing a good university education. He was only too glad to enlighten Sinclair where he could concerning the ways of the country and what might be expected of him in the free trade. He was even prepared to introduce him to those who might be able to assist him, particularly Andrew McDermot and Chief Factor James Curtis Bird—the eccentric, but influential and affluent leader of the retired company colony.

Most doors in Red River were opened to Thomas Bunn, for he was highly respected for his integrity and had been given ample reward for his long and able service with the company. Retiring to Red River in 1822, he had been given a good pension and granted one hundred pounds a year for seven years, besides being allowed to hold as much land as he could effectually cultivate.[10]

With a singularly alert mind trained in logical perception and reasoning from his studies at Edinburgh, and with a good general knowledge of history relative to the New and the Old Worlds, Sinclair listened attentively to what Bunn had to tell him, especially regarding what would be expected of him in the free trade now that his indenture with the Hudson's Bay Company had expired. Bunn informed him that the free trade in Red River was not all it appeared to be, particularly in relation to the Hudson's Bay Company. Much of this had come about since Governor George Simpson's rise in power and the drastic changes wrought in company policy in recent years.

Since the Old Company and the Nor'Westers had resolved their differences by union in 1821, the revitalized "new" Hudson's Bay Company had not only retained the old name but many of the methods and a large part of the personnel of its former rival. To these considerations had been added an exclusive "license to trade" in Rupert's Land and the Northwest, granted to the Hudson's Bay Company by the British crown. Since the appointment of Simpson as governor, great improvements had been wrought, especially when in 1825 he had been placed in authority over the company's southern department and the vast region west of the Rocky Mountains in the Oregon and New Caledonia, in addition to his duties as head of the company's northern department.

At the time of the company's union but six years before, Simpson had been comparatively unknown in the North American fur trade, and there had been much jealousy in the company's ranks when he had been elevated to the position of governor. Bunn pointed out to Sinclair that should an opportunity come for him to meet the Governor some time when he was in residence at Fort Garry, where he usually came during the summer on regular tours of inspection, he would find him a hard man to impress. Simpson must be handled with the utmost discretion, tact, and formality; he was an unpredictable and arrogant man, and his initial dislike—even if entirely unwarranted or unwittingly incurred—could prove damning to a man's future in Rupert's Land, for his finger was on everything.

In all fairness to Simpson, Bunn revealed to Sinclair that he had tried to deal justly in most matters throughout Red River, and he appeared to govern wisely. His best efforts, however, were often little appreciated, except by some of the company's officers of the old school, still loyal to the organization they had once served. There was also much ill-feeling, for some officers of higher rank, along with certain other privileged citizens in the settlement like Andrew McDermot, had received much larger apportionments of land than had some others. Nevertheless, by and large the division was based on the estimated ability of an individual to cultivate the land allotted to him and in recognition of his former services to the company. It was said that Governor Simpson and the company's executive were fairly well pleased at the way in which their retired servants were settling down as farmers, and their officers—like James Curtis Bird—as "squires" on the land along the Red River, although they were less pleased with the problems wandering *Métis* were posing—many of whom were hostile and resentful toward Simpson.

It was the natives who caused Simpson the greatest difficulty. Unfortunately, he had let it be known in certain quarters that he had not too much love for the half-breeds. He realized that their growing numbers presented grave problems for the future. There were dissenting elements and troublemakers among them, who threatened insurrection and challenged openly the Hudson's Bay Company's title to the soil of Rupert's Land and its exclusive right to deal in furs. They considered themselves to be privileged native sons, not subject to restraint by the company or even by the British crown. These sentiments were traceable to their long association with the Nor'Westers, and the natives felt that their old "bourgeois"—partners or proprietors in charge of North West Company forts or districts—had not been done justice. They particularly resented Simpson's rule over them and impudently called him "the little emperor," defying his restrictions at every turn, particularly in the free trade in fur.

As a matter of fact, however, while Governor Simpson may not have liked, or may even have distrusted the *Métis*, he did what he could for them apart from restricting their participation in the free trade in fur. Employment was provided the half-breeds at good returns for manning the company's York boats and canoe brigades to carry goods and fur on the northern waterways. Their liberty to hunt the buffalo on the plains was unrestricted, and most of the produce of their hunts was purchased by the company. Indeed, they were almost entirely unrestrained so long as they brought their furs and spoil of the buffalo hunt for trade with the company at Fort Garry, or to Andrew McDermot's shops, and did not seek illicit traffic in furs with the Americans south of the line.

Since the flood of 1826, Simpson had continued in residence at Fort Garry for most of the winter to remain in close consultation with Governor Donald McKenzie, so that they might deal as effectively as possible with the problems that had arisen during this critical period. They had striven to formulate practical plans for the country's future, as well as to deal sensibly with problems closer at hand, despite the criticism leveled against them for measures taken—particularly proclamations issued against the illicit free trade.

Chief Factor Donald McKenzie was the officer now in charge of the company's business at Fort Garry. He also served as governor of Assiniboia and administered the affairs of the Selkirk Settlement generally. McKenzie was known to be an amiable, tolerant man of wide experience—a former Nor'Wester who had been employed at the beginning of the century by John Jacob Astor in the Oregon adventure and was blamed by the Americans for the taking of Astoria by the British. Here in Red River, Donald McKenzie was empowered to use his own judgment in much of the administration, subject, of course, to Simpson's final decisions. It would be necessary for Sinclair to win McKenzie's favor, for he was known not to be too ardently opposed to *controlled* free trade, and was on particularly friendly terms with Andrew McDermot and, especially, Alexander Ross, for he had known him in the Oregon in earlier days.

Simpson's present task was to increase efficiency, cut costs, and make profits for the Old Company. Above all, he must maintain its monopoly of the fur trade against any illicit traffic in that preserve, whether within or without the Hudson's Bay Company's territories. There were, however, a number of ways to accomplish this, and some free traders were now in fact tolerated by the company itself as a deterrent to other, less desirable elements. Under the Hudson's Bay Company's monopoly, therefore, there was actually a considerable free trade in Rupert's Land—both *illegal* free trade and a free trade countenanced by the Old Company as a check on the former and to the benefit of British control of the vast Northwest of America.

It was known, for instance, by those well informed, that Andrew McDermot was enriching himself under a "special protective license to trade," [11] which he had secured directly from Governor Simpson. He was protected, also, by the good will of Chief Factor Donald McKenzie, under whose immediate authority he carried on his private business in his own shops close by the main gate of Fort Garry.

McDermot had set up his own effective, if not very impressive, shops at the forks of the Red and Assiniboine rivers immediately after he had relinquished his position with the Hudson's Bay Company as a clerk in 1824. His shops, in the very heart of the Red River Settlement, were most conveniently placed close to his residence near the company's wide reserve at Fort Garry, where he could easily meet visiting Indians and halfbreeds in their camps. The Hudson's Bay Company had considered it desirable to have shops of the kind run by McDermot in Red River to supply the settlers' demands for a number of articles that it was not usually possible for the company to fill at its regular, utilitarian shops within the fort. It was, therefore, considered by the company an advantage in the long run to have private persons, such as McDermot, undertake a "petty trade" on their own account. They were permitted to purchase assortments of trade goods at wholesale prices in London on private charge to them for the purpose of retailing the merchandise to the settlers—such goods being brought into the company through York Factory on the company's annual ships. For this business McDermot and those others so preferred by the company were allowed to purchase their goods at an advance of 33⅓ per cent on the current London prices. As a private merchant, McDermot had to provide his own means of transportation from York Factory to Red River and satisfy the company that he was a man of responsibility prepared to make satisfactory payment with "good bills upon London." [12] McDermot had filled these requirements; and when Sinclair reached Red River the Irishman was prospering, his shops were running satisfactorily, and he had acquired his own brigade of York boats to carry his goods from York Factory to the Red River Settlement to be retailed in his shops.

In point of fact, when Sinclair reached Red River there was no problem about trade in ordinary goods outside the regular company shops, the colonists possessing the right to purchase necessities from such men as McDermot if they so desired. The problem was one of the company in its position of authority and monopoly in Rupert's Land being able to control the trading of such goods or liquor for furs, which were solely and legally theirs throughout Rupert's Land.

Other problems of great seriousness confronted the Red River Settlement when Sinclair arrived in 1827. The Red River people had begun to produce grain and cattle beyond their immediate needs, and they would have been even further advanced in this direction but for the setback to their industry by the flood of 1826. Andrew McDermot had been fully conscious of the real difficulties that the disposal of this surplus produce would impose upon the settlers. Unlike certain officers at the company's trade store within the fort, the canny Irishman turned no man, woman, or child away from his shops if they wished to trade and had something to trade. He took farm produce as freely as the pemmican of the buffalo hunt, and gave his patrons greater variety in exchange for their commodities than the company could afford to give them. The people, therefore, had come to look upon McDermot as their friend and a man who understood their particular problems and who would never see them want. He was a good general merchant who gave fair equivalent for goods exchanged, offering articles that the company refused to bring in as additions to their regular staples. In view of this, business was coming increasingly to McDermot's door.

The Irishman, however, was not merely a "petty trader" supplying colonists. He had been given his special license to engage in the fur trade in 1824 in order that he might be able to compete with an American trader at Pembina. This McDermot did so successfully that the American withdrew after one season's trading. McDermot, nonetheless, continued the free trade in furs to his own profit and to the benefit of the company, for he kept the half-breeds from turning to the American traders on the headwaters of the Mississippi and Minnesota rivers, or even further afield on the Missouri. The company, therefore, could afford to tolerate him, for McDermot was able to buy at prices in goods that still made it possible for him to resell to the company at a profit. Thus, the furs ultimately came to the company; the half-breeds were kept quiet; and the Americans deterred from coming up to the border. But only a shrewd dealer like McDermot could play such an astute and complicated role.

This, then, was the somewhat remarkable character with whom Sinclair was to seek employment in the free trade. McDermot, it was said, was becoming the richest man in the country—even richer than Chief Factor James Curtis Bird, with whom there was rivalry for social prominence in the settlement. Actually, McDermot had become first both in popularity and in enterprise in a surprisingly few years. As his means increased, his inspiring genius expanded. He was talking of becoming a general freighter, with his brigade of York boats and a line of Red River carts. He was coming to be the company's right-hand man in the framing of contracts and a number of undertakings. He talked of speculating in houses and lands, of building mills, and encouraging local manufacture. The man had unusual vision. He was also possessed of peculiar personal charm, as well as a somewhat erratic and roguish temperament, which seemed to draw all and sundry to him. Such was the man for whom Sinclair was prepared to work.

As to Sinclair's own family, Thomas Bunn had some shocking revelations to make, especially concerning Sinclair's sister Betsy. Betsy had borne a child to Governor George Simpson [13] in the summer of 1820—the same summer that Margaret Taylor,[14] the daughter of the company's schooner master at York Factory, had borne Simpson another child. However, Bunn assured Sinclair that Betsy was not badly off. Simpson had seen to her marriage to the chief accountant at York Factory, who had replaced Bunn himself there, after the union of the Hudson's Bay Company and the North West Company in 1821.

Betsy's husband was Robert Seaborn Miles, who had been in

the Athabaska with Simpson and was under some sort of obligation to him to do what he was told. Miles was an educated Englishman from Oxfordshire. He was able at his accounting, if somewhat eccentric. He was clever enough to realize that his advancement meant accepting Simpson's terms—one of which had been that Miles bring up Simpson's daughter to Betsy as his own. Odd as was this arrangement, Betsy seemed happy enough with Miles, was bearing him a child a year, and was provided with a good home within the fort at York Factory.

Although this unhappy affair between Simpson and his sister was difficult for Sinclair to accept, he was nevertheless sophisticated enough to realize that such complications were not unusual in Rupert's Land. It was also obvious to Sinclair that although he might feel resentment toward Simpson for the treatment of his sister, he was master of the country, and this fact must never be forgotten. To incur his displeasure could mean ruin to a man's career. Whatever his personal feelings might be about Simpson, his power had become almost limitless over the Hudson's Bay Company's vast North American possessions, reaching from Hudson Bay to the mouth of the Columbia River, and from the American border to the Arctic Ocean. And although there were many in Red River who disliked Simpson heartily, he had to be accepted for the larger good of the land.

The truth of the matter was that Simpson, since his first visit of inspection to Fort Garry in 1822, had inaugurated many valuable reforms for the general welfare of the colony as well as for the protection of company interests. After the recent flood of 1826 and other vagaries of fortune such as a pioneer settlement must inevitably face, it was unlikely the colony could have reached its state of growing prosperity by 1827 had it not been for Simpson's personal direction. He strove continually to pacify and unify the dissenting elements in Red River, and he honestly wished to bring lasting concord and good government to the land.

There were much greater issues at stake in Red River than the petty, illicit trafficking in fur among the half-breeds. The

Métis quite naturally felt indignation at some of Simpson's more pointed edicts. They believed that these infringed upon their native liberties as "children of the new nation," and their indignation could lead to serious trouble were it not cautiously handled. Therefore, it was the long view that counted, no matter what a personal opinion of Simpson might be, nor how personal the cause for resentment. It was from this standpoint that Sinclair must consider matters for the sake of his own future; and it was on this basis that Thomas Bunn was prepared to introduce him to Andrew McDermot at once in order that Sinclair might find a livelihood for himself and help support his family as a petty trader in Red River. Later, Bunn would introduce him to other prominent men in the settlement, such as Alexander Ross and Chief Factor Bird—not to mention Governor Simpson himself, who would hasten his advancement toward success.

3. SINCLAIR THE FREE TRADER

I

James Sinclair was introduced to the wealthy, eccentric Andrew McDermot by Thomas Bunn, as the son of their mutual friend, the late Chief Factor William Sinclair; and the merits of James's education and native ability were not disregarded in the introduction. McDermot accepted Sinclair as an assistant in his business, and in his warmhearted Irish way considered it an opportunity to repay some of his indebtedness to the elder Sinclair, who started him upon his own career with the propitious present of the chest of tea that day at Oxford House in 1813.

From the moment of their introduction, Sinclair found McDermot to be a most unusual and impressive character, distinguished by his confident bearing, as well as his shock of flaming red hair, beginning to lose the astonishing brilliance of his youth and now worn to his shoulders in the fashion favored by the not less impressive Dr. John McLoughlin of Fort Vancouver. McDermot's shrewd, penetrating blue eyes were set wide apart under shaggy red eyebrows. And while his features radiated joviality, there was a firmness to his face, evident in a very square jaw, wide mouth, large beaklike nose, and high, broad forehead—some of these characteristics evincing the regal ancestry he claimed in relation to the mighty Elochaid Mignedoin, the Irish chieftain who had died at Tara in A.D. 365.[1] McDermot did not affect the rough garb of a frontier trader, as might have been expected, but the clothes that Sinclair's own father had favored as a chief factor—low-cut waistcoat, a shirt of fine lawn with pleated bosom, and frock coat, of the best black broadcloth, with wide lapels.

An agreement that Sinclair should work for him was soon made in McDermot's curious trade shop—a series of poor-looking sheds,[2] whose contents were disclosed only by the light of an open door, with lanterns used at night and on dull days to reveal and facilitate the sale of the contents. There were no serving counters in the sheds that served as shop, but only rough trestle boards. There were no shelves, and everything was left in a shocking state of disorder, in striking contrast to the neatness of the company's Indian shops. A strong odor of tanned hides filled the confined space. A pair of rusted "balances" served in place of scales. There was a pile of buffalo parchments on the floor and another of dressed buffalo hides. Stacks of moose hides and mounds of "Indian shoes" were scattered among boxes of tea, tobacco, and bunches of assorted beads, and bright cotton handkerchiefs were heaped on crude wooden trays. There were unopened kegs marked "flour," and a number of bales of brownish stuff varying in length and thickness, but about three feet long, five to ten inches wide, and a quarter to a half an inch thick, which Sinclair recognized as dried buffalo meat, prepared by the Indians on the plains for trade. Such were to be Sinclair's stock in trade in the free trade he was about to undertake for McDermot.

Sinclair was impressed by McDermot's house when he was invited there by the Irishman to seal their agreement over a glass of wine. He saw that it was furnished with good English pieces such as might have befitted a gentleman's house in the Old Land,

and the sight of it aroused the thought that if he should prove as lucky as the Irishman in this business of Red River trading, he might one day hope to own a similar establishment.

McDermot did not hesitate to inform Sinclair that for the time being he was to go about his business in the settlement as if he were strictly about his own affairs, without revealing the fact that he was in any way connected with McDermot. Sinclair would draw his company rations [3] along with his mother and sister at Fort Garry as a legal beneficiary of his late father. He would continue to live at his mother's house when in the settlement and farm her little allotment of land. He would be required to be away from the settlement for long periods of time, carrying on trade at the *Métis* camps, and if by chance he should secure any fur—McDermot had a special arrangement for the return of pelts to the company—he must try to avoid detection and search by company men authorized to arrest anyone found bearing illegal pelts.

All in all, Sinclair must try to make friends with all and sundry in the settlement as well as among the Indians and half-breeds outside it, and he must try to discover prospects of trade wherever they might be found. He would thus get to know the important *Métis* hunters as well as the agents of any American traders who might venture so far north. In due time he would be introduced to Governor George Simpson when he was in Red River on an official visit, who might have special assignments for him. In the meantime he would meet Governor Donald McKenzie, in charge at Fort Garry, who understood the various aspects of the free trade, who cooperated with McDermot, and who was likely to issue Sinclair himself a protective special license to trade once he had proved worthy to receive it. So it was arranged between Sinclair and the Irish merchant.

That same day Sinclair was introduced to another remarkable Red River character—McDermot's neighbor and friend, Alexander Ross. Sinclair liked this Scotsman well upon their first meeting. Ross was introduced as one of Red River's outstanding citizens, who was both adventurer and schoolmaster. He was told that Ross had gone to the distant and dangerous Columbia River country with John Jacob Astor's party in 1811, and had built the first Fort Okanagan. At the time of the famous "deal" between the Pacific Fur Company and the Nor'Westers in 1812, Ross had been in charge there and had stayed with the North West Company until the time of its union with the Hudson's Bay Company in 1821. He had also helped Donald McKenzie in establishing Fort Nez Percés—later known as Fort Walla Walla. When McKenzie took the first of the great Snake River expeditions into the Oregon mountains in an effort to thwart the westward movement of the American traders, Ross had remained in charge of Walla Walla for three years, until he succeeded McKenzie as leader of the Snake River parties. In 1824, Governor Simpson had "withdrawn" Ross to Red River from the Oregon on the pretext of making him the local schoolmaster. In fact it had actually been a banishment "east of the mountains," as a condemnation for a misadventure in which Ross had been involved through no fault of his. It did not take Sinclair long to realize that Ross was a knowledgeable, kindly man whom he could trust and who could teach him much he needed to know of the free trade and Red River generally. But he did not guess at the time that Ross would become the closest friend and confidant of his life.

II

It may be supposed that Sinclair made his first real venture in the Red River "petty trade" in the autumn and winter of 1827. It is likely he was supplied with sufficient money by McDermot to bargain advantageously with the *Métis* for pelts that would otherwise have fallen into American hands, and which, through this peculiar arrangement with the Irishman, ultimately found their way back to the Hudson's Bay Company where they legitimately belonged. When Sinclair began these efforts behind the scenes on behalf of Governor Simpson and the Hudson's Bay Company through McDermot, it would seem that any illicit trading in furs being carried on between Red River people and the American traders was still slight. Nevertheless, it was a growing possibility, even if it did not reach dangerous proportions until Norman Kittson, the astute American Fur Company trader, appeared at Pembina in 1844.

In point of fact, the situation was such that when Sinclair began his trading in 1827 the Hudson's Bay Company, although alert to the danger that an abused traffic in illicit furs might ultimately present, was yet not too concerned so long as aggressive American traders were kept out of the valuable Rainy River, Upper Red, and Souris River countries. This was accomplished between 1828 and 1844 with comparative success, and any really serious threat to the company's monopoly of the fur trade in the Red River sphere was prevented during that time. With this state of affairs—particularly the fact that the Hudson's Bay Company had created a sort of vacuum in the fur trade from the Rainy River to the Souris—the American Fur Company was partially content for the time being. However, the time was to come when this situation would be drastically changed, and Sinclair was to find himself embroiled in a peculiar set of circumstances over which he had little control, when the rivalry between the American and Hudson's Bay Company to obtain the half-breed furs became intense.

At the outset of his trading, Sinclair must have been supplied with enough American dollars by McDermot to purchase such tempting articles to advance the Irishman's trade as could not be imported on the company's ships from Britain and must be secured from the Americans to the south of Red River. As time passed and the settlers prospered, there was naturally an increasing demand for luxury goods, although it would appear that no great quantity of American goods found its way to Red River before 1844. On that year an uproar was raised in regard to the danger such traffic presented to the company's monopoly of trade. However, there can be little doubt that from the year 1827 to 1844 Sinclair did a little lucrative smuggling for McDermot to satisfy the growing demand of Red River women for such folderols as buttons, bonnets, ribbons, and laces, which

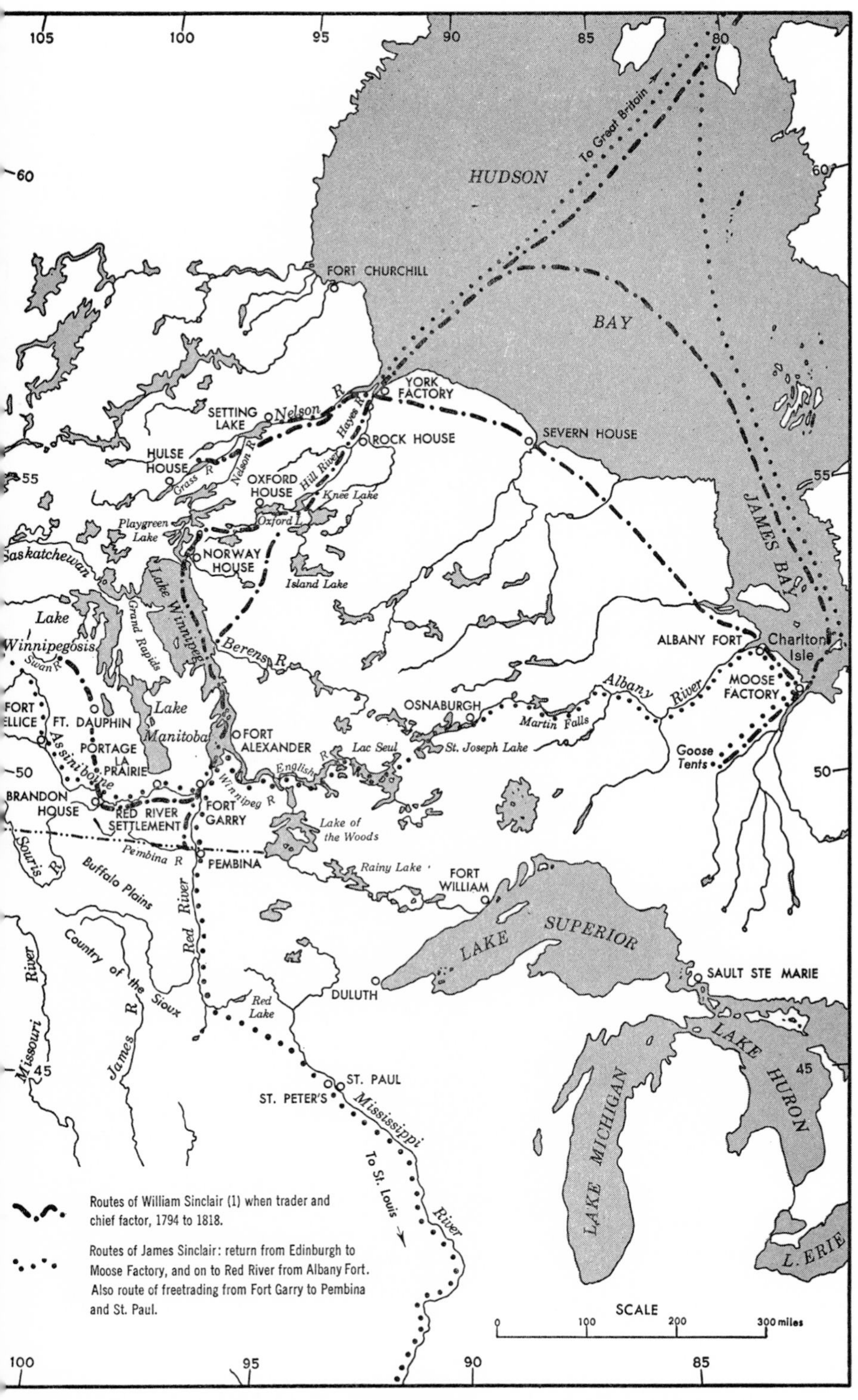

Map 1. Trading routes of William Sinclair and James Sinclair

were naturally not forthcoming from the company's regular stock in trade at Fort Garry.

The pursuance of this undercover work for McDermot and Simpson, along with his later effort on behalf of his half-breed friends, was ultimately to lead Sinclair far afield and into curious adventures—the extent of which he could have little guessed at the beginning of his career in Red River. From the outset he seems to have traveled widely with parties of trusted *Métis*, who ranged the country ceaselessly, and he often went south of the border to visit friends and relations settled about the American posts. His traveling with the *Métis* provided some measure of protection through the increasingly dangerous country of the truculent Sioux in the region to the south of the forks of the Red and Assiniboine rivers. It is, therefore, possible that at a comparatively early date Sinclair may have ventured as far as St. Peter's and Prairie du Chien, and even on to St. Louis, for his curiosity was always insatiable, and distance seems to have held little meaning for him. One thing is certain: as the years went by, Sinclair came to know the country well; and through his many dealings with them, he came to know and sympathize with the half-breeds, championing their cause—his bond with these people strengthened by his own native blood.

In addition to all this, from his frequent conversations with his new friend, the Red River schoolmaster, ex-trader, and historian, Alexander Ross, Sinclair had been provided with a useful background concerning the status and difficulties of the Red River half-breeds. For instance, it was made known to him that Governor Simpson was conscious of the *Métis* numbers and the problem their uneasiness posed as an increasing danger to the peace and profits of the Hudson's Bay Company. He was also informed as to the power of the *Métis*' colorful leader, Cuthbert Grant. Simpson, for his own reasons, had recently appointed Grant "Warden of the Plains"—an office that placed him in the position of local magistrate and justice of the peace for his people, whom he ruled like a native lord at his "seigneury" near White Horse Plain.

Grant, Sinclair discovered, was still held responsible by some of the Selkirk people for the part he was assumed to have taken in the unhappy "Seven Oaks Massacre" some years before. Nevertheless, upon acquaintance, Sinclair found Grant to be a man of superior intelligence and culture, possessing a good Edinburgh education like his own, with some knowledge of medicine, which he shared generously with those in need of it. Grant had a proud manner—said to have come from a father of some breeding. But there was also said to be some mystery concerning the anonymity of his native mother, about whom legends had grown throughout the country. Certainly he possessed a peculiarly magnetic personality and much native ability, which placed him securely in a position of influence among his fellows. Besides all this, Sinclair learned that the Hudson's Bay Company had come to depend upon Grant and his followers for the supplies of pemmican needed for their outposts and brigades, as well as to sustain the settlement itself in large measure. Above and beyond this, Grant's well-disciplined bands of half-breeds now afforded the settlement its only real defense against the possibility of attack by the Sioux, increasingly on the warpath south of Fort Garry. Serious as the loss might one day be to the Hudson's Bay Company through their illicit trade in furs with the Americans, many of the *Métis*' unruly ways had to be overlooked in the larger view of the real advantage these people afforded the company and settlement in the way of protection and food. However, the uncertainty of the temper and actions of the Red River half-breeds was beginning to pose a very real danger to the company's property and profits, even before Sinclair became a force among them.

It early became apparent to Sinclair that Cuthbert Grant's power over the uneasy half-breed majority lay much deeper than any mere accident of his native birth, although in recent years he had come to epitomize in himself many of their faults and virtues; his influence touched the very core of the entire inflammable half-breed question. It was also obvious to Sinclair that in his dealings with these people he must act cautiously and tactfully at all times, and especially so with Grant. First and foremost he came to recognize the fact that the future of Rupert's Land rested with this unpredictable majority, who rightly or wrongly felt that they were the heirs to the soil and that all others in the land were intruders. The half-breeds asserted that through their native mothers and their long association with the land they had a prior claim to the soil. They also claimed original occupation of the land and felt that this claim was reinforced through their sires, the earliest French explorers and traders who had come first as independent traders out of Montreal, and later as the *engagées* of the North West and XY companies.

The *Métis*, Sinclair also knew, were an innately proud people. They never forgot an insult, and they were insulted at being called half-breeds because of their descent from the French and the Indians. They accepted in good part such names as *Métis*, *gens libres*, and—jokingly—the *bois brûlés;* however, they preferred the title of "Citizens of the New Nation." There were also to be recognized the striking differences in personality between the *Métis* and the English or Scotch half-breeds—one of whom Sinclair was proud to call himself.

It was undoubtedly Grant's acceptance of the peculiar characteristics of his people and his particular care to respect their pride and differences that had brought about the half-breeds' acquiescence in his leadership. But aside from such acceptance, in himself Grant possessed outstanding ability and the personal magnetism that enabled him to forge his followers quickly into an effectual guild of hunters who could become as dangerous as they were useful to the company and country generally—a fact that Governor Simpson had not been slow to recognize.

Unfortunately, Grant had become in his own mind a peculiarly privileged person, as head of his nation and lord of a chosen race, possessing a rich heritage in fur, horses, guns, carts, and buffalo herds, which must be jealously guarded. In the three years of Grant's acknowledged position as chief of the *Métis* before Sinclair arrived in Red River, he had awakened in his people a growing sense of unity and even of destiny. Sinclair soon realized, therefore, that Grant was likely to be deeply jealous of him should he show too much rival influence among these people of his own blood. But above and beyond any personal feeling of rivalry for leadership, Sinclair recognized the fact that it was to be hoped that Grant and his followers would continue to accept British law and justice, as administered by the Hudson's Bay Company for the British crown through the terms set forth in the Old Company's original charter. It would appear that at this time Cuthbert Grant was the one person who could hold his people in check should a crisis arise in Rupert's Land. Rightly led, his disciplined bands of *Métis* hunters could not only provide food for the settlement but also its greatest protection. Wrongly led, they could set the land aflame with violence.

III

As a matter of fact, with the passing of time Sinclair's understanding of many matters broadened enormously, not only from his participation in the Red River petty trade, in his association with the wandering, volatile *Métis*, but through his friendship with Alexander Ross. Ross was able to provide Sinclair with an intelligent presentation of the political background and its implications in regard to the interests he now served, and he could relate something of the actual conditions then existing south of the border. For example, Ross was particularly well informed concerning the activities of the great John Jacob Astor, who was becoming a serious thorn in the flesh of the Hudson's Bay Company, especially in the region west of the Rockies, where Astor was threatening the profits of the Old Company through his aggressive traders following up the Missouri to cross the mountains and penetrate the Oregon.

Something of the personalities and successes of the powerful General William Henry Ashley and Pierre Chouteau, Jr., of St. Louis was also known to Ross. He recognized the fact that these gentlemen, although seeking to serve their own private interests in an intensified effort to secure a portion of the rich profits from the North American fur trade, were peculiarly united—even with Astor—in common cause to defeat the Hudson's Bay Company, particularly in the Rocky Mountain region and in the Oregon where a permanent border had not yet been established between British and United States territory.

From what he heard of these matters, Sinclair became intrigued by the outstanding success of General Ashley, who had recently acquired a mysterious fortune in the Rocky Mountains and was said in some quarters to have gained it at the expense of the Hudson's Bay Company. The story went that he had discovered a cache of the Old Company's fur in the region of the Great Salt Lake, then considered American territory but where Hudson's Bay Company men had inadvertently wandered to their great loss.

General Ashley had not actively entered the fur trade from St. Louis until 1822, and at first he had suffered serious financial reverses. In a desperate effort to recoup his fortune, Ashley had traveled with his parties of so-called Mountain Men up the Missouri River to its junction with the Yellowstone to feel out the prospects of the Indian trade. As a result of this expedition, the General had formed the highly successful Rocky Mountain Fur Company and had outfitted it at his own expense in cooperation with the famous frontiersman, Andrew Henry. It was this latter trader-explorer who was reputed to have been the first American to enter the unexplored regions of the Rocky Mountains west of the Great Divide and south of the forty-ninth parallel of latitude, since the important Lewis and Clark expedition had found its way across the Rockies earlier in the century. Henry had discovered an important branch of the Snake River, which was to bear his name—along with a fur post that, incidentally, was the first planted by the Americans in that part of the Rocky Mountains since John Jacob Astor's hapless venture in the building of Astoria.

After forming the Rocky Mountain Fur Company with Andrew Henry in 1822, Ashley had headed a large party of young men up the Missouri, taking with them two keelboat loads of trade goods to do business with the western Indians. This trip and a similar one in 1823 were not successful, through unfortunate encounters with the warlike Arikaras. Despite his personal losses in his effort to secure trade with the western tribes, Ashley had gained much valuable information concerning the Rocky Mountain region—in particular, the possible existence of valuable mountain passes—which he was able to give his government in Washington, and which later proved of inestimable value to the Americans in hastening their settlement westward.

In the autumn of 1823 and the spring of 1824, Ashley's Mountain Men penetrated the rich beaver country of the Green River Valley—perhaps the first white men to reach the region of the Great Salt Lake. It was in that same eventful season of 1823–24 that Ashley dispatched yet another party westward under the capable leadership of the trader Étienne Provost. To him Ashley attributed the first crossing of the highly important South Pass by white men. It was also about this time that fortune suddenly turned in Ashley's favor: he formed a valuable working arrangement with the other great frontiersman of his day, Jedediah S. Smith, who had returned to St. Louis in 1824 to present to Ashley the information he had gathered firsthand concerning the operations of the Hudson's Bay Company in the Columbia River country. It was Jebediah Smith who had accepted Alexander Ross's hospitality the previous winter at Ross's Flathead Post. Details of this peculiar encounter—that had, perhaps, saved Smith's life, and that led to Ross's banishment east of the Rockies to serve as Red River's schoolmaster—had been recounted bitterly to Sinclair by Ross himself before Sinclair had set forth on his first trading ventures, and certainly before he had an opportunity to hear the American version of the story, perhaps in St. Louis.

Here it may be said that it seems beyond a question of doubt that a man of James Sinclair's ability and inquiring, educated mind should have taken the first opportunity to visit the exciting fur capital of St. Louis. While we have no direct evidence of this, it seems quite possible that Sinclair should have arranged matters so that he would have made such a trip to St. Louis at least once or more—to secure trade goods, to see "the lie of the land" for Simpson's ultimate information, and to satisfy his own curiosity. The entire tenor of his life and later cumulative events point to the fact that he was only too conscious of what was occurring on the American side, cut his cloth accordingly, and opportunely played his cards to what he conceived to be the best advantage, ultimately and incidentally losing thereby.

Be that as it may, Sinclair was certainly not unmindful, even at an early date in his career, of what was happening on the American side, nor was he ignorant of the methods used by American frontiersmen, as the safety with which he learned to travel testifies. The point at issue seems to be that history, until a more careful study of Sinclair's somewhat unusual life could be made and available facts verified, has been inclined to consider Sinclair as an uneducated half-breed, restrained by circumstance to a comparatively limited area of thought and action. It has been reluctant to consider that he was a man of education; that his perception, experience, travel, influence, and even depth of conflicting loyalties may have been beyond the concept of his time and place, or, for that matter, beyond that of a hundred years later. Added to this, Sinclair had the peculiar advantage of his friend Alexander Ross's bitter experience, and that of Chief Factor Donald McKenzie with John Jacob Astor, which provided him with sufficient evidence to piece together a fair appraisal of what was occurring at this critical period south of the border.

For instance, Sinclair must have heard of General Ashley's fabulous life of luxury at the time in St. Louis, based on the fruits of his personal fur empire established at the Hudson's Bay Company's expense and upon Chief Trader Peter Skene Ogden's alleged unfortunate blunder or accident near the Great Salt Lake. Sinclair must have known that Ashley was protected in all he did by powerful political interests in Washington, for certainly Ross knew a good deal of such matters and would have so informed Sinclair. Then too, it must have been known that Ashley was in possession of two highly important fur posts in the American Far West—one at the mouth of the Yellowstone River, the other at the entrance of the Big Horn—both of which were threatening to take the valuable Blackfoot trade away from the Hudson's Bay Company at Edmonton House, as John Jacob Astor was planning to do with his own posts along the Missouri River. Fortunately, up to this time the Blackfeet had remained comparatively loyal to the British trade; but when Sinclair entered Red River free trading both Astor and Ashley were threatening to press their interests dangerously to the north and west, thereby jeopardizing more than ever the Hudson's Bay Company's position and profits in those regions.

A significant factor in Ashley and Astor's threat to the Old Company and British possessions was the fact that Ashley himself had taken part in his mountain enterprise with astonishingly imaginative forethought. As late as 1824 he had succeeded in reaching personally the Green River Valley, where he had remained for the winter with his Mountain Men. This had been the start of Ashley's truly remarkable innovation, the Rocky Mountain "rendezvous," which was later to prove so costly to the British west of the mountains. To these extraordinary gatherings of traders, trappers, and Indians came the men of rival fur companies scattered throughout the Rockies—not even excepting the traders from the Hudson's Bay Company's western outposts. Here was done an enormous amount of trade in the exchange of goods for fur to the highest bidders. This kind of annual trappers', traders', and Indians' festival—so Ashley believed, and not without profit to himself—would prove a unique method of doing business. It appeared to have definite advantages over the old established method of the Hudson's Bay Company that had compelled its men to bring their furs each season to its chief trading posts and receive in return their trade goods, which they had to carry back with them to their hunting grounds at great loss in time and labor.

All this was proving a decidedly expensive problem for the

Hudson's Bay Company to solve. Indeed, Ashley's introduction of the rendezvous had quickly changed the entire prospect of the North American fur trade west of the mountains. The unreliable free men in the Oregon—men who had left the ranks of the Hudson's Bay Company after completing their period of contracted service—were now deserting the Old Company to serve the more tempting American interests, and valuable fur that had once reached British hands was now falling all too easily to Ashley and Astor. The profits of the Old Company were falling off badly from its once remunerative Flathead Post, Fort Okanagan, Fort Colvile, and Fort Walla Walla, and ways and means had to be discovered to offset this growing danger.

It was in 1825 that Ashley had returned to St. Louis with such a valuable cache of beaver that he was said to have become overnight the wealthiest man in the American fur metropolis. But by 1828 Ashley was in a position to retire from active participation in the fur trade to devote himself to politics—leaving the field more or less open for Astor to fight the Hudson's Bay Company for domination of the North American fur trade. However, much of Ashley's damage was done, for already the march of American settlement had begun to move westward, as a result of his shrewd advertising of the fact that his South Pass was the logical entrance for settlers to reach the rich Columbia River country.

These and many other interesting facts concerning the American fur trade were presented to Sinclair by his friend Alexander Ross, and later gathered firsthand on expeditions south of the border. For, as time passed, and he came to know the *Métis* and their wanderings better, Sinclair—from the little evidence we have of his doings in the late 1820's and throughout the 1830's—was not idle nor were his activities too circumscribed.

In regard to these *Métis* wanderings, it was said that by 1828 parties of these Red River half-breeds might be met almost anywhere throughout the vast, largely unsettled region extending from the forks of the Red and Assiniboine rivers to the American outpost of Prairie du Chien, and even much farther afield. In-

James Sinclair, about 1850 (*Courtesy Miss Barbara Johnstone, Archivist, Hudson's Bay Company Archives, Winnipeg*)

ork boat on Cross Lake, Manitoba. Used to ship fur and trade goods in Rupert's Land
ourtesy Hudson's Bay Company)

Cree encampment, such as Sinclair visited in the free trade (*Courtesy Public Archives of Canada*)

Trading post at Fort Garry. Cart and oxen are like those used by Sinclair's 1854 party (*Courtesy British Columbia Provincial Archives*)

deed, a number of the Red River *Métis* had espoused the American cause and by this time were living near the military bases that President Jefferson and his successors were establishing in the Upper Missouri country and in northern Louisiana. This provided the *Métis* in Red River with an incentive to cross the border frequently to visit American relatives and friends, with the possibility of their carrying a quantity of fur to eager American traders. Governor Simpson issued a series of unpopular proclamations at Fort Garry threatening severe punishment to anyone caught carrying contraband fur south of the border. These proclamations seemed rather to serve an adverse purpose, making the *Métis* defiant and tending to increase the traffic, as well as bringing personal animosity to Simpson and the company.

IV

With widening experience through these travels with the *Métis*, and from his many elucidating conversations with his friend Ross, it seems to have become apparent to Sinclair that North American rivers and their tributaries linked Fort Garry in a singularly effective way to the American fur posts, and that all trails—no matter how obscure—seemed to ultimately lead to St. Louis. From that great fur center one might proceed westward, and certainly not without danger, up the Missouri River and on to the Rocky Mountains, where a way had almost miraculously opened to the Oregon by Ashley's recently discovered South Pass.

Indeed, Fort Garry lay at the very core of the North American continent. Water systems converged here from almost every direction, while the forks of the Red and Assiniboine rivers—as Governor Simpson had realized when he placed his headquarters here—provided a most useful point of departure for any part of the vast North American continent. Certainly Fort Garry had become a nerve center of the enormous territory over which Governor Simpson now held sway for the Hudson's Bay Company and therefore for the British crown.

From Fort Garry the great North American plain extended westward as far as the foot of the Rocky Mountains, and beyond was New Caledonia and the Oregon, presenting a rich prize for those able to claim it first by proof of original exploration, occupation, and diplomatic treaty, if not direct resort to arms. The powerful John Jacob Astor looked upon this region with envious and hopeful eyes for his own flag, in contest with the Hudson's Bay Company for the British. Therefore, the situation resolved itself into a strange rivalry for command of the North American river systems. This rivalry fashioned a curious pattern of destiny beyond the immediate vision of those engaged in the fur trade—the progress of Ashley's Mountain Men to be followed, at some not far distant date, by wagon trains of settlers, traveling along the banks of the great streams and their tributaries westward to new homes. Preferably, they would choose to follow the wide Missouri from St. Louis, taking one of its feeding streams up to the strategically important South Pass, over which would inevitably flow a flood of humanity across the difficult continental divide to reach the promised land of the Oregon.

It was inevitable that Governor Simpson would finally recognize this danger. Occupation of the Oregon by American settlers would mean serious loss to the Hudson's Bay Company's valuable fur trade in that region and possible ultimate conquest of the land presently held by a useful "joint occupation treaty," which served both American and British interests tolerably, if not too satisfactorily, until permanent settlement of a boundary could be reached.

It was recognized by all who knew anything of such matters that a restlessness now gripped the people of the eastern United States—part of a great upsurge of national confidence following the War of 1812. Many Americans now desired to move westward at any cost to establish new homes, discover new freedoms, and realize the promise of fortunes in the still largely uninhabited wilderness west of the Mississippi. Fortunately for such hopeful Americans, the mighty Missouri River, the chief artery of their fur trade, flowed entirely within United States territory. Its main tributaries—such as the Yellowstone, the Cheyenne, and the Marias—provided useful means of entry to the Rockies and on into the Oregon. And a difficult way it was, largely through uninhabited plains and deserts, over rugged mountains, sadly lacking in game and water, with the greater part of the distance from St. Louis to Fort Walla Walla infested with warlike Indian tribes—such as the Arikaras and Blackfeet—who were resisting fiercely the inroads of white settlers with every means at their command.

Surely such a possible influx of American pioneers into the Oregon presented serious threat to British interests in that region, well founded as they were upon certain valid claims of early exploration. However, in order to reach the rich Pacific regions west of the mountains, the British traders and settlers had to follow the Red River from Fort Garry in its flow northward, as the beginning of the roundabout British Route to the Oregon. Continuing up Lake Winnipeg, this route entered the great Saskatchewan River system, following its northern branch to Fort Edmonton, and from that post westward travel overland by Jasper House, over the Athabaska Pass to reach the Boat Encampment on the Columbia River. There bateaux must be taken down that great treacherous stream to Fort Vancouver, the Hudson's Bay Company's fine western depot, ruled by Dr. John McLoughlin and at this time the chief prize of the Oregon.

This British route to the Pacific, though circuitous and longer, was comparatively easy and safe in contrast with the American overland route. By this British way, for the most part, could be found sufficient game and water to sustain any party of travelers, while the Indians encountered were as a rule not too hostile to company men. But the British route could be greatly simplified if new mountain passes across the Rockies could be found within British territory.

That such passes did exist was revealed to James Sinclair by Alexander Ross, who had also considerable knowledge of such matters from his sojourn in the Far West in earlier times and through his association with such experienced men as Chief

Factors James Curtis Bird and John George MacTavish and Chief Trader Peter Skene Ogden. It was also known that Governor George Simpson was ambitious to discover such passes himself in order to achieve some glory as an explorer. But in 1828 they had not yet been found, and the only British means of entry to the Oregon was either by sea around the Horn or by the old route up the Saskatchewan to Edmonton House, over the Athabaska Pass to the Boat Encampment, and by bateaux down the Columbia River to Fort Vancouver.

V

It would appear that the possibility of discovering new passes across the Rocky Mountains north of the forty-ninth parallel early whetted James Sinclair's appetite for exploration, directing his thought and ultimate career toward such actual discovery in later years. To further this end, he seems to have sought upon every opportunity the company of Chief Factor James Curtis Bird—considered to be the authority on such matters in Red River. Through Bird's long position as chief factor of Edmonton House early in the nineteenth century, he had acquired much valuable information concerning the western plains and Rocky Mountain region. Through the good offices of Thomas Bunn, and because Bird had also been a close friend of Sinclair's father, this wealthy and influential retired company officer welcomed the acquaintance of James Sinclair. The entree of Sinclair into Chief Factor Bird's affluent home on a social footing did much for the young trader's prestige, for Bird was recognized throughout Red River as the unofficial leader and spokesman of the company's settlement of retired servants and officers. Many important decisions rested on his word. While a deep personal jealousy existed between Bird and Governor Simpson, as a result of the latter's appointment in place of Bird as head of company affairs in Rupert's Land, Simpson nevertheless often followed Bird's advice in matters of importance relative to the colony and in affairs even further afield.

No man, for instance, knew better than did Bird the importance of sustaining the Columbia River fur trade and the necessity of holding as much as possible of that valuable region west of the mountains for the British. Indeed, as early as 1806 Bird had insisted—and had so advised Governer William Auld at York Factory at the time—that an overland route to the Oregon should be established as early as possible, utilizing a pass well within British territory, thus linking the chain of Hudson's Bay Company posts from the Atlantic to the Pacific oceans. So, with a common interest, it was not unnatural that a close friendship should grow up between young Sinclair and the clever, if somewhat irritable and eccentric, chief factor.

It is unlikely that any man in the fur trade of his day had greater knowledge of the plains Indians and the eastern slopes of the Rocky Mountains than had Bird. Up to the time Sinclair entered the free trade, the Blackfeet had barred the way across the Rockies to most white men, thereby hindering the discovery of the southern passes within the British domain north of the forty-ninth parallel.

Chief Factor Bird had first learned of these passes from his trusted Indian scouts at Fort Edmonton, at the beginning of the nineteenth century, when the brilliant North West Company trader and explorer, David Thompson, had been in the Rocky Mountain region endeavoring to discover new passes for the organization he served. This effort had brought the existence of such passes to Bird's attention as head of the rival Hudson's Bay Company's North Saskatchewan department. It had also been revealed to him that other North West Company men, such as John George MacTavish and Peter Skene Ogden, knew of these untrodden passes. (The latter, crossing such a pass at a later date was inclined to feel it was his discovery, but it was actually found by Sinclair, as we shall later prove.)

Some of Bird's knowledge of such passes came to him from his son, who had taken on the ways of the Indians and regularly traveled with bands of Blackfeet across the Rockies into the Snake River country. He discovered and used passes well to the south of Edmonton House, but was never given credit for them.

As a matter of fact, some of the important Blackfeet chiefs, who came to deal with Bird at Edmonton House early in the nineteenth century, on more than one occasion had told him of at least two such mysterious mountain passes. One of these, they revealed, was used regularly by the Kootenay Indians—sworn enemies of the Blackfeet—who crossed annually to the east side of the Rockies to hunt buffalo on the plains and, if possible, steal Blackfeet horses and women. This particularly useful pass was reached by following the Bow River, an important tributary of the South Saskatchewan, so Bird had revealed to Sinclair.

The powerful Blackfoot Confederacy, consisting of the Blackfoot tribe and the related Bloods and Peigans, was not regarded with the same fear by Chief Factor Bird as by many other white men. He had dwelt among them since his youth and had succeeded in getting on admirably with them in trade at Edmonton House. Despite the general opinion of Blackfoot ferocity, Bird had found them to be, for the most part, forthright and honorable men. He had traveled with them extensively and had visited their encampments on many occasions. Once he had even gone with them to a point well within their dangerous territory near Red Deer Crossing, where he had caught a glimpse of the Great White Stone Mountains, as the Blackfeet called the Rockies.

Bird also confirmed what Sinclair had heard elsewhere: that the Americans were now penetrating the Blackfoot country from the south and were using every inducement to lure the valuable Blackfoot trade from the Hudson's Bay Company at Edmonton to their posts along the Missouri River. Indeed, Bird had become seriously alarmed at this development within the Blackfoot territory by the year 1828; with the securing of more guns and ammunition from the Americans, the Blackfeet were now seriously disrupting the old balance of trade, which the Hudson's Bay Company had long striven to maintain along the Saskatchewan. The Blackfeet were now driving their age-old enemies, the Crees, far to the east of their usual trading grounds, thereby making it exceedingly difficult for the Old Company to do its usual business at Forts Edmonton, Pitt, and Carlton. This was the very condition that Bird had sought to prevent when he was in command of the Saskatchewan country, with his headquarters at Edmonton. According to Bird's way of thinking, Governor Simpson had not awakened to the seriousness of the situation and the growing danger it presented to all the company's trade and traders in the Far West.

VI

Besides learning much relative to the Far Western trade, the way to deal with the Blackfeet, and the possibility of discovering new Rocky Mountain passes from Chief Factor James Curtis Bird, Sinclair received a welcome to Bird's fine home and enjoyed a close friendship with the old Chief Factor's family, especially with Bird's daughter, Elizabeth. This soon developed into romance, and the marriage of James Sinclair and Elizabeth Bird took place at Red River in December, 1829. They were married in St. John's parish church,[4] the ceremony performed by another of Sinclair's new and congenial friends, the Reverend David Jones, Anglican missionary and Hudson's Bay Company chaplain. The pair settled down to what proved a most happy married life, in a house McDermot had built for them on the eastern bank of the Red River.

VII

Sinclair's participation in the Red River petty trade with McDermot prospered for a time, but all was no longer peaceful in Rupert's Land. Resentment was rising among the *Métis* against Governor Simpson because of certain enactments they felt had been deliberately aimed at them. Despite any feelings of animosity that Sinclair and Alexander Ross might have harbored against Simpson for injury done them, both of them were wise enough to see that Simpson alone could cope with the larger problems of the country's administration. Certainly he alone was in a position to provide adequate diplomatic liaison between the company and the government of Britain—because of actual experience in the trade—with any degree of wisdom or foresight. Disliked as Simpson was in several quarters of Red River—particularly by many of the *Métis*—there was at this time no one capable of replacing him. If his handling of local affairs was not always tactful, it was at least tolerable.

Nevertheless, there were bound to be serious repercussions if Simpson did not soon recognize the trend of sentiment against him and the Old Company, for some of the more competent Red River settlers as well as the more restless *Métis* were beginning to feel themselves oppressed by demands for the repayment of advances made during the periods of stress and disaster that the Red River Settlement had undergone since its inception. Resentment was also being expressed against the restrictions being imposed to control or eliminate altogether the illicit traffic in furs becoming increasingly widespread among the *Métis*. Indeed, there were not by this time many settlers of Red River who did not indulge in the traffic, to a greater or lesser extent, thereby committing an infraction against the chartered privileges of the Hudson's Bay Company.

Sinclair, for the time being, was protected by McDermot's special privileges as a petty trader, and had become recognized throughout Red River as a favored junior partner in the prospering Irishman's numerous dealings. That these operations were legal was set forth plainly in a general regulation that read:

> . . . private persons should undertake this business on their own account . . . they may be allowed to purchase assortments of goods in wholesale for the purpose of being retailed to the settlers from the stores at York Factory at the advance of 33⅓ p.ct. on the London prices, and they will, of course, have to provide their own means of transport from York Factory to Red River. Such sales will, of course, only be made to men of responsibility and upon satisfactory payment of good bills upon London.[5]

Through McDermot's generous sharing of his profits with him, things went well for Sinclair; and by 1832 he was able to secure a good property and build a fine residence between those of the Irishman and Alexander Ross, in the heart of the settlement. Sinclair now came and went as he pleased and was received in what were recognized as the best circles of Red River "society." He was also welcomed into the humbler homes of less prosperous settlers and in the shanties of the *Métis*, although less affably in the limited and exclusive coterie of Governor Simpson and his young wife when they were in residence at Fort Garry.

Sinclair had a happy life at this time with his wife and young children, and they enjoyed the society of their good neighbors, the Rosses and the McDermots. In fact, conditions for Sinclair seemed most propitious, but such good fortune was not to last; in the early winter of 1833, Sinclair's good and protective friend, Governor Donald McKenzie, was finally removed from office at Fort Garry. The days of his tolerant and popular administration as chief factor and governor of Assiniboia were over, and he was to be succeeded by a man who, if perhaps as capable and just in his own way, was to prove much less to the liking of the general populace of Red River.

4. THE COMING OF GOVERNOR CHRISTIE

I

It was in the year 1834 that fortune seemed to turn against James Sinclair, both in his personal life and in his free trade. In September of that year a terrible epidemic struck the settlement, and Sinclair's family did not escape. The sickness took the form of a virulent dysentery; in a matter of hours it reached epidemic proportions, and scarcely a home in Red River was untouched. On September 19, 1834, Sinclair's eldest daughter, Elizabeth, died of the disease,[1] and the following day his only son—an infant of nine months—was taken. This child had been christened on February 28, 1834,[2] at St. John's church by Sinclair's friend, the Reverend David Jones, and had been given the name "Alexander" in honor of Chief Factor Christie, who had replaced Donald McKenzie in charge at Upper Fort Garry. This fact discloses that Christie and Sinclair were on friendly enough terms until this time but such a happy relationship was not to continue for long.

By the spring of 1835, Sinclair had every reason to believe

that general prospects for the fur trade were none too encouraging, and that the petty trade in Red River was likely to fall off drastically with the new restrictions placed upon it by the Hudson's Bay Company. In regard to the North American fur trade, word had reached Sinclair from St. Louis that those there in a position to know were convinced that the greatest days of fur trading were past. Not only were the beaver becoming exhausted in the Rocky Mountain region but a great settlement westward was active throughout the United States—an element in itself likely to defeat fur trading. It appeared that the short but colorful and expansive era of Ashley's Mountain Men and unique Rocky Mountain rendezvous was over. These fears for the future of the fur trade also seemed confirmed by the fact that the astute John Jacob Astor—grown old and extravagantly rich—was devoting himself almost entirely now to the even more remunerative sphere of New York real estate. Astor, with characteristic business acumen and foresight, had recently written to confreres in St. Louis, who spread the word abroad, that "he very much feared that beaver in the future would not sell well unless very fine; and it appeared that the most recent innovation, the silk hat, was about to replace permanently the accepted beaver head-piece." This change of fashion was certainly destined to affect seriously the Hudson's Bay Company's profits and business. Indeed, so convinced was Astor of his surmise that he had quietly sold out his predominant share in the American Fur Company in 1834, disposing of his interests to his old and faithful aide, Ramsay Crooks.

Drastic changes were also becoming evident during this season of 1835 in Red River. The Administrative Council of Assiniboia had been reorganized thoroughly by Simpson on February 12 of that year. This had been a direct result of the "reconveyance" of Lord Selkirk's enormous grant of land, which gave the tract back to its original owners, the Hudson's Bay Company. The change of legal ownership of Assiniboia had necessitated a wider representation of the Red River people on its governing body. Even Andrew McDermot and Alexander Ross had been invited to be present at this first session of the reorganized Council, with Ross officially appointed as sheriff of Red River.

Nevertheless, the old conservative Hudson's Bay Company officers—both active and retired—still dominated the Council and determined its course. Simpson himself was in attendance at this important first session, as was Chief Factor Alexander Christie. Simpson, in his opening address, expressed the thought that the chief purpose of the reorganized Council was to maintain order and tranquillity in the land; and to further this purpose very definite legislative and administrative powers, within the terms of the Hudson's Bay Company's original charter, were granted the Council.

II

By 1838 Sinclair must have known from his many sources of information—as Governor Simpson must surely have known—that the interests of the Hudson's Bay Company and the British claims west of the mountains were being increasingly jeopardized by the accelerated movement of American settlers westward out of St. Louis toward the Oregon. At this time the feeling was abroad in the United States that it could soon wrest the entire rich Columbia River country from the British by preponderance of settlers, if they could be poured in before the settlement of the prolonged boundary dispute placed in continuation of a permanent border line from the Great Divide of the Rocky Mountains to the Pacific Ocean.

In recent years the movement westward of American settlers had been greatly intensified by the activities of the exotic, mysterious Louis Eulalie de Bonneville in the Rocky Mountain region. This adventurer was a friend of the revolutionary hero, Lafayette, and also of the prominent author, Washington Irving. He appeared to enjoy some special favor of the American government, for wherever he went he was magnificently equipped for his exploration and scientific investigations. Peculiarly enough, his footsteps as early as 1832 seemed to lead him straight for the Hudson's Bay Company's important post at Walla Walla. He had apparently found this a particularly good outpost and key point at the western end of the newly opened Oregon Trail, over which American settlers were beginning to pour westward from Independence, Missouri, to the valley of the Columbia.

It was Captain Bonneville, also, who had at last accomplished the seemingly impossible feat that General Ashley and the Sublette brothers had earlier foreseen of taking wagons over the Rocky Mountains to the Oregon. This achievement alone was of singular importance to the continuing Hudson's Bay Company profits and security west of the mountains, for it brought one step closer the inevitable march of American settlers to the Oregon in ever increasing numbers, and thus the ultimate demise of the fur trade.

It was now quite generally felt that the United States was entering upon an interesting new phase in its expansion, especially with the opening of the entire region west of the Mississippi River. An epoch of importance had dawned between the period of the fur trade and the establishment of permanent settlement from coast to coast. A struggle was about to take place for the possession of all the verdant lands along the lower Columbia River and the rich Willamette Valley. The deciding factor would be the ability of either the British or Americans to pour the most settlers first into the region under dispute, before the final boundary were settled by diplomatic treaty and political negotiations in London and Washington.

Added to all this, a great surge of religious enthusiasm had been sweeping the eastern United States, spurring missionary effort among the western Indian tribes. American religious leaders were sending out devout and patriotic men to convert the natives. The Presbyterians and Congregationalists, through their commissions for foreign missions, had undertaken to carry Christianity to the Indians of the Oregon, led by such dedicated men as the Reverend Samuel Parker and Jason Lee, who in 1833 had preached the first Protestant sermon west of the Great Divide, to a little group of Indians and trappers gathered on the banks of the Snake River. Lee had continued westward to create a permanent settlement of his followers in the beautiful Willamette Valley south of Fort Vancouver, where Lee had begun at once a political ferment on behalf of the Americans' right to that region.

Lee was followed by the no-less-formidable Christian leader and physician, Dr. Marcus Whitman—a remarkable visionary who made his first trip across the Rockies in 1835 with a party of Mountain Men from Missouri. Whitman—like Ashley, the Sublettes, and Bonneville before him—was convinced that a wagon trail should be established as a practical entry over the Rocky Mountains into the Oregon to assure possession of that valuable territory for the Americans. Since their arrival in the Columbia River country, Whitman and his beautiful wife Narcissa had accomplished remarkable things in their Christian and medical endeavors. In 1836, they had set up an efficient mission station—known as Waillatpu—not far from the Hudson's Bay Company's Fort Walla Walla. The master of that place was an equally interesting character named Chief Trader Pierre Pambrum, who, despite his British affiliations, had become friendly with the Whitmans and had given them every aid possible in establishing their mission.

At the same time, Dr. John McLoughlin, the powerful Hudson's Bay Company officer in charge of the headquarters at Fort Vancouver, had also become friendly with the Whitmans, and apparently saw nothing alarming in the growing number of Americans now pouring into the Oregon. Nor, indeed, did McLoughlin seem to feel that there was any great danger to Hudson's Bay Company interests with their presence. Rather, he appeared to feel it would be to the company's advantage and ultimately increase business.

In all this, however, the kindly doctor's attitude was at striking variance with that of Governor Simpson, who saw in this invasion of the Oregon by American settlers and missionaries cause for the gravest concern for both Hudson's Bay Company and British interests. Simpson, with his astute mind, realized that it was only a question of time until the settlers themselves would decide the form of government under which they cared to live, and whether the final placing of a permanent boundary line should be along the Columbia River, the forty-ninth parallel, or north of it.

5. SINCLAIR AND THE UNREST IN RED RIVER

I

By 1838 James Sinclair seems to have been accepted into the inner circle of the Red River *Métis*. There was room for his growing leadership among them since Cuthbert Grant, their colorful chief, had more or less retired to the comparative quiet and comfort of his estate near White Horse Plain. He had been provided with a good competence by the Hudson's Bay Company as "Warden of the Plains," with a seat on the Council of Assiniboia. This still gave him a preferred, if less vocal, position among his fellows, for policy prevented him from playing too conspicuous a part in any public remonstrances on behalf of the half-breeds against the laws and privileges of the Old Company.

It was about this time also that a decided animosity seems to have grown up between Sinclair and Governor Alexander Christie. Christie had let it be known generally that he held Sinclair personally responsible for "sowing seeds of discontent and disaffection" [1] among the Red River half-breeds and suspected him of arousing a spirit of insubordination against the established authority of the Hudson's Bay Company in Rupert's Land.

Christie was a company officer of the old school, imbued with tradition and respect for the letter of the law. He was a thoroughgoing and conscientious man,[2] who did not always comprehend the expansive tactics that Governor Simpson exercised with results beyond an imagination of less far-reaching perspective. Christie prided himself on standing firm on matters of policy, and he was exceedingly loyal to the Hudson's Bay Company he served.

Christie regarded the Old Company's charter as something almost sacred and inviolable. He considered the company's exclusive license from the British crown to deal in furs, and, for that matter, the right to all forms of trade in Rupert's Land, as privileges that must be upheld at all cost, no matter what sacrifice this might demand from any individual. This, then, was precisely Christie's stand against the free trade and against persons like Andrew McDermot and James Sinclair, whom he felt were abusing the special liberties afforded them as petty merchants in Red River; this was actually the basis of the bitter quarrel that was to develop from this time forward between Christie and Sinclair personally.

II

Early in the summer of 1839 another important personage arrived in Red River to assist with the Hudson's Bay Company's administration at Fort Garry. This was Recorder Adam Thom, who had been sent to Rupert's Land by Governor Simpson to serve in the capacity of judge and legal advisor to the company and Council of Assiniboia, and who was prepared to uphold Governor Christie in his stand against the free trade.

Thom's reputation had traveled before him to Red River, and a somewhat unfriendly reception awaited him. Despite the feeling of resentment displayed toward him from the outset, Thom was a gentleman of no mean attainment. He had been educated at King's College in Aberdeen, Scotland, where he had not only been trained as a teacher but was also learned in the law. He had taught for a time in the north of Scotland, and upon his arrival in Montreal he had practiced law for a while before becoming an editorial writer for the *Montreal Herald*. During this period he had incurred the displeasure of the French-Canadians for his stand against the so-called "Papineau rebellion." News of his activities had reached the sympathetic French-Canadians and *Métis* of Red River, who were not prepared to receive him with much enthusiasm.

Prejudice also formed from the start against Thom for his inability to speak French as well as English when performing his judicial duties. It was felt that he might be biased in his judgments in favor of the Old Company, and therefore not inclined to render entirely impartial verdicts where the *Métis* or Red River French-Canadians were concerned. Unfair as such opinions may have been, they were nevertheless held toward Thom by many, from the moment he arrived in Red River until the time of his departure some years later.

III

Not long after Thom's arrival at Fort Garry, in 1840, a vexing question arose that brought James Sinclair into prominence on behalf of the half-breeds, and that ran counter to Governor Christie's adamant attitude. This was the matter of the shipment of tallow, and it seemed destined to lead to widespread trouble throughout the country if the company persisted in its arbitrary stand regarding it. The whole thing resolved itself to this: the produce taken from the annual buffalo hunts—such as pemmican, dried meat, hides, and tallow, much of which provided the essential sustenance and trade of the *Métis*—had reached such large proportions that the Hudson's Bay Company had neither the facilities to store or dispose of it to any advantage. Governor Christie, for some peculiar reason, did not appear to realize the basic importance of this trade to the general economy and well-being of the country, nor did he realize that an unwise handling of this touchy problem could easily provide tinder for a general uprising if the *Métis* were tested too far or too long regarding it.

However, apparently ignoring the warnings, Christie arbitrarily refused to accept any more of such produce at the company's warehouses in Fort Garry. As a further aggravation, he also threatened to deny the *Métis* and some other Red River settlers who had a surplus of domestic tallow the privilege of shipping it on the company's ships sailing from York Factory to Britain. This was somewhat in line with an earlier company policy regarding the denial to ship buffalo hides, which were said to contaminate the valuable cargoes of furs sent from York Factory to the London warehouses.

A short time after this, Christie also threatened—should he finally agree to limited shipments of tallow to Britain at a later date—to raise the freight rates so high that it would be entirely impractical to carry the stuff from Fort Garry to York Factory over the arduous waterways and portages. Here, it seemed, Christie had at last struck upon an effectual plan to prevent McDermot and Sinclair from using further the privilege they had previously enjoyed, through a special arrangement with Governor Simpson personally, of transporting tallow for the *Métis* and certain Red River settlers in their private brigade of York boats from Fort Garry to York Factory, and for shipment of the tallow from that place to Britain on company ships.

It was also in the year 1840 that Sinclair sought redress from this troublesome situation by a direct appeal in writing to Governor Christie. This took the form of a formal petition, with Sinclair recognized now as personal representative of the *Métis*. A fair reduction in the freight rates for the shipment of tallow to Britain on the company ships was asked. This aggressive action seems to have angered Christie, and he does not appear to have condescended to even acknowledge the petition. However, Christie is said to have made a statement at the time to the effect that, while he had afforded every facility to the new class of petty merchants who had sprung up in Red River, in accordance with a previous policy of the company, these same petty merchants, meaning especially McDermot and Sinclair, had taken advantage of the position that their credit system afforded them, and he was now stepping in with his authority as Governor of Assiniboia to withdraw such privileges. He was also said to have added that he would see to it that in future the regular shops of the company within the walls of Fort Garry were in a position to carry all the goods the people of Red River might require, which were now being supplied by these petty merchants with too much advantage to themselves. What was more, the Hudson's Bay Company's shops within the fort would, in future, supply these goods at cheaper rates than the Red River petty merchants could afford to meet. Thus the Old Company would recapture the lucrative business that had been lost to McDermot and Sinclair. While this might mortally incense these petty traders who would raise a hue and cry against the Old Company—accusing it of exercising an unfair monopoly of trade as it had in the matter of furs—the re-establishing of the company's rights as set forth in the original charter and its license to trade from the British crown would be to the decided advantage of the company and the people of Red River as well.

It was not long after this that Christie went even further in his efforts to curtail, if not completely destroy, the petty trade of Red River. He threatened to prevent such merchants as McDermot and Sinclair from importing any further trade goods from Britain by York Factory in the company ships, as Governor Simpson had permitted them to do in the past.[3] In this new stand, Christie had a firm backer in Chief Factor James Hargrave,[4] who had succeeded him in charge of York Factory. Hargrave had recently written to Fort Garry that if petty traders were permitted to import trade goods at pleasure on the company's ships, the Hudson's Bay Company's own regular indent for essential trade goods, required to carry on effectually the regular company business throughout Rupert's Land, would be dangerously reduced. The Old Company was now losing the best part of the cash annually collected at Red River; and Hargrave had been particularly incensed that McDermot was permitted by Governor Simpson to transport some forty-three "pieces," or ninety-pound bales of trade goods, out of every one hundred pieces carried in the company's regular annual "outfits." He was also angered that both McDermot and Sinclair had been allowed a boat cargo apiece each fall on the same terms as the summer freight, thus hampering the company's legitimate business and traffic.

Chief Factor Hargrave had further complained of the difficulties caused at York Factory by the necessity of sorting and repacking McDermot's and Sinclair's goods brought from Britain on the company's ship each year, in order that an impost tax might be levied on it at York before it could be carried inland by these traders' private brigade of York boats. It was most peculiar, Hargrave insinuated, that these privileged traders should be allowed to bring in their goods from England in the company's ships and then be permitted to place themselves within the limits of the Hudson's Bay Company's territory in competitive trade to the manifest injury of the Old Company's legitimate business. These petty traders were now spoiling the company's trade by the low rates at which they were disposing of their goods to the *Métis* and Indians near Fort Ellice,[5] where Sinclair had recently set up a private trading post for McDermot, and where the Irish merchant and his partner were now usurping much of the company's valuable business in the Qu'Appelle Valley.

IV

Before the quarrel over the free trade between Governor Christie, Recorder Adam Thom, and those engaged in it—with James Sinclair now in the forefront of the trouble—several changes in the company's administration at Fort Garry occurred, and some unforeseen developments took place that changed Sinclair's position definitely for the time being. Chief Factor Duncan Finlayson, Governor Simpson's brother-in-law, who had earlier served as a company officer of lesser rank at Fort Garry, was to replace Governor Alexander Christie temporarily while he was away on furlough in Scotland.

It was not long after Finlayson took office at Fort Garry, early in 1840, that word reached the settlement that at long last Governor Simpson was about to take a journey around the world. He expected to be away in London, England, for a time, to make final preparations for this momentous trip before actually setting forth upon it from Fort Garry. It was rumored that Simpson planned to cross the plains and Rockies early in the summer of 1841, using a pass previously untried by white men to reach the Oregon. From Fort Garry, Simpson planned to travel by company trading ship to the Sandwich Islands, and from there to cross the ocean to Asia, then across Siberia and Europe to London, returning to his headquarters at Lachine by swift packet across the Atlantic via New York. This somewhat astonishing world-circling journey was to take Simpson something more than a year to complete.

Interesting as was this news, it was the announcement that Governor Simpson had invited Alexander Ross, the Red River historian and schoolmaster, to conduct a party of Red River settlers to the Oregon that really stirred the settlement. These settlers were to be placed near Fort Vancouver, on Hudson's Bay Company farms already being prepared for them by Chief Factor Dr. John McLoughlin at Cowlitz and Nisqually.

As early as 1832, Dr. McLoughlin had seen the possibility and necessity of introducing British agricultural development into the Oregon as a corollary to the decreasing fur trade. He had even suggested the formation of a joint-stock company, under the auspices of the Hudson's Bay Company, to be largely financed as an investment from the savings of company officers who might care to participate in such an undertaking. But it was not until 1838 that Governor Simpson seemed inclined to consider the matter seriously, when he wrote: "American immigration might seriously imperil the Company's position in the Columbia," and "counter-immigration by British subjects to be settled north of the river seems to offer possibilities to encourage the gradual migration of settlers from the Red River Colony to the Columbia River." [6]

At first the company's London governor and committee had not looked upon the scheme with too much sympathy, but the undertaking was finally given more serious consideration in order to foster the production of wool, hides, and tallow for the British market. It was then proposed that several agricultural communities be set up between Fort Vancouver and Puget Sound, at the Cowlitz Portage and in the Nisqually meadows. In furtherance of this plan, the company's London committee had written to Governor Simpson on March 20, 1839:

> We deferred carrying the plan into effect until we were secured in the possession of the country by a renewal of the exclusive licence from the Government which was obtained last year [1838], for the term of 21 years. The [British] Government is favourable to the object for political reasons, and after giving the subject matter consideration and obtaining the best legal advice, we are of the opinion that it can be better done under the protection and auspices of the Hudson's Bay Company by a separate association than if undertaken by the Company in conjunction with the fur trade; the Association to be styled "the Puget's Sound Agricultural Company"; a Deed of Settlement being prepared for Simpson's signature while he is in London.[7]

On December 31, 1839, the London governor and committee wrote Dr. John McLoughlin at Fort Vancouver, stating:

> With the view that our settlement on the Cowlitz may not be overawed by the presence of so large an assemblance of strangers, and as a means of protection to the depot and trade, we have directed Chief Factor Finlayson to encourage the gradual migration of settlers from the Red River Colony to the Columbia River, and the facilitating of such migration by making advances and affording passage to persons who may feel disposed to proceed thither. We think it is probable several families may next year avail themselves of the encouragement thus held out, and as those people have been reared about the Company's establishments, we should hope they will find themselves attached and useful.[8]

Peculiarly enough, although Dr. McLoughlin had conceived the original plan for this project, he appears to have been none too enthusiastic as to its fulfillment once the London committee had approved the plan and set it into motion, for the doctor now wrote of it thus:

> If there were more prairie land at the Cowlitz it would be possible to encourage emigration to that place, but the Puget's Sound Association

requires all there is, and though the soil is equally as good as that of the Wallamette, the larger extent of the prairies of the Wallamette and the great abundance of deer in them and their more beautiful scenery causes them to be preferred to the Cowlitz, and the Settlers will never settle on it till the Wallamette is settled, or till the wood at the Cowlitz comes into demand. . . . Still I consider it very proper to encourage people to come from the Red River to settle in the Wallamette, but I hope that they will not be led to suppose that they have any claims on us beyond our good will and the sale or loan of a few head of cattle and seed grain, if convenient. I regret to see you intend to send 20 families to this place. I hope you will have altered your intention as we have no prairie land on the Cowlitz on which to place them; and as to placing them on wood land, it would be worse than useless as our timber is so heavy that besides the difficulty to cut it down, (which I might say is impossible to accomplish by men unaccustomed to the axe), it requires several years to rot the roots before the ground can be cleared. As to the plains of Nisqually, at present they are only adapted to sheep pasture. . . . Sgd. McLoughlin.[9]

However, by this time the plan was so fully advanced there was nothing for it but that McLoughlin should see it through.

As a follow up of all this, Simpson wrote to Chief Factor Duncan Finlayson at Fort Garry in September, 1840, giving instructions and terms of preparation for the sending of an expedition of Red River settlers to the Oregon, arranging for them to set forth from Fort Garry as early as possible in the summer of 1842, under the suggested leadership of Alexander Ross. Simpson's instructions to Finlayson read:

The emigrants to the Columbia are to take farms on halves; houses will be erected for them; stock such as cattle, sheep, horses, etc. provided; likewise agricultural implements without any advances being required from them. In fact, the Company is willing to provide them with capital; their proportion of the capital being labour, and the Company looks to be repaid for their advances in the shape of produce, say half the increase of stock and produce of every kind. Allottments will be made to each family of at least 100 acres of land, (besides the use of common pasture lands), part thereof will be broken up, with the necessary buildings erected for them and livestock advanced to each family of a bull and 10 or more cows, 50 to 100 ewes, with sufficient number of rams, hogs, and oxen for agricultural purposes, and a few horses; in short, as many of these different stocks as they can be equal to the management of, all valued at low money prices; the expense of erecting the buildings being a charge upon the farm each; and other stock in proportion; the credit given to them from year to year for their increase, produce or returns at such prices as the state of the market can afford. . . . I have promised to the emigrants whose signatures are affixed to this sheet that as soon as the boundary line will be settled on the west side of the Rocky Mountains between the British and American governments, and that the Hudson's Bay Company can legally effect sale of land in that country, the system of holding land on halves will be abolished, provided always, and it is hereby understood that such will not take place until all debts and other expenses contracted by and incurred on account of the emigrants are paid by them to the Hudson's Bay Company or to their representatives on the Columbia.[10]

Honored as he was by Governor Simpson's returned confidence in him, which favored even a temporary return to his beloved Columbia River country, Alexander Ross no longer felt he was able to undertake such an arduous adventure as conducting a party of Red River settlers across the plains and mountains from Red River to the Pacific. Ross was too old for such a strenuous undertaking, and his interests and ties had become too deeply rooted in Red River to leave it even temporarily. As an alternative, therefore, he at once suggested that his friend, James Sinclair, be permitted to replace him as leader of this expedition, knowing that Sinclair had become a recognized authority on prairie travel, was able to deal competently with any Indians met on the way, and was compatible with the *Métis* who were to make up a large part of the migrants.

Besides this, Ross well knew Sinclair's long desire to make a crossing of one of the still untried Rocky Mountain passes to the Oregon, even if such an attempt be without Simpson's consent or knowledge. Also, Sinclair's leadership of such an expedition would remove him for a time from Red River, thereby not only excluding him from participation in the tempting free trade but retarding his growing influence upon the *Métis*. Thus, Sinclair would be removed from any possible trouble in Red River, and at the same time he would have the opportunity for a new life and adventure west of the mountains.

PART II: SINCLAIR, THE LEADER AND EXPLORER

6. ACROSS THE ROCKIES

I

By Easter, 1841, preparations were well under way for Sinclair's first conduct of a party of Red River settlers to the Oregon for the Hudson's Bay Company. Chief Factor Duncan Finlayson's instructions from Governor Simpson had been carried out with dispatch; and Sinclair for his part faced the numerous problems of leader with experienced and efficient detachment, realizing full well that he would be held responsible for the safety of this large party.

From the outset he sought to instill in his prospective followers a sense of confidence, and the knowledge that although they were about to travel across more than half a continent—for the most part through country little traveled and over untrodden paths across the mountains—the difficulties confronting them were not likely to prove more arduous or dangerous than the life led by the wandering *Métis* on their hunting expeditions. Fortunately, most of the people prepared to undertake this trip with Sinclair were Red River half-breeds, many of whom were well known to Sinclair personally in the free trade and most of them hardy buffalo hunters with some knowledge of stock raising and farming. A number of these men had families accompanying them to make new homes west of the mountains.

All of these people were prepared for what they might expect on a venture such as this, and knew how to cope with most conditions likely to be met on the trail and in the pioneer life of the Oregon. Certain of the men had grown weary of the severe restrictions lately imposed in the free trade, and felt that in joining such an expedition they were leaving the restraint placed upon them by the company in Red River. Oregon seemed to promise greater liberty of action. Records give the following names of some of those accompanying Sinclair as John Tait, William Flett, David Flett, Charles McKay, John Cunningham, Archibald Spence, John Spence, Henry Buxton, James Birston, Alexander Birston, Horatio Nelson Calder, and Touissant Joyalle [1]—other names seem to have been misplaced or lost in official lists of the 1841 party.

As time wore on toward the day of departure some seeds of discord seem to have been deliberately sown among the people leaving. Certain of those who had signed the agreement binding them to make the trip suddenly expressed dissatisfaction with the terms presented to them, and some even suspected that the company had ulterior motives in wishing to see them removed from the settlement.[2] However, with some difficulty Sinclair managed to silence most of the murmurings, and nearly all of those who had signed earlier decided to carry out the terms of the contract. Therefore, by May 1, 1841, Chief Factor Finlayson was able to write Governor Simpson at Lachine:

> Although there is a strong desire to remove yet there is some reluctance in leaving their old quarters. Mr. Ross has refused to conduct the party but has in every other respect given me all the assistance I could desire. James Sinclair has, therefore, undertaken to be the conductor, and if the necessary facilities be afforded him will be back here in sufficient time to conduct another party next spring.[3]

Upon this more hopeful note the party set forth from Fort Garry on June 3, 1841. Less than a week later, on June 20, when Simpson reached Red River to make his official start on his trip around the world, the Governor wrote to the company's London office:

> Chief Factor Duncan Finlayson has been successful in carrying out instructions in reference to the removal of settlers from this Colony to the Columbia, having provided twenty-three families, amounting to one hundred and twenty-one souls under the care of James Sinclair . . . a few days previous to my arrival of June 9 at this place. It is intended they shall proceed by the Saskatchewan and across the Kootonais Portage, and unless any unforeseen difficulties occur to prevent it, I am in hope they will reach Vancouver in the course of the month of October next. I expect to be there a month or six weeks before their arrival so that I shall be able to make the necessary arrangements with Chief Factor John McLoughlin for their location previous to my departure for the Sandwich Islands.[4]

There seemed to be little more concern for Sinclair's party than if they were proceeding to the annual buffalo hunt. This quiet departure had been deliberately arranged by Sinclair and Finlayson, since it was considered wise for the cart train to assemble a little way beyond the settlement, at a rendezvous near Cuthbert Grant's headquarters at White Horse Plain. Each head of a family in the party had been instructed well in advance to bring two or three Red River carts as well as sufficient horses and cattle and a few dogs. The men and boys were required to ride horseback, while the women and children traveled in slow-moving, creaking carts, drawn by strong *Métis* ponies and covered with a rack for canvas or buffalo hide as protection against rain and the blazing sun as the party progressed across the plains. No surplus belongings were permitted. To meet the barest necessities for the trip, which was likely to extend well through the summer and into autumn on the long distance between Red River and the Oregon, the company had advanced the settlers such essential supplies as pemmican, buffalo hides, shot, powder, guns, flints, knives, blankets, and tobacco. The number of buffalo hides, robes, and oiled ground sheets was estimated on those likely to be required for adequate bedding and protection for the loaded carts, as well as to convert the carts into boats when streams that could not easily be forded must be traversed by this other means. Each group was allowed enough, but no more, kettles, frying pans, tin plates, mugs, water pails, wooden kegs, butcher and hunting knives, axes, shovels, and shaganappi, or rawhide rope. Enough clothing was allowed to be carried, apart from what they wore, to provide necessary comfort and protection in any kind of expected or unexpected weather from early summer to late autumn, the length of time the party was likely to be on the trail.

While individual preference was given members of the party in some matters, Sinclair had advised the men to revert to the clothing affected by the *Métis* when at their hunts. This garb consisted of buckskin shirt and jacket worn with heavy, homespun trousers obtainable from the regular company stores at Fort Garry. Capotes were carried for the cold weather likely to be encountered when crossing the mountains. Women and girls in the party were clad in the simple clothing customarily worn in Red River that consisted of practical, dark homespun dress and drab trade shawl, to which might be added a bright kerchief worn about head or throat. The wearing of "Indian shoes" or moccasins was definitely the choice of almost everyone in the party, since sore, blistered, or swollen feet on such a lengthy expedition as this could give rise to real concern and much discomfort.

While the party was expected to live largely off the country in transit, to insure against the eventuality of insufficient game being found, the company provided pemmican to the amount of some fifty pounds for each member of the party—this being considered enough to last one person two months. Should it be necessary to use this emergency ration, Sinclair was empowered as leader to renew the pemmican stocks at the several company posts along the way. However, every member of the party was carefully warned and was expected to be provident in all things and to see that their supplies of food, weapons, and ammunition

Andrew McDermot's store near Fort Garry (*Courtesy Public Archives of Canada*)

"Red River Settlement," by Paul Kane. Fort Garry on the right and St. Boniface on he left. Here the *Métis* crossed the river, rejoicing at the conclusion of the Sayer Trial (*Courtesy Royal Ontario Museum*)

"Half Breeds Running Buffalo," by Paul Kane, from *The Beaver*, Sept., 1850 (*Courtesy Hudson's Bay Company*)

were well husbanded and carefully guarded at all times. This was especially true for the limited amounts of flour, sugar, and tea that members were allowed to bring with them, and which were to be considered as luxuries to be used wisely to relieve the monotony of the regular diet along the way.

Before finally setting out from the rendezvous at White Horse Plain, Sinclair organized his expedition thoroughly in accordance with the methods he had found most profitable from long experience on the trails with the *Métis*. First and foremost, he established his own position as unquestioned leader of the expedition, with power delegated to him by the company that he should assert the authority thus vested in him at all times. It had long since been recognized throughout Red River that Sinclair was a fair but firm leader who could be trusted to bring such a party as this through safely if given a normal chance under most circumstances. Insubordination would not be tolerated, and, as at the annual buffalo hunts, no lapse from a leader's reasonable rules would go unpunished. To break carefully prepared regulations on the trail, would not only bring upon an offender painful ostracism by his fellows and assignments of double camp duties but in the worst extremity the miscreant might even be compelled to turn back and find his way home as best he could. Strict discipline was necessary if the destination over unknown country were to be reached in safety.

Naturally there would be occurrences that would demand facing certain hardships with courage, self-denial, and resourcefulness. In an emergency, every member of the party must be counted upon to conduct himself with fortitude, restraint, consideration, and good humor. Everyone must do his share of the ordinary day's work—no more, no less. Fortunately, there were few if any *moonias*, or greenhorns, in the party. It was expected that every man would know how to make camp efficiently, repair carts, negotiate streams, build bridges, handle horses, and hunt game, both large and small, for the general support of the company. In short, everyone should know what to do at the right time under most circumstances, anticipated or otherwise.

It was also understood that each unit in the party should consider the carts as their homes on the way. In view of this, even more than normal good care must be given them to avoid unnecessary accident or breakage. Consideration must be given all stock with the party. Some of the men brought along their best buffalo runners to be used to secure fresh meat if herds of buffalo should be encountered on the way. There were also essential replacements of draught animals. It was thought wise to bring a few good oxen, and while they were inclined to retard the progress considerably, they were also considered a safeguard against famine. All members of the expedition fully appreciated their dependence upon the livestock, for if lost or stolen, grave danger could ensue for everyone. Young men and boys, therefore, were instructed to take charge of the stock at all times, taking it to water and pasture at regular intervals, seeing it properly rounded up at night and placed securely within the protective ring of carts, when a proper guard of mature and responsible men would be set to watch from sundown to sunrise, after which the younger men and boys would again resume their duties to guard the animals on the march all day—such duties being assigned in fair rotation.

At all times the men were to see to it that their guns were in good order and ready at hand for the protection of the party and to secure game. But guns must be used with discretion and conservation of ammunition. Special consideration must be given the storing of gun caps, kegs of gunpowder, bags of shot, and chunks of lead—it being considered advisable to keep such articles in various carts, well spaced for security against the possibility of explosion or theft by skulking Indians.

As leader of the expedition, Sinclair—like the chief factors in earlier times—was entitled to possess the best equipment he could possibly afford—a good gun, toilet articles to make himself presentable to company officers at the various posts visited along the way, and clothing worthy of his position. In addition, he carried in his cart a compact, well-equipped medical kit, containing such standard remedies as calomel, castor oil, laudanum, surgical knives, and instruments for cauterizing wounds likely to be suffered on the trail. Sinclair's position as leader also demanded that he carry a good magnetic compass should the party become lost in unknown country, as well as a good English spyglass to scan the horizon for approaching buffalo or Indians so he might alert the men in time for appropriate action.

Another point upon which Sinclair was adamant from the outset related to carrying liquor. Under the circumstances, this could not be permitted except in the limited amount required for emergencies, to be issued by Sinclair if he considered it necessary. Drinking on the trail would not be permitted, nor would trifling with Indian women be tolerated, in case displeasure be incurred with tribes met on the way and unpleasant consequences result to the danger of the party.

The route chosen by Sinclair was the only one possible in that day; for the most part, it followed the dim tracks used by the wandering, buffalo-hunting *Métis*, which by 1842 linked the widely separated Hudson's Bay Company posts at Fort Ellice, Fort Carlton, Fort Pitt, and Edmonton House. Beyond this point, expediency was to dictate Sinclair's route. The distance to be covered between Red River and Edmonton was some nine hundred miles, broken into three main parts. The first stage was estimated to be about two hundred miles, from Fort Garry to Fort Ellice. The second was a little over three hundred miles, from Ellice to Carlton House. The third, from Carlton to Fort Edmonton, was something less than four hundred miles—this way leading through country where the powerful Blackfoot Confederacy was now driving dangerously north and east into previously unchallenged Cree territory.

II

Two days after the appointed time of meeting at the rendezvous near White Horse Plain—with preparations for travel completed, the most able men chosen to assist Sinclair with various duties, the carts allotted their respective places in the line of march, and the leader's final instructions given—the last farewells were said to *Métis* friends. Then the cart train creaked forward toward the west, beyond the most outlying of the small, whitewashed log shanties of the Red River half-breeds, partially hidden in the little clumps of aspen trees scattered over the prairie. Indeed, that late afternoon of May, 1842, these little *Métis* houses were almost the last human habitations the party would see for some months to come, save for a few scattered Indian tepees and the buildings clustered about Forts Ellice, Carlton, Pitt, and Edmonton, before finally reaching Fort Colvile in the distant Columbia River country.

The first night's camp made on the way west of the rendezvous was set up on the shores of what was known as Long Lake, not far from the Assiniboine River to the west of Fort Garry. Here could be found sufficient dry firewood and good feed for the stock. The members of the party slept comfortably enough that night in and beneath carts, placed in a circle for safety from the prowling, thieving "bungies" or members of an interbred tribe sometimes encountered in this region, with buffalo robes spread beneath and over them for shelter. This method of making temporary camp proved simpler and quicker than setting up tents or tepees, and it was much easier to break camp quickly again at dawn the next morning.

The party's first stop of any importance was made near Portage la Prairie, the old "carrying place" of the Nor'Westers, where as early as 1738 there was said to have been a site of a trading post placed there by the French explorer, La Vérendrye. However, when the Sinclair party went through this country in 1841, no Hudson's Bay Company post had as yet been established in the vicinity. After several days' rest at this point, the party's next camp was made at Rat Creek, some ten miles beyond the portage. Here the trail forked—one fork leading to the Turtle and Moose Mountains, the other trending toward Fort Ellice and on out to the limitless plains as far as the Rocky Mountains. This was the trail the party would follow.

Not far beyond Rat Creek they entered the dreaded Bad Woods, a stretch of thick poplar woods at the foot of an escarpment, where they had to watch for another band of pilfering Indians about whom they had been warned before leaving Red River. Happily, they experienced no trouble from this quarter, perhaps because of the size of the party. But as they progressed the narrow, winding way through the Bad Woods they were annoyed by the bothersome swarms of bulldog flies and mosquitoes—so vicious their attacks that at the camps made in the region they were required to set smudge fires of grass and green brush to ward off the insects whenever the party tried to rest.

Once out of the Bad Woods the party must traverse the rough terrain of an escarpment where there was danger of breaking cart axles by striking hidden tree stumps in the burnt-out brush. However, it was not long until traveling was somewhat better, and when they reached Pine Creek the worst part of this section of the country was over. Here was a favorite camp site of traders and hunters traveling to and from Fort Ellice. Beyond this point they emerged on what was known as the Big Plain—an open and rolling region with the violet outline of Riding Mountain clearly seen to the north of the way they traveled.

Every day that passed now seemed to become more like the one preceding it, but the slow progress of the creaking cart train was not actually as monotonous as might have been expected. Sinclair wisely broke the routine to allow opportunities for hunting the plentiful ducks and geese to be seen almost constantly on little sloughs or for shooting prairie grouse in the thickets to replenish the party's larder and renew the stocks of pemmican. As a still more pleasant diversion, when a good camp site was found, the carts in place, horses hobbled for the night, and an early supper eaten, the more experienced members of the party would recount past exploits of the hunt or tales of encounters with Indians. Pipes were smoked as the people relaxed, with sometimes a song or two to the accompaniment of a *Métis* fiddle before it was again time to retire in and under the carts, with guards set carefully for another night's watch. And so the time passed for the most part on the trail.

At Bog Creek a somewhat uncomfortable camp was made in

an undulating country of sand-dune ridges covered with light vegetation. From the top of a large dune could be seen a wide, parklike expanse of country studded with groves of wild oak and other trees, creating a vast panorama of considerable beauty that extended to Riding Mountain at the north and to the Blue Hills of the Souris at the south. In this vicinity it was known that fires were sometimes deliberately set by unfriendly Indians in order to disorganize parties of the wandering, buffalo-hunting *Métis*, and this danger had to be watched for constantly. Such fires were "put out," as the *Métis* phrased it, meaning that they were set by Indians not only as signal fires and to turn the buffalo herds for their own hunting, but in order to trap unsuspecting parties they desired to accost and rob. If the grass were dry such a fire could race across the land faster than any man could ride the fleetest horse, and would run wild across the plains for miles, destroying everything before it until a river or drenching rain could stop it. Certainly there would be little chance of escape if caught in such a holocaust, so constant vigilance had to be maintained whether fire encountered had been set by evil intent, lightning, or through negligence when they were traveling across the plains.

The party had now reached a point some one hundred miles out of Fort Garry. Several inconveniently wide and deep creeks had to be crossed in this region, and if the banks were too high and steep to negotiate in the usual manner, it was often necessary to ease the carts down the grades with rawhide ropes. Sometimes the men had literally to put their shoulders to the wheel and with bodily strength heave the heavily laden carts through the mud of mirey streams and sloughs. At other times they waded waist deep in water before a cart could be extricated and the train move on again.

It was with a certain sense of relief that the party reached the sweet, swift-flowing, Little Saskatchewan River—the first stream of any size encountered since leaving the Assiniboine. This was a small river—some forty to fifty feet wide and about three feet deep at the ford—and its banks cut deep through the encircling plain to form a valley of much beauty clothed with abundant grass. Twenty-five miles beyond this ideal camp site they came upon a small salt lake—one of a number found on the way to Edmonton—its water bitter with a soda deposit, which concentrated to a whitish crust at the slough's edge as its water evaporated slowly in the summer sun.

The next encampment was made by a shallow body of water called Shoal Lake, which possessed a good beach and was welcome for bathing and washing soiled clothes. The point was now reached some twelve miles from the end of the first lap of the journey at Fort Ellice. From the dominating crest of a hill above the Assiniboine River could be seen this river's junction with the Qu'Appelle a short distance beyond. From here the waters flowed as one, slowly cutting peculiar patterns of land, which were covered with soft greensward and a parklike growth of willows that made delightful vistas of each bow and island in the river's wide valley. In the distance, some three miles away, the several white buildings at Fort Ellice could be seen on the opposite bank of the river. This was a Hudson's Bay Company post that had gained considerably in importance since Sinclair's first visit to the country some fourteen years before; he had helped its growth through the competition he had set up with McDermot's private post in opposition to the company's establishment. The Americans working up into this country from the Missouri were also forcing the Hudson's Bay Company to intensify its efforts here to secure business wherever they could get it by establishing smaller outlying posts on Riding Mountain and Touchwood Hills. Fort Ellice had also become noted for its horse trading and for the securing of some of the best buffalo robes in the country, as well as for extremely good, berry pemmican made by the squaws in this region.

Fort Ellice appeared quite impressive to the Sinclair party, with its pointed spruce-picket stockade some fifteen feet high, its two-story main building facing the main gate that served as officers' and clerks' quarters as well as shops and offices, and also included the main hall where some notoriously hilarious dances were held. On the west side of the post's square stood a row of small, one-story dwellings that housed married men and their families, while workshops were placed conveniently near the front gate. On the opposite side of the square stood provision shops and storage buildings for fur and trade goods, while in the center of the courtyard was the customary squalling fur press. The high flagstaff flew the company's flag to welcome the party, word having reached the post of its approach some time before by company scout. But at this season of the year there was no resounding celebration, for most of the *Métis* who frequented this post were now some hundred miles farther up the Qu'Appelle River, hunting the buffalo that were still plentiful in this country. For this Sinclair had little reason to be sorry. With few people about the post there was less reason for celebration causing unnecessary delay, and it was daily growing more urgent that the party hasten on its way as soon as possible. Also, with most of the Indians up country there would likely be few on the trail from Fort Ellice to Carlton House. This would avoid the necessity of paying a somewhat excessive tribute to these tribes, who at this time were inclined to demand "presents" to permit the passage of a party like this through what they considered to be their territory. Therefore, it was decided the party would remain at Ellice only long enough for a short rest and refreshment, and to make necessary repairs to carts and other equipment, replenish stocks of pemmican, and exchange worn-out horses for fresh ones.

III

Within three days they were on their way again. The cart train ascended from the floor of the lovely Assiniboine Valley, traveling for a time through a rich undergrowth of willow and delightful thickets of prairie dogwood and wild rosebushes that had thus far escaped the ravages of Indian fire. Indeed, there was a singular beauty to the land at this season of the year, with the vivid greensward and the shining young leaves of birch and poplar reflecting the bright clear sunshine. In those mid-June days the turquoise sky was almost cloudless, and there was an unforgettable, exhilarating sparkle to the entire landscape that might well be lost in the usual dryness and dust of the late summer weeks not far ahead.

Once out of the valley and beyond sight of Fort Ellice the party traveled for a time on the high plateau south of the Qu'Appelle River through a country of sloughs swarming with waterfowl. Here and there a few scattered spruce began to appear among the poplars, and boughs of these evergreens provided comfortable springy couches for the weary travelers at their next few encampments.

The trail now sprung northwest, and soon another steep, slippery descent had to be made, from the uplands into the valley of the Qu'Appelle. This crossing was considered somewhat dangerous—as was the ascent from the other side of the valley up to the plains again. Sinclair had reason to be grateful when the crossing and ascent were made without incident. They entered one of the finest buffalo countries in all Rupert's Land of that day, and despite the fact that most of the *Métis* and Indians were still up country after the larger herds, enough straggling buffalo were to be found here to keep the party supplied with fresh meat for a time.

The next stage of the journey carried them over twenty-five miles of beautiful terrain. The aspens appeared to grow larger on the lovely gentle hills of the Little Touchwood range, but the water was harsh and unpleasant for drinking, and casks carried in the carts had to be filled whenever sweet water could be found. Many of the sloughs in this region were also badly tainted with buffalo excrement and decaying vegetation. Deeply indented trails led to the buffaloes' favorite drinking holes and wallows, and some of the *Métis* also informed Sinclair that the foul stench that sometimes filled the air came from the rotting remains of abandoned buffalo pounds, where Indians had recently left numerous carcasses to rot in the sun when they moved on to new hunting grounds farther afield.

The summit of the range of Touchwood Hills proved to be

a series of fine upland prairies sixty to seventy miles wide. These hills overlooked the great level plains that extended on either side of this decided rise. It was a pleasant, gradual climb to the top of this range—the party following a dim trail that wound through most beautiful country. Little streams of sweet water wandered through small valleys clothed with aspen groves and interspersed with lush meadows dotted with wildflowers. Here and there were little lakes from which duck, geese, plover, and even some large crane rose to take flight as the cart train passed by.

The top of the Touchwoods had to be crossed before a descent could be made to the great sweep of plains beyond. Here, except in this hunting season, the Cree, Ojibway, and "bungies" usually roamed far up the Qu'Appelle. Their comparatively recent camps were marked by old tepee poles and rings of medicine lodges; the torn boughs of maskotima or saskatoon berry bushes evidenced the squaws' pemmican making.

The descent from the fine uplands of the Touchwoods was some fourteen miles in length to the seemingly endless expanse of unbroken prairie below. It was difficult and unpleasant country, and Sinclair had been warned to prepare well for it at Ellice. He had therefore ordered that extra wood be placed in the carts while the party was still in the wooded country of the hills they had left behind. In this present bit of wasteland there was not even enough deadwood to repair carts or make campfires. The way they must cross was full of boulders and ruts that could snap cart axles like matchwood, and if this occurred even temporary repairs could cause unpleasant delays.

This country was made even more uncomfortable through lack of water for man or beast. Before the descent from the hills was made Sinclair had insisted that the kegs be filled at the last possible opportunity with fresh water. But none could be carried for the stock, and the animals must go without water until sloughs could be found beyond this wasteland. Fortunately, this portion of terrain was crossed without too much difficulty, although some axles snapped and had to be mended with temporary binding of shaganappi dampened in some of the precious drinking water. Horses and cattle suffered during the two days it took to cross this barren spot, but gradually the party emerged into better country, and the South Saskatchewan River was reached late on the third day from the descent of the Touchwoods.

The first sight of the South Saskatchewan revealed a torrent some two hundred feet wide, swollen with mid-June flood waters that poured down in melting freshets of the river's tributaries, which took their rise in the Rocky Mountains far to the west. The banks of the river appeared to be a good 150 feet high. The valley, although decidedly narrower than either the Assiniboine or Qu'Appelle valleys, seemed about a mile across where the Sinclair party first viewed it—its banks lined with a fair growth of poplar, white birch, and other trees. The water at this time of early summer flow was an unattractive milky gray, but fresh and cool to the taste.

Crossing this wide and swiftly flowing river was a formidable task, and Sinclair had to rely upon the experience of his most trusted men to see the party over safely. Without delay the carts were made into strong, buoyant rafts. The shying horses were driven into the river amidst shouts, yells, curses, laughter, and even the throwing of stones to force the animals across. Some of the creatures struggled to combat the sharp current; others took to the stream more steadily and sensibly. The river for a time seemed a strange melee of horses' heads—a curious sight, as impressive as it was terrifying. But by the *Métis*' good management all stock and people were brought across in safety.

However, additional delay was caused at this crossing for the making of a crude log raft—something like a primitive ark—to ferry the party's few oxen across, along with the more timorous women and children, unprepared to face the frightening trip over in the converted cart boats. Those with nerve enough to take this other way were piled on their crude ferry with the precious belongings and were poled over by men in the party who had earlier seen service with the company's York boat brigades. Sinclair waited until all were across before making his way over the stream himself—watching with restrained anxiety and marveling that all was accomplished with such astonishing dexterity and lack of concern by his men.

Once the South Saskatchewan River was traversed without loss or mishap, the distance of some eighteen miles to the great stream's northern branch was crossed easily. This was over a low plateau, not more than three hundred feet above the level of the river itself, that provided little but an unbroken vista of prairie grass studded with wild flowers. Over all arched an endless expanse of clear blue sky, never so beautiful as when seen above a low horizon such as this bit of unrelieved plain.

IV

The party had now reached Fort Carlton, or La Montée—the "Place Where Horses Are Taken Overland," as translated from the Cree. It was considered the roughest and toughest of all the Hudson's Bay Company posts, due to the fact that it was the regular stopping place for the brigades of York boats that traveled up and down the Saskatchewan each year between York Factory and Fort Edmonton. The boatmen demanded a short respite from their arduous labors on the waterways, and Fort Carlton provided them with plenty of buffalo meat, liquor, the opportunity to gamble, and a chance to frolic with the pretty half-breed girls and Indian squaws of the district—all of this giving rise to much rough sport and brawling.

Sinclair's party was only too eager after the long days on the trail from Fort Garry to partake of some of this post's hospitality, but such celebrations were not to be prolonged. Time was running out in this curious race across the continent, and no unnecessary delay could be allowed if the Rockies were to be traversed by a new and previously untraveled pass before the first fall of autumn snow.

Carlton proved to be a crude but substantial fort situated on the south bank of the North Saskatchewan River. It had an especially strong palisade and a well-armed gallery surrounding it, with fortified towers at each corner, for this area was now in almost constant danger of Blackfoot attack. The usual volley of gunfire and wild shouting greeted the party's arrival, for word of its approach had gone well ahead by Indian "grapevine." The inhabitants of this post also realized that the Sinclair party was inaugurating a new era of prosperity for Carlton House, which could bring regular cart brigades this way to augment its already lucrative and exciting trade from the company's boat brigades on the Saskatchewan.

After three days at Carlton, spent in some lively celebrating and preparing for the next lap of the journey to Edmonton, the party was once more ready to go forward. The next stretch would take them to Fort Pitt, through country Sinclair had never traveled before, although company men had come this way for a considerable length of time. Trails, however, were dim beyond Carlton in 1841. In fact, two trails led from this post westward to Edmonton. One followed the south side of the river, but this was now in greater danger of Blackfoot raids; so Sinclair chose the northern route, although it included many streams to be crossed, which would mean greater delay.

To reach this chosen track the North Saskatchewan had to be crossed, but this crossing proved less troublesome than the crossing of the South Saskatchewan had been. At Carlton House the Hudson's Bay Company was able to provide a crude ferry —at a comparatively stiff tariff—to transport the carts and settlers to the other side of the stream. However, there were certain definite compensations in this route, above and beyond the greater safety it afforded from Blackfoot Indian attack; for while the same vast plain extended generally westward, the country through which the party was about to pass was more heavily wooded than that which lay to the south of the river. It therefore provided greater comfort for both stock and people when camping and resting, although here again treed watersheds gave rise to some annoying crossings of the various streams that flowed south into the North Saskatchewan River from the height-of-land to the north. One such stream was the Jack Fish River, some fifteen miles north of the main course of the North Saskatchewan where the trail led, and not far from the site chosen by the Cree and Salteaux Indians for one of their annual sun dances. However, none of these Indians were met here—being far out on the plains to the south of the Saskatchewan River in pursuit of the large buffalo herds—and for this the party had reason to be thankful.

Some twenty-five miles farther on they reached the Tortoise River. The trail now wound through hilly country and once more approached the main course of the North Saskatchewan at a point known as the English River. To cross some of the larger streams in this vicinity bridges had to be built by those accustomed to such work. Large logs were hauled into place with some difficulty and fastened together securely with lengths of shaganappi, making a kind of trellis strong enough to bear the weight of the heavily laden carts, stock, and people. Added vexation was often caused when men slipped at their work on the wet banks of the streams and oxen balked as they were urged to cross these crude bridges.

The party had now reached what was known as the Red Deer Hills—still well to the east of Fort Edmonton. Here was a range some four hundred feet above the level of the North Saskatchewan, which provided yet another height-of-land to feed more aggravating streams that had to be crossed by one means or another. One hill, known as Frenchman's Butte, stood out with striking prominence; it was shaped like a giant beehive. It was here that Governor George Simpson caught up with the Sinclair party, making extraordinarily swift progress on this first lap of his journey around the world.

Unencumbered by a large party of settlers and wandering stock as was Sinclair, Simpson traveled light and superbly equipped, served by skilled attendants and riding the best horses. His rate of travel across the plains was rarely less than fifty miles a day, and when on the waterways in his swift canoe he boasted that he could often cover as much as one hundred miles a day.

Indeed, Simpson's exploits in the year 1841 were quite phenomenal. He had traveled almost continuously that year, starting from London, England, on the morning of May 3. He had crossed the Atlantic Ocean by swift packet, reached his headquarters at Lachine near Montreal, and from that place had set forth almost immediately in his ably manned canoe to continue up the St. Lawrence and Ottawa rivers to Lake Nipissing. Then he had gone down the French River to Lake Huron, crossed it to Sault Ste. Marie, and traveled up Lake Superior to Fort William. From there he had journeyed by Kaministiquia, Rainy River, Fort Frances, the Lake of the Woods, and down the Winnipeg River and up the Red River to Fort Garry, which he reached on June 9. He had been detained there for more than a week at company headquarters, which gave Sinclair's party a head start on the trail as far as Frenchman's Butte where he had overtaken it.

The Governor and his nimble entourage had camped near Sinclair's people for one night and were ready to depart at sunrise the next day. There had only been time for a short interview between Sinclair and Simpson, and there could have been few if any confidences exchanged; for old resentments still rankled deep, and the "Little Emperor"—grown even more arrogant with the years of his proud authority—tolerated no show of familiarity from one of Sinclair's standing, even on a trail in the northern wilderness. It would appear that as a result of this meeting Sinclair parted with Simpson more determined than ever to find his own way across the Rocky Mountains with his followers by some still untrodden way, and that he had not in any way betrayed his intention to the Governor at this meeting. However, Simpson had bluntly informed Sinclair before he left his camp that final instructions would await him at Fort Edmonton as to how he was to take his party across the mountains.

Nevertheless, Sinclair could not have had any way of knowing that Simpson had studied him and his party carefully at this meeting, for while the Governor's memory was still fresh with recent impressions he wrote the following passage for his manuscript, later entitled "A Narrative of a Trip around the World": "Each family had two or three carts, together with bands of horses cattle and dogs. . . . As they marched in single file their cavalcade extended above a mile long. . . . The emigrants were all healthy and happy; living with the greatest abundance and enjoying the journey with great relish. . . . There were more members in the party at the finish than when they started!"

This last comment was only too true, for several births had occurred to *Métis* women in the party on the way, causing further delay in the expedition's progress.

V

The excitement of the Governor's visit past, the plodding party resumed its way, striving to maintain its best rate of not less than twenty miles a day—certainly a poor record in comparison with Simpson's pace. Surprisingly few incidents or injuries had occurred thus far, and only a few minor bands of friendly Cree had been met with on the way—fortunately no warlike Blackfeet, who chanced to be farther to the south hunting the buffalo and trading with the Americans this year along the Missouri.

The rough and rowdy outpost of Fort Pitt was found to stand some one hundred yards back from the banks of the North Saskatchewan. This post was little more than a few log buildings placed within a pathetically inadequate crude palisade, for the place stood dangerously close to the country being fiercely fought over by rival Cree and Blackfoot bands on a number of occasions. Fort Pitt had only been established some ten years before the Sinclair party arrived, but its importance had recently been enhanced as an exchange base for the company's horses. A large horse-guard or wintering camp had been established near the post. This place was also of value to the Old Company for the amount of pemmican produced each season in this region by Indians and *Métis*, from the great herds of buffalo that seemed to range in this vicinity annually. Because of this post's excess of waste buffalo flesh, the company also kept a large number of its valuable sleigh dogs here in the summer, to get them in prime condition for the strenuous winter transport. As the Sinclair cavalcade approached, the yelping and barking of these dogs could be heard for a considerable distance.

Certainly a somewhat inappropriate time had been chosen for their arrival at Fort Pitt. There was a tense attitude of expectancy here for fear of attack by roaming Blackfoot bands returning from their trading and hunting far to the south at any moment—the post's usual complement of men for its defense unhappily absent. When the Sinclair people arrived, the danger was accentuated by the unexpected advent of some hundred tepees of Cree, who had encamped just outside the post's stockade, eager to trade their pemmican, hides, and grease for company trade goods and ammunition—the latter mostly to continue their retaliatory skirmishes with the Blackfeet. This in itself provided a special inducement for Blackfoot attack upon the post, and the fear was intensified by the fact that a serious brush between Blackfeet and Crees had recently occurred not far from the post at Horse Hill, with considerable loss to both sides. As a consequence of all this, Sinclair and his people were most anxious to finish their business at Pitt quickly—replenishing food supplies, making necessary repairs to equipment, and exchanging worn-out mounts so they might be on their way again without delay or involvement.

It was essential for Sinclair to secure a competent guide at Fort Pitt to lead the party the rest of the way to Fort Edmonton, since it would be incurring unnecessary danger in this unpredictable Indian country for him to attempt to find the way unguided through a region that was poorly marked and that he had never crossed before. If the party should become lost it would make a most desirable target for surprise Blackfoot attack. Therefore, while he considered the price for such a guide somewhat excessive, he secured the services of Michele, a full-blooded Iroquois

Indian from Quebec, one of a number who had come to serve the company as guides in the west, to take the party as far as Edmonton House, even if such an arrangement irked some of the *Métis* in the party who thought the hiring of the Indian unnecessary.

Beyond Fort Pitt the party traveled through a pleasant, hilly, well-treed country, crossing many more streams by devious means and passing landmarks with appropriate descriptive names given by earlier traders, such as Dog Rump Hill, Riding Lake, and Snake Lake.

As the party approached Edmonton House there were still more streams to cross with some difficulty—Pine Creek, White Mud Creek, Smoking Lake Creek, and Vermilion Creek. Some of them were still in freshet from rains at the height-of-land; others had deep banks or fords, which required the construction of bridges. Sinclair had cause for worry at every delay, for the days were passing swiftly, thus increasing the danger of crossing an unknown pass in the Rockies too late. However, most of this annoyance was past with their arrival at Fort Edmonton, and with the realization that they had crossed the great plains from Fort Garry without molestation from the Blackfeet or any untoward incident. Now the decision must be made whether they should take the unknown way or that which Governor Simpson expected them to follow.

VI

Sinclair's weary emigrants reached Edmonton House early in August, 1841, after having been more than two months on the trail from Red River. Fort Edmonton was a fine establishment, with a high picketed stockade, bastioned and battlemented, and certainly built better than many a post. It was situated on a high bank that dominated a beautiful expanse of the North Saskatchewan River. Its large main gate was surmounted with most peculiar weathervanes. All in all, it appeared to Sinclair—as it later did to the artist Paul Kane, who was to one day become a friend of Sinclair's and to paint his portrait [5]—as a strikingly different establishment from any he had seen before.

Surprisingly enough, the gates at Fort Edmonton were quietly and unceremoniously opened to let the Sinclair party through without the firing of guns or shouts of welcome. There was a kind of restrained decorum about this place of which Sinclair had heard and which proved consistent with the dictates of the post's able governor, the powerful if somewhat eccentric Chief Factor William Rowand. Indeed, there was a very genuine welcome awaiting the party. The company's flag was formally broken on the high staff in the center of the large square, symbolizing the fact that good will awaited them, along with every hospitality the post could afford.

The official residence of the governor, called the "Big House," where Sinclair went at once to present his credentials from Simpson and Finlayson, was a somewhat extraordinary structure —a massive wooden building at least seventy-five feet deep by sixty wide, three stories high, with a gallery opening from the second story at the front. Instead of being whitewashed in conformity with other such buildings at Fort Garry or York Factory, the "Big House" was painted a durable warm brown that seemed to be obtained from a mixture of ground vermilion smeared with earth and primed with oil. It was decorated inside and out with striking barbaric designs—Indian carvings and curious symbols in other strong earth colors that added a unique appearance to the place.

The importance of Fort Edmonton had increased perceptibly under the governorship of Chief Factor Rowand, according to what Sinclair had learned of the place from Chief Factor Curtis Bird who had been governor here some thirty years before. Sinclair was deeply disappointed to discover that Rowand was not at Edmonton House but had gone across the Rockies with Simpson, and would accompany him as far as the Sandwich Islands on the company's ship. Simpson—so it later proved—had availed himself not only of Rowand's company and wit on the journey but of his practical knowledge of the Rocky Mountain region to assist him in the discovery of his new pass.

With Rowand gone, Sinclair was informed that the papers Simpson had left for him as he passed through Edmonton were awaiting him in the hands of Simpson's former trusted servant, Trader Colin Fraser.[6] Simpson had brought Fraser from Scotland some years before to act as his personal piper, and he later served as an interpreter along the Saskatchewan, but was now postmaster at Jasper's House where he had been stationed for the past five years. Simpson still trusted him to carry out some of his special commissions, and before he left Edmonton the Governor had instructed Fraser to hand Sinclair his letters in person. Simpson's orders to Sinclair read:

> I leave three of my people here to assist in getting the boats up from Fort Assiniboine in the mountains, and it will be necessary that six or seven of your people should be separated from your party, as with the three men left by me to bring the boats back to Fort Assiniboine in time to transport the Columbians going from York Factory who may be expected there by the latter end of August. It is of the utmost importance that every expedition should be used to get your people up to Jasper's House in order that the boats may be available in time for Mr. Manson and his party. Your blacksmiths should be set to work in nail-making immediately upon their arrival here, and they remain a day or two after their families take their departure from Fort Assiniboine so as to complete their work as they may easily overtake the main party before they get to the Athabasca River, and are immediately on landing at Jasper's House, Bernier, Spence, and any other handy men you may have should be despatched with all expedition to the Boat Encampment to prepare wood and build boats by the time they reach the Boat Encampment.[7]

His plans forming in his own mind as to what he intended to do, in complete disregard of Simpson's explicit instructions, Sinclair went about preparing his party for crossing the Rockies by a completely new overland route he now meant to discover himself. As he went about this, Sinclair also found that this Edmonton House was indeed an extraordinary company establishment apart from its outside appearance. It proved to be a well-organized place of business that was everywhere stamped with Rowand's dominating personality. Edmonton was in truth another actual factory such as York Factory. Normally this post housed from forty to fifty men—a number with wives and families—who were engaged in all manner of essential labor. Even the women at Edmonton, whether Indian or *Metis*, were kept usefully employed in making moccasins and buckskin garments, as well as with sewing many bright cotton shirts—a special feature of Edmonton's valuable trade with the Blackfeet. The women also performed other special duties in keeping the post neat and clean, with certain chores peculiar to the season, such as sweeping snow from the courtyards in winter—all this apart from the domestic duties of their own households. In all this, Rowand had set an exemplary pattern in his own private establishment, where Madam Rowand—a woman of exceptionally fine character and attainments, and held in the highest regard—had helped Edmonton earn an enviable reputation above many other company posts for its efficiency and the moral rectitude of the people generally within its gates.

Apart from all this, Edmonton's importance as a trading center under the wise supervision of Rowand was now widely recognized. One of its achievements, especially in winter, was the building of a large number of good York boats for carrying fur and trade goods on the Saskatchewan. In the year 1841, about twice as many York boats were required to take the fur down to Rock House—the important exchange point on the water route to York Factory—as were needed to bring the trade goods back upstream from York. Empty York boats at this time were never brought all the way inland again from York, so construction was continuously carried on at Edmonton for replacements.

Indeed, under Rowand, Edmonton House had become almost unrivaled in a number of respects. Not only was trading carried on with the friendly Cree and Assiniboine Indians but also with their inveterate enemies, the Blackfeet. Rowand, like Chief Factor Bird before him, was compelled to maintain, by shrewd and tactful bargaining, a precarious balance of trade with both sides. The Indians who now came to Edmonton to trade often presented a most striking and sometimes terrifying spectacle in their barbaric native regalia—some appearing at the post as naked as Greek gods, with perhaps the adornment of a top hat secured by some peculiar bargaining and regarded as of great value by any native able to obtain one. Most of the Indians trading at Edmonton sought blankets, beads, cottons, strouds, Prussian blue and pink calicoes, pink and blue shirting, blue druggits, large silk and cotton handkerchiefs in bright colors, Paisley woolen shawls, and quantities of vermilion powder for decorating their persons, horses, and tepees, to mention but a few of this post's important trade items, apart from the brisk business in tea and fire arms. Such commodities were sought in exchange for large quantities of pemmican, buffalo hides, and wolf skins from the Blackfoot country to the south of Edmonton, as well as the valuable fur from the wooded regions long claimed by the Cree and other northern and western tribes.

Edmonton House was a busy place at all seasons of the year in the middle of the nineteenth century, and was particularly so when the overland brigades of pack horses arrived bringing in the rich fur from the company's farther outposts to the north and west, such as those in the Athabaska and distant Columbia River country. It was the sight of these pack trains that suddenly suggested to Sinclair the way he might convey his party across the Rocky Mountains to the Oregon, and brought to mind the fact that his people must not tarry too long at this place if they meant to get across in safety without being trapped by early winter snow at the height-of-land.

VII

It was apparently quite by chance that Sinclair met at Edmonton House an interesting Indian chief named Mackipictoon, who belonged to the Wetaskiwin band of Cree. This most unusual Indian was also known as "Broken Arm" from a conspicuous infirmity. Curiously enough, this cognomen had been given to several Indians, half-breeds, and even white men at Edmonton House throughout the years, which has caused some historical confusion; but this particular Cree was somewhat distinguished by his unusual exploits. In conversations with him, Mackipictoon confirmed for Sinclair the fact that there were negotiable passes in the Rocky Mountains that were still untrodden by any white man, and over one of these he was prepared to guide Sinclair and his party in safety.

Sinclair soon discovered that this Indian was widely traveled. It was reported concerning him at Edmonton that he had once gone far to the south on a trip that had taken him to the capital of the United States, where he had been received in special audience by President Andrew Jackson. Mackipictoon was considered by his Cree brethren to be a very great warrior—as was his father before him, who had been feared and respected even by the Blackfeet. Mackipictoon was known to have an ungovernable temper, and it was said that he had once scalped his own wife for suspected infidelity—the unhappy woman having survived in some miraculous manner this harrowing ordeal. Mackipictoon, however, was said to have greatly improved in temperament since his conversion to Christianity by the Wesleyan Missionary, the Reverend R. T. Rundle,[8] only the year before Sinclair met him, in 1841.

Sinclair also learned that Mackipictoon's keen desire to lead his party across the Rockies resulted from the chagrin he felt that Governor Simpson and Chief Factor Rowand had not let him lead their party over their new pass to the Oregon in the summer of 1841, but had chosen instead a rival half-Cree chief named Peechee. The wily Mackipictoon saw in this chance to conduct Sinclair's party over the mountains an opportunity to restore his own prestige as guide. He informed Sinclair that he would follow Simpson's trail from Edmonton as far as the foot of the Rockies, or to the Long Narrow Lake, Imna-stoh, which other Indians called Lake Minnee-wah-kah,[9] or the Lake Where the Spirits Dwell—the Devil's Lake of the white men. From here he would lead Sinclair's party by another track never before followed by white men over the Great Divide of the Rockies. It was, he assured Sinclair over and over again, a safe course. The only possible danger lay from Blackfoot attack between Edmonton and the base of the Rockies, which actually lay in their country, but it was unlikely that any serious trouble of this sort would arise this season, since it was known to Mackipictoon that the main body of Blackfeet were still far to the south hunting the buffalo and trading with the Americans along the Missouri and the Marias River.

After careful consideration and in full consultation with the members of his party, it was finally agreed that all who were willing to follow Sinclair and the Indian chief over the new way to the Oregon should set forth from Edmonton as early as possible. Vigorous preparations were therefore undertaken at once for this unprecedented venture. Good horses for both riding and packing were chosen, with only a few carts to be taken as far as convenient. Warm clothing was secured, for it was apparent that cold weather would surely overtake them at the height-of-land; and in case sufficient game was not to be found on the way, enough pemmican must be carried with them to sustain the party over the mountains. With every apparent eventuality carefully considered and every possible precaution taken, the party was ready to depart from Fort Edmonton by the second week in August—some two weeks later than Simpson himself had set forth from that place on July 28, 1841, for his own adventure in pass finding.

VIII

The Sinclair party set out from Edmonton House fully reorganized and confident in its new mode of travel. Most of the people rode horseback, even the women, with children up behind them, and some with infants carried on their backs papoose fashion. The party's few possessions had been cut to the minimum, with only the barest necessities retained of blankets, sacks of pemmican, and the simplest kind of camp equipment carried on the extra pack ponies. Sinclair had seen to it that his most trusted men were trained in the art of packing by experts at

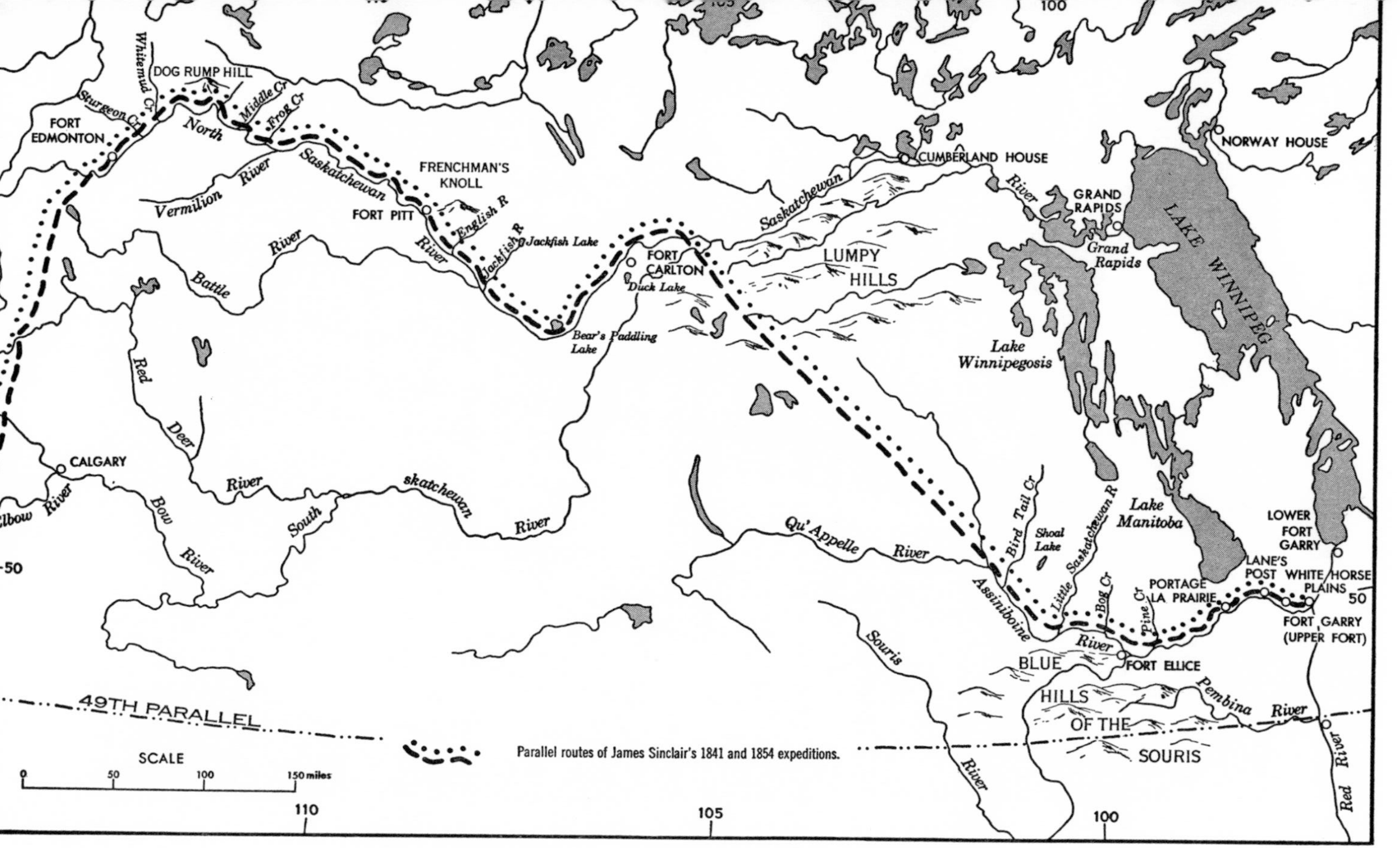

Map 2. Routes of James Sinclair's 1841 and 1854 expeditions

Edmonton, retained there for the preparing of pack trains to carry the company's trade goods and fur back and forth to the outlying posts to the north and west.

Once the great gates of Edmonton House were closed behind them, the party took—in direct defiance of Simpson's orders—not the usual path westward toward the Boat Encampment, but a trail leading to the company's ferry, which carried the party as quickly as possible across the North Saskatchewan River to the south bank of this stream. Once on its way the party quickly adjusted to the new mode of travel and, with characteristic *Métis* adaptability, as quickly forgot the former dependence upon carts for transport and shelter. They soon devised comfortable and ingenious ways of making camp, sleeping after the manner of the Indians with crude shelters constructed from the buffalo hides, and apparently most of them relished the change and freedom this form of pack-train travel afforded.

The Cree guide led them for several days almost due south from Edmonton at a varying rate of from twenty to thirty miles a day. He rode at the head of the train beside Sinclair, pointing out the landmarks familiar to the Indians traveling in this part of the country, and selected suitable camp sites until they reached the body of water known today as Gull Lake. Here was a fine sheet of water some twenty miles in length by five or six in width. The weather continued warm, and the party was subject to the vicious attacks of bulldog flies, mosquitoes, and sand flies—as bothersome to the stock as they were to humans.

It was near the crossing of the Red Deer River that the party caught its first glimpse of the Rocky Mountains—at about the same spot as Chief Factor James Curtis Bird had witnessed them some thirty years earlier. The mountains presented a clear serrated line against the western horizon, dark blue at their base in the early morning sun with their snow peaks shining in bold relief against the characteristic arch of blue sky beyond them. Gradually, as the party traveled toward the southwest, the mighty barrier of the vast range, extending as far as the eye could see from north to south, became larger and bolder in mass and outline.

The Indian Chief said that the crossing of the Red Deer River that must be made was the only good crossing of this stream at most seasons of the year. It had long been used by both Cree and Blackfeet traveling north and south to trade, fight, or visit with other tribes. The season was swiftly approaching when the Indians would come north from their hunting and trading, but no bands of either warlike or friendly Indians were encountered here for fight or parley.

Mackipictoon now led the party for some time in the same southwesterly direction and followed up a stream he called "La Biche," or the Little Red Deer River—a branch of the main Red Deer, although no game of any importance, deer or otherwise, was met with in this country, and the party had to resort to some of its precious stock of pemmican. Advancing up the Little Red Deer, they were compelled to cross it and its many smaller tributaries no less than forty times before leaving the country drained by it. But such fords proved of little difficulty to the pack train in comparison with the trouble the party had experienced when traveling with their carts between Fort Garry and Edmonton.

Now they followed an old Assiniboine or Stony Indian trail that kept them well to the wooded country in the Rocky Mountain foothills for some time, where fortunately their campfires were better hidden from the watchful eyes of any Blackfoot scouts that might have been lurking about. As the train drew closer to the main range of the Rockies, a great gray escarpment seemed to loom directly before them as if to block all entry to the mountains. But the Cree guide pointed out that there were actually three ways into the mountains in this vicinity. One was called the Devil's Gap; another, the Kananaskis Gap; and the third, the Gap of the Minnee-znee-wap-tah, or Gap of the Cold Water River—also sometimes called the Bow River Gap, because the prairie Indians were said to come to this place to secure wood for their bows and arrows.

The Devil's Gap,[10] the Indian said, was the way taken by Simpson's party some weeks earlier and would lead them directly toward a peculiarly shaped mountain that seemed to stand out sharply from the rest, called by various Cree names meaning the Devil's Nose, the Devil's Head, or the Devil's Thumb. This dominating mountain remained curiously dark throughout the year while other peaks were covered with snow, and it seemed to stare ominously in all directions with a similar face. In fact, the Cree Indians so feared this peak they made propitiatory offerings to its *Manitou* in the form of pipes, tobacco, and decorated tomahawks on certain of its ledges.

In this country, upon the advice of Mackipictoon, Sinclair kept the party fully alerted against surprise Blackfoot attack, for many severe brushes had taken place in this country between those Indians and their enemies, the Cree and Kootenays. As the party drew closer to the Devil's Head, a passage suddenly appeared to open. This was the Devil's Gap, marking the entrance to the Rockies, and once through it the party proceeded for some time through comparatively thick woods in a lovely valley some two or three miles wide, containing four beautiful lakes linked together by small streams. The largest of these lakes was the Minnee-wah-kah,[11] of the Assiniboine tongue—the Spirit Water—or the Much-Manitou-sa-gi-agun—the Devil's Lake of the Cree. Here the party rested for a few days to make ready for the next step in crossing the Rockies.

Lake Minnee-wah-kah was a leaf-shaped body of water some thirteen miles in length and not more than two miles in width. It was an amazing, changing blue, taking its hue from the vagaries of passing clouds and the shadows of the mighty peaks that surrounded it—the first mountains of any great height the party had yet seen.[12] The trail that Simpson and his party had traveled some weeks earlier through this region followed the north and west side of the lake. The trail over which the Cree guide now took the Sinclair party led half-way down the east and south side of the lake, then through a picturesque little gorge that struck directly away from the lake to emerge in the valley of the Bow River.[13] Here the trail, singularly enough, turned for a little while to the east in order to find a good ford of the Bow River; and on the opposite side of this stream it struck an Indian trail, leading them west and southwest again to the entrance of the new pass.

The Bow River was forded without too much difficulty, and the southwesterly trending trail led them slowly upward and on through the mountains, past a great rocky ridge known as the Goat Range, which possessed some especially fine peaks—one particularly impressive with a beautiful triple summit.[14] The party now entered a country of fine lakes,[15] the trail passing many more majestic peaks [16]—some with curious Indian names, and most of them little less than nine thousand feet high, and some even higher. Travel was pleasant in this high, exhilarating country with glorious August weather, as the party climbed toward the summit of the Rockies. They traveled now almost continuously in a southwesterly direction, following the course of a stream whose rapid waters led them to the top of the Great Divide.[17]

Once they had crossed the Divide—almost imperceptible but for the change of flow of the mountain streams that took their rise at that height—the difference of vegetation was perceptible on the western slope of the mountains. The very atmosphere was different—softer and more moist. The change was also evident in the more abundant growth of trees and other plants, certain species of which had not been seen on the eastern slope of the mountains. As the Cree guide had said, the party followed one of the fine streams taking its rise near the great shining mountain pyramid,[18] which could be seen in the distance to the right of the trail along which the party descended from the height-of-land. The trail now trended southwest once more, following this river's northern bank and passing many fine waterfalls of smaller streams that poured into it from the southeast.

They at last reached the Kootenay River, which flowed through an enormous trough running parallel with the Rocky Mountain Range, which the party had left behind, although another great range farther to the west had still to be crossed before they reached the Columbia River valley.[19] It was when they came to the banks of the Kootenay that the Cree guide announced triumphantly that he had brought the party safely over the new pass of the Rocky Mountains. From this point onward they would again be following in Governor Simpson's footsteps, since it had been necessary for him to come this way some weeks before, after having made his own crossing of the Rockies by his newly discovered pass.[20] Here their trails converged again to reach the Columbia River.

The Cree guide led the Sinclair party to a comparatively safe crossing of the Kootenay River itself. They then followed a trail that led for a time in a northwesterly direction up the Kootenay Valley to a point where they struck a fine stream flowing into it from the west; and they followed the stream up to the next height-of-land on the same trail Simpson had used some weeks before. At the summit of this pass[21] they came upon a delightful lake surrounded by a forest that seemed to cast upon its waters a peculiarly scintillating sheen of green shot with gold.[22] But such beauty was soon replaced by the spectacular and awe-inspiring sight called by the Indian, Red Rock Gorge.[23] It was a terrifying cut through the mountains, with high, overhanging cliffs the color of clotted blood that reached up more than a thousand feet and nearly met overhead to create an eerie semidarkness that all but obliterated the sky above the narrow passage through which they must travel. Their trail led through this gorge, following dangerously near a roaring mountain stream[24]—the only one that would take them to the valley of the Columbia not too far beyond.

It was a pleasant relief to leave this oppressive canyon and to follow the river into a wider passage where at least some sun could break through upon them between the overhanging cliffs. The river then took them down from this height-of-land to an interesting hot springs,[25] which the Indian guide said was often visited by his and other tribes in order that the medicinal waters might relieve many of their maladies.

It did not take long to reach the valley of the mighty Columbia River,[26] the waterway used for many years by the company's bateaux to reach Fort Vancouver from the Boat Encampment. This was the way that Simpson had expected Sinclair to bring his party. However, in defying the Governor and bringing his people overland to this point where the Columbia widened from the mountains into a series of lakes, Sinclair discovered an overland route much simpler and easier to follow than anyone might have expected in this curious race to find a new way across the mountains.

The party had emerged into an entirely different terrain of the Upper Columbia River country—a region first discovered by white men when the exceptional Nor'Wester, David Thompson, was believed to have reached this country at the beginning of the nineteenth century. Thompson had established a series of posts in this vicinity, calling each in turn "Kootenai House," in honor of the Indians with whom he traded.

When the Sinclair party reached this region they encountered a few of the Kootenay tribe, but most of them were still on the eastern side of the Rockies hunting buffalo and raiding Blackfoot encampments to steal horses and women. The Kootenays, like the Cree, were the bitter enemies of the Blackfeet; and David Thompson had helped this age-old feud by supplying the Kootenays on the west side of the Rockies with guns before the Blackfeet could secure enough firearms to carry on an even struggle. For this the Blackfeet had never forgiven Thompson nor any other white man. However, the Sinclair party did meet in the Upper Columbia River country a few wandering Shuswaps, or "Shee-waps" as Mackipictoon called them—members of a somewhat unusual tribe of Indians with distinctive traits and customs, and a people most skilled as mountain travelers as well as fearless hunters of grizzly and wolf.

This country was pleasant and different from any Sinclair or his people had previously seen on the trip, and it seemed particularly so during the delightful early autumn days. The air was clear, dry, and stimulating as they progressed toward

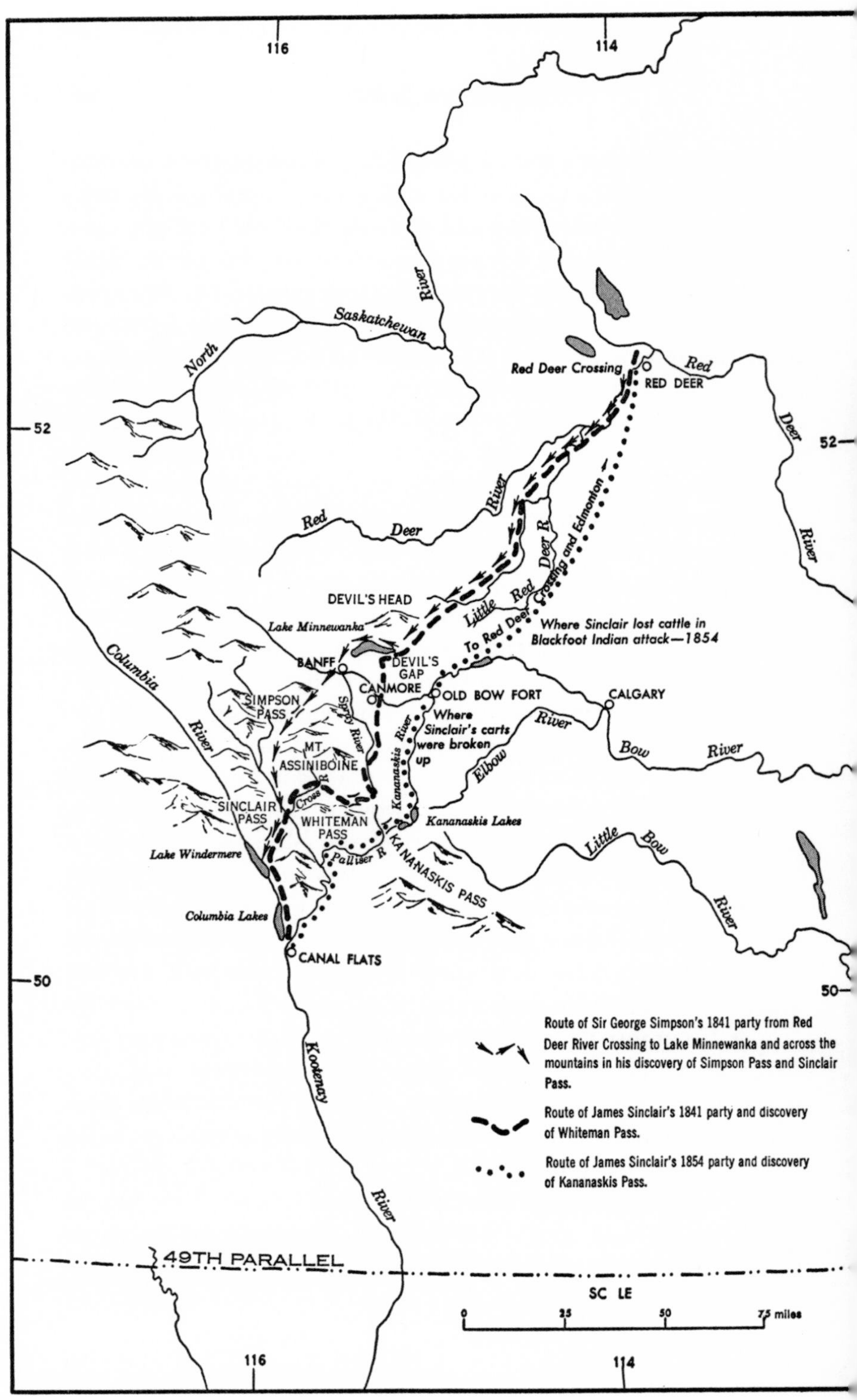

Map 3. Routes of Sinclair and Simpson, and passes discovered by each

the Kootenay Portage. The land, for the most part here, was a parklike plateau—the landscape broken by tall spruce trees along the high sandbanks on the eastern side of the lake.[27] To the south was a strikingly high mountain peak,[28] beyond which the Kootenay River flowed, with the Columbia River sweeping near it to the north, shortly to mingle their waters and flow on together to the sea.

In this vicinity was to be seen the remains of an old canal, dug many years before by the Nor'Westers before they joined with the Hudson's Bay Company in 1821, to link the flow of the Kootenay and Columbia, thus facilitating the transport of fur and goods. After crossing the flats[29]—which marked another height-of-land between the two great rivers—the party proceeded along the course of the Kootenay once more, then struck overland by another old Indian trail to reach Grand Quête Lake.[30] This was a favorite gathering place of the Kootenay Indians for their annual celebration upon their return from their autumn hunting trips, but in 1841 they had not yet returned to this spot.

From this point the Sinclair people continued along another stream that flowed from Grand Quête Lake to the Kootenay Traverse. Somewhat more difficult terrain was encountered before the party reached Fort Colvile, passing on the way a site of Thompson's old Kullyspell House on the eastern shore of Lake Pend d'Oreille. Here still another watershed had to be crossed to reach the Kootenay River again, with another hard bit of traveling through dense forest and brush in a swampy valley, at the height of which two more streams flowed in opposite directions from surprisingly close proximity.

The Cree guide then led them along a better-marked trail that had once been the old North West Company fur track between what had been its old Kootenay Post and the Hudson's Bay Company's present important establishment at Fort Colvile. Here it was that the guide left the party to return alone to Fort Edmonton by the way he had come.

IX

A genuine welcome awaited Sinclair and his people at Fort Colvile. This was a most pleasant post with a good master. It was ideally situated near the beautiful Kettle Falls, about one mile from the junction of the Columbia and Colvile rivers, and about seventy-five miles north of the famous old Spokane House founded by David Thompson for the North West Company in 1810. With the abandonment of Spokane House on Governor Simpson's orders when he visited Fort Vancouver in 1824, the site for Fort Colvile had been chosen and named for Simpson's friend and sponsor, Andrew (Wedderburn) Colvile who stood high in the London councils of the Hudson's Bay Company. Fort Colvile had been a more advantageous location than Spokane House after bateaux travel was established on the Columbia River between the Boat Encampment and Fort Vancouver for carrying back and forth goods and furs over the mountains.

Fort Colvile, when the Sinclair party visited it in 1841, had become a flourishing, well-defended, comfortable post that was almost completely self-supporting from the favorable nature of its situation. There were some nineteen buildings placed within a good stockade of large cedar logs. Colvile boasted a good trade shop, blacksmith and carpenter shops, a flour mill, a saw mill, a bakery, a dairy, a fine residence for its chief trader, excellent quarters for single men, and neat cottages for married men and their families. There were some 130 acres of land under cultivation around the fort, including fields of wheat, oats, corn, beans, potatoes, and other garden produce to amply supply food for the establishment. The country was capable of yielding almost anything if given proper cultivation and some irrigation. There were also at Colvile some good herds of cattle and horses, and the proximity of forests afforded sufficient lumber for any building requirements for an indefinite period of time. Indeed, Sinclair was so favorably impressed with Colvile and its location, he felt that he might one day settle here.

He was soon to learn he was not alone in this estimation, for already the Americans were casting envious eyes on this region, as well as on the fruitful and pleasant Willamette Valley to the south of Fort Vancouver.

In 1841, Fort Colvile was commanded by an able officer of the company, Chief Trader Archibald McDonald, who had been a friend of Sinclair's father many years before, and was also well known to a number of his friends. A well-educated Scot from Argyllshire, McDonald had been second in command of the party of Selkirk settlers whom the elder Sinclair had befriended when they had passed through his post at Oxford House in 1813, and Andrew McDermot had been a member of the same party. McDonald was also well known to Alexander Ross from the time when they had served together earlier in the Columbia River country, and Ross had assisted Chief Factor Donald McKenzie in establishing Fort Walla Walla. Trader McDonald had also accompanied Governor Simpson on several of his most hazardous expeditions, including his adventures on the Fraser River in 1828. He therefore knew Simpson's failings and better qualities; and he at once sensed the indignation the Governor would feel when he learned of Sinclair's defying his orders.

The truth of the matter was that McDonald had been greatly astonished to see Sinclair leading his party into Fort Colvile by pack train instead of arriving by boat brigade. Sometime earlier McDonald had received his own instructions from Simpson regarding this matter, to the effect that he was to be prepared to expect the Sinclair party down the Columbia by bateaux. In accordance with this information he had despatched a party of his own men upstream to meet the party and escort it down to Colvile. These men would be seriously disturbed when they found no members of the Sinclair party on the river, and would come to the conclusion that some tragedy had befallen them—perhaps at the treacherous Dalles du Mort below the Boat Encampment, where Governor Simpson's own daughter, Maria, born to Betsy Sinclair, had been drowned along with her young husband and members of their party just three years before in 1838.

At their meeting, McDonald handed Sinclair the letter that Simpson had left for him some weeks before, dated at Fort Colvile, August 19, 1841, which read:

> I arrived here yesterday after a very laborious journey across the mountains where we found the travelling exceeding bad; so much so that I considered it most fortunate that your party did not attempt to pass that route. . . . Mr. McDonald will forward from hence [Fort Colvile], as much flour and Indian corn, with a little grease for the use of your party as can be conveniently taken without overloading the craft which would be unsafe in the present state of the water, and wishing you a safe and speedy passage, I remain, dear Sir, Yours truly, George Simpson [31]

It appeared that Sinclair had been singularly fortunate in his decision to bring his people overland instead of risking their lives by taking bateaux on the swollen Columbia River. But his insubordination was sure to have unpleasant consequences in the future.

Sinclair learned something of conditions generally in the Oregon from McDonald and of the company politics being played behind the scenes between Simpson and Dr. John McLoughlin. It was obvious that Simpson resented the manifest prosperity that McLoughlin had achieved in the Oregon since Simpson's last visit to Fort Vancouver some sixteen years before. McLoughlin now exerted unbelievable power in the Oregon, and Simpson's anger was bound to be aroused when he saw McLoughlin's evident sympathy for the American settlers who were now flowing into the Oregon in ever increasing numbers.

At Fort Colvile, Sinclair was also told more about Alexander Ross's old Fort Walla Walla, especially concerning the disastrous condition into which it had recently fallen since its master —the extraordinary Pierre Pambrum—had been killed four months before in a fall from his horse on May 15, 1841. The report of Pambrum's death shocked Sinclair considerably, for he had been anticipating a meeting with this interesting trader and carried personal messages for him from former friends in Red River. Most serious consequences from Pambrum's death were already being felt—well beyond the normal activity of his fort—especially here at nearby Fort Colvile, and, indeed, all through the Columbia River country and in the Snake River region. Since his death Pambrum's old fort was managed by a trader named Archibald McKinley. McKinley was unable to cope with the exacting situation now confronting him at Walla Walla and could not handle effectually the warlike Indians of this vicinity who were constantly threatening attack. By contrast, Pambrum had been an exceedingly able and forceful officer who had kept the Indians well under control—particularly the unpredictable and treacherous Cayuse tribe. Indeed, it had been largely through Pambrum's personal efforts that a serious Indian war had not broken out in this region earlier, which could have set aflame a general state of war against all whites throughout the Oregon.

Fort Walla Walla was at the core of the most dangerous Indian country. A number of the natives accustomed to trade at this post since Alexander Ross's day had become increasingly restless since Pierre Pambrum's death. These troublesome tribes included the Flatheads, Snakes, Klickitats, Nez Percés, Cayuse, and others—some of whom were almost continually at war with each other, although it was becoming increasingly evident that they would not be adverse to making common cause against all whites in the Oregon if they so dared. Some of their more vicious warfare was carried on in open attack, but more often in treacherous secrecy—waiting for an appropriate moment for an unexpected assault upon some isolated settlers.

Before leaving Red River, Alexander Ross, who had dwelt for a considerable length of time among these treacherous tribes, had warned Sinclair what to expect of them. Ross had said that Walla Walla was a place that no white man could hold without adequate defenses; and he must make every show of fearlessness while exercizing the greatest care and tact in all dealings with these Indians. A white trader at Walla Walla must realize first and foremost that he had "the Nez Percés behind, the Cayuse before, and the Snakes everywhere!" Of them all, Ross had most disliked and mistrusted the Cayuse. There were, however, several more trustworthy tribes about Walla Walla who usually remained on fairly friendly terms with the white traders. The Snakes, for example, had certainly proved more reliable since Pierre Pambrum had come among them than in Ross's own day, although they still caused concern in their persistent quarrels with the Blackfeet, in which white traders might easily become involved. The Snakes could not resist sending war parties across the Rockies each year to hunt the buffalo and steal horses in Blackfoot country; naturally, the Blackfeet retaliated with raids on the Snakes. Nevertheless, regarding such matters from the long view, it was the Nez Percés who actually held the balance of power in this region; for these Indians, while a comparatively warlike tribe, did not often support the Cayuse in their intrigues since they mistrusted that tribe's treachery almost as much as they resisted the white man's entry into their domain. If peace were to be maintained along the Columbia from this time forward and security were to be assured for all whites in the Oregon, the Nez Percés must be dealt with tactfully to maintain this balance of power among the several other tribes about Walla Walla. They commanded the situation from Fort Walla Walla to the Chutes of the Columbia farther down the river toward the sea—a distance of almost three hundred miles. The Nez Percés' country also bordered the region dominated by the Snakes. Yet the greatest danger to all the Oregon lay in the fact that the Nez Percés might one day be incited to make common cause with the Snakes and Cayuse against all whites in the country.

With Pierre Pambrum's death it seemed that real trouble was brewing with the Indians along the Columbia River. In view of this unrest, Dr. John McLoughlin had recently issued orders that all traders were to exercise the greatest caution and to control their actions and tempers carefully in all their dealings with these Indians, no matter how aggressive or aggravating the natives might be. Chief Trader Peter Skene Ogden, second in command under McLoughlin at Fort Vancouver, was one of the company's most able men, both as trader and in his dealings with the Indians. His dictum for negotiating with the Indians was, "never let go, never oppose force with force until the last extremity," and to use every alternative before capitulating, especially in councils with the leading chiefs of these tribes and before resorting to the use of arms. Unfortunately, such advice was not always possible to follow, especially when a trader was caught unawares; and relationships with the Indians along the Columbia seemed to be deteriorating day by day.

So serious had conditions become when Sinclair and his party reached Fort Colvile in the autumn of 1841 that they were informed before they moved on to Fort Walla Walla that the Indians were no longer permitted to come within the walls of that post to trade. Business was now conducted there through an eighteen-inch aperture in the wall of the fort, with traders covered by another armed man at all times for their protection. This action in itself was irritating to the Indians, who were accustomed to Pierre Pambrum's more tolerant if nonetheless careful ways of transacting business.

Added to this difficulty with the Indians about Walla Walla, the influx of American settlers passing through this post at the end of the Oregon Trail had increased unbelievably since the year 1838, thus presenting new problems for the Hudson's Bay Company to solve in this part of the country. Pambrum, because of his versatile and capable personality, had been able to cope with the situation fairly well, and had even offered these American immigrants rest and needed supplies to see them on their way to their usual goal in the Willamette Valley. But his successor McKinley was a man of another stamp, and in addition he was in no position to offer the same facilities Pambrum had been able to afford in his day. McKinley was not entirely at fault in this, nor was he completely ungracious in his attitude to the strangers. He simply had neither the means nor supplies to offer under the constant threat of Indian attack. Furthermore, normal trade had fallen off alarmingly since Pambrum's death. The post's former fine showing of some two thousand beaver pelts a year—largely secured from the rich Snake country—had dwindled to veritably nothing. Such were the conditions facing the Sinclair party at this next stage of its journey to the Oregon.

X

Refreshed, their supplies once more replenished, their weary stock replaced, the party left Fort Colvile for the imminent dangers of Fort Walla Walla, reaching this troublesome outpost one exhilarating autumn day in 1841. To the southwest could be seen the crisp line of the Blue Mountains, of which Alexander Ross had often spoken to Sinclair—telling him of the dangers that range had held in his day, both for traders and for the settlers coming across the difficult Oregon Trail from Independence, Missouri.

By the time the Sinclair party reached Walla Walla, uncertain gusts of hot dry wind whipped clouds of sand in the weary travelers' faces, and the general atmosphere of the post seemed quietly ominous. The stories Sinclair had heard of Pambrum's happy, comfortable establishment vanished at the actual sight of this peculiar appearing outpost, threatened by drought, blowing sand, and hostile Indian attack.

The country about Walla Walla was a kind of undulating plain trending toward the mighty Columbia River. At a distance from both sides of the post rose rocky and somewhat picturesque ridges, comparatively well brushed, which under normal conditions might have afforded fairly good shelter for stock if anyone dared face the possibility now of theft and destruction by the Indians. The vegetation on the plains was largely bunch grass, excellent for raising good horses, with some wormwood scrub and a few willow thickets to be seen farther along the Walla Walla River. But Sinclair quickly recognized the fact that if this country were properly irrigated and kept at peace it could yield handsome returns to any energetic stockbreeder.

The fort itself had once been an impressive establishment of unusual design. It stood on the left bank of the Columbia River near the mouth of the Walla Walla River, some five miles from the Columbia's junction with the Snake, where Alexander Ross's career as a trader had been sealed some seventeen years earlier in 1824. But in the few months since Pambrum's death, although the more salient features of his somewhat fantastic structure still remained, it had been sadly neglected and was quickly becoming dilapidated. Fort Walla Walla was a pseudo-Spanish mission fort, largely constructed of locally made adobe brick, more typical of California and somewhat incongruous in the Oregon —its bastions, walls, and buildings curiously reminiscent of Moorish architecture. The once graciously watered soil of Pambrum's fine domestic gardens was swiftly reaching a state of sterility—the soil thoroughly dried out, the small irrigation channels already silted up, with only a few struggling, self-seeded turnips, potatoes, beets, and melons striving to survive in the parched earth where the seeds had fallen, for Pambrum had died before his gardens for this year were planted. A few miserable turkeys and chickens scratched about within the walls of the post, and some swine, goats, and cows lurked hopelessly and timid in the shadows. All in all, Fort Walla Walla presented a desolate enough prospect to Sinclair's weary people as their entry to this promised land of the Oregon.

Indeed, the greeting awaiting the party was little more hopeful than the prospect that met their eyes at this outpost. Trader McKinley was bedeviled by his own problems. He made it quite apparent that this unexpected visit of even Hudson's Bay Company-sponsored Red River people was none too welcome at this inappropriate moment, and that their compulsory stay of even a few days must not be prolonged in preparing the company's bateaux to be found here for continuing their journey down the Columbia to Fort Vancouver.

XI

Sinclair's party left Walla Walla with little regret. It was again fortunate that a number of the *Métis* in the group were accustomed to river travel and had served in the York boat brigades out of Fort Garry. The company's bateaux found at this place were similar in most respects, if somewhat larger, to the usual Red River York boats, so the party was able to proceed on its way the remaining two hundred miles to Fort Vancouver without too much trouble or delay.

Gradually the landscape became more and more impressively rugged as the great Columbia River down which they traveled flowed through a strangely beautiful land. They had reached the beginning of the peculiar obstructions in the river, and a difficult portage of some fourteen miles must be made around the falls and the Dalles, for there was as yet no wagon trail from Walla Walla to Fort Vancouver to circumvent these obstacles.

The party, however, was ill prepared for the wild majesty of the scene that now confronted it. This awe-inspiring place was known as the Celilo Falls. Here the fiercely rushing water fell more than eighty feet in the twelve miles of the river's run about which the party must portage before they could reach the next obstruction, known as the Dalles, the Big Shoot, or the Five Miles Rapids. These falls actually provided the entrance from the sandy plains about Walla Walla into the impressively grand country of the mighty Cascade Range, which paralleled the Pacific Ocean from Alaska to California.

When the Sinclair people reached the Dalles another weird and terrifying spectacle awaited them. It was as if some tremendous upheaval in ages past had tossed huge masses of rock into the river to force the rushing waters through a channel not more than 150 feet wide. The channel was actually deeper than wide and like a gigantic mill race, concentrating the rush of water and continuing straight for about two miles to a point where another great rock obstruction flung the racing water against a huge cliff, to send it crashing with unbelievable fury upon a lower reef of still another rock mass.[32]

After this fierce fall of water at the Dalles, the river became curiously calm and deep and almost sullen in appearance. For fifty miles or so the river continued thus peacefully to the next barrier at the Cascades. Here, after more violent rapids and amidst overhanging banks, the river became calm once more, flowing through a country that seemed one continual vista of unexcelled beauty, relieved at some places by volcanic cliffs, grassy plains, and enormous forests. The gigantic mountain peaks sometimes in sight seemed singularly different from those through which the party had passed in the Rocky Mountains.

These Cascade mountains were no less impressive than the Rockies in many respects, and they possessed a singular isolated grandeur. Some of the peaks bore curious Indian names, such as Kulshan,[33] the Great White Watcher; Tachoma,[34] the Fountain Breast of Milk White Water; and Winjeast,[35] the Pinnacled Crest.

After the arid country above the Dalles, with its clear air and abundant sunshine, the land below the Dalles seemed almost overblessed with water-laden breezes from the sea, which gave a soft and almost languid atmosphere to this land, somehow oppressive to these wandering overlanders from the plains, and almost overwhelming with its superabundance of vegetation and mammoth trees—lofty fir, spruce, cedar, and pine that slid by the bateaux for miles on end—only here and there interspersed with lush meadows.

At last the journey's end was reached at Fort Vancouver, the Hudson's Bay Company's great western depot. Sinclair, true to his word, had brought his party safely across the Rocky Mountains after almost five months on trail and river, crossing half a continent between Fort Garry and the Pacific Ocean—most of it via routes previously untraveled by white men.

XII

Fort Vancouver, situated on the northwest side of the mighty Columbia River, was considerably different from any other company post Sinclair had ever visited, both in the nature of its environment and the somewhat peculiar arrangement of its good buildings. It stood back on a small plain about a quarter of a mile from the river bank at a point where this great stream flowed almost a mile wide and exceedingly deep, still some ninety miles inland from the sea. Behind the fort stood the vast primeval forest of fine cedar and pine, interspersed with clearings made by the company's servants under Dr. John McLoughlin's direction for well-cultivated fields of grain, vegetable gardens, and orchards.

The fort itself was built in the shape of a large parallelogram, surrounded by a strong stockade some twenty feet high, well buttressed, bastioned, and mounting formidable twelve-pounders as well as some still larger cannon that commanded a wide field of fire to protect this somewhat extravagant outlay. Inside the palisades were two courtyards, instead of the usual one large square found at most Hudson's Bay Company establishments. Surrounding these courtyards were as many as forty well-constructed buildings, including Dr. McLoughlin's good residence, which also housed the gentlemen's dining room and a good bachelors' hall. Other buildings included the officers' and clerks' living quarters, warehouses to store large quantities of fur and trade goods, shops of various kinds, and—rather unusual for such a place as this—a good schoolhouse and an attractive chapel. It was generally known that the individualistic Dr. McLoughlin respected religion highly and encouraged it for his people of whatever denomination; further, he encouraged learning for the children of his officers and servants.

All in all, Sinclair found himself deeply impressed with Fort Vancouver from his first look at it. It appeared to be a most commodious and well-managed establishment—obviously the result of McLoughlin's able and dominating personality, for he had succeeded in making it a great trading center and meeting place for the entire Northwest Pacific region in the comparatively few years in which he had been in command of this important area, leading to Governor George Simpson's considerable chagrin and jealousy. All fur and other articles secured in trade with the Indians of the Pacific slope were now brought to Vancouver for shipment to Britain by company sailing ship around the Horn. Here also were brought large quantities of trade goods and ships' stores from Britain for distribution to the various company posts west of the mountains, to be carried from Fort Vancouver to their various destinations, either by company bateaux, pack train, or coastal ships. Under McLoughlin's regime Vancouver had become the great company emporium west of the Rockies, from as far south as California, north to Alaska, and even to Kamchatka in Russian Asia, and the Sandwich Islands far out in the Pacific Ocean.

XIII

The arrival of Sinclair's party at Fort Vancouver caused little commotion; the people of this place were long used to comings and goings of all kinds, and the party, therefore, was cared for with dispatch and efficiency—the emigrants provided with shelter and food after the manner of all others who chanced to come within McLoughlin's gates. Sinclair himself received some special consideration, for a definite if somewhat unusual relationship existed between his family and McLoughlin by marriage. Sinclair's eldest brother, William, had married McLoughlin's stepdaughter, Mary Wadin McKay, the offspring of Madam McLoughlin's first unhappy marriage.

While McLoughlin, the busy and powerful executive, treated Sinclair well enough, he had little time for excessive sociability. Nevertheless, Sinclair had reason to be grateful for a number of fortuitous circumstances. He was, for instance, especially thankful to find that Governor Simpson had left Fort Vancouver for some weeks on a tour of inspection to Alaskan waters. This would give Sinclair time to study conditions generally in the Oregon and to try to become fairly well entrenched at Fort Vancouver should Simpson upon his return be especially displeased to discover that Sinclair had deliberately defied his orders.

At his first meeting with McLoughlin, Sinclair was greatly impressed by this unusually forceful character. The doctor was close to sixty years of age at this time—a physically striking figure, some six feet four in height and proportionately well built, possessing great poise and dignity of bearing. He had a florid complexion, exceedingly bright blue eyes, and a generally benevolent countenance. But perhaps his most unforgettable feature was his shock of snow-white hair, which distinguished him as an almost legendary figure to the Indians, to whom he had become known as the "Great White-headed Eagle," symbolizing to them power and wisdom.

Sinclair also discovered at this first meeting confirmation of the attitude McLoughlin had earlier displayed in the letters shown to him at Fort Garry, namely, that he did not altogether welcome the arrival of this party of Red River people to his Oregon domain, and from the outset seemed to evade placing these people on the farms at Cowlitz and Nisqually in accordance with their contract with the company. This, Sinclair realized, might well have been because McLoughlin felt that it was Simpson's prerogative to arrange such matters, since he had come to the Columbia country headquarters at this particular time. Until Simpson's return from the north, therefore, Sinclair and his people were compelled to remain restlessly within the fort, committed to labor that they felt unjustified in accordance with their earlier agreement at Fort Garry.

It was also noticeable to Sinclair that upon Simpson's return to Fort Vancouver the entire atmosphere of the place changed perceptibly. It seemed veritably charged with the Governor's nervous and aggressive presence. In the officers' mess there was a forced attitude of extreme courtesy and cold reserve, especially between superiors and the lesser ranks. The strictest protocol was observed, with McLoughlin displaying an obvious example of good breeding and correct demeanor, while Simpson was curt and officious. It was only too apparent that the Governor was physically exhausted, although he would have been the last to admit it; consequently, he displayed a certain bravado before the assembled officers, especially at dinner in the great hall, where he appeared to take every occasion to relate how he had traveled to Fort Vancouver from Lachine in a matter of some twelve weeks—the entire journey being made in canoe and saddle, with but a week's rest at Fort Vancouver before setting out again for Stikeen by boat, and returning to Vancouver by October 22.[36] Surely this was a feat of endurance exacting of any man, and especially of Simpson, past the peak of physical health.

Sinclair's own dealings with Governor Simpson at Fort Vancouver appear to have been brief and to the point. The Governor apparently did not deign to show his displeasure at Sinclair's blatant defiance of his explicit orders as to how he should conduct the Red River party across the Rockies. But Sinclair had reason to believe that he had escaped Simpson's wrath lightly. He was told that the placing of the Red River people on company land must now rest with McLoughlin, and until such a decision was reached, Sinclair must be prepared to hold the party in check as he had done when conducting them to the Oregon—to see they made themselves useful at tasks assigned them within the fort. Simpson then commanded Sinclair to be prepared to return to Red River as early as possible after the people were placed on the land, for he wished him to stand ready to conduct another such party from Fort Garry across the Rockies in perhaps a year's time, if conditions warranted another such expedition. Sinclair was then dismissed from the Governor's presence as if he had been any other lesser company servant.

Sinclair was deeply annoyed that the fulfillment of the Red River people's contract had been temporarily sidetracked, for as the days wore on and nothing was done to place them on their promised land, the people grew increasingly restless and disgruntled, and Sinclair was in no position to help them further. He had also discovered that there were a number of American sympathizers within Fort Vancouver who had lost no time in making an issue of the Red River settlers' position, and were using every means to turn them to their cause. There was also a disturbing rumor going around Fort Vancouver that neither the Hudson's Bay Company nor the British government had any legal right to bestow land upon these emigrants; and with the boundary dispute still unsettled west of the mountains, as well as with the arrival of so many American settlers in the Oregon, the country would soon become American territory.

If this occurred the Red River people were unlikely to possess land of their own in fulfillment of the company's contract with them. In confirmation of this, several members of the party quoted to Sinclair the words of a man named "Fitzgerald," who was going about the fort stating that the Red River people were receiving poor treatment by McLoughlin, and were not even being given enough to eat. When an attempt was made to find the man who made such statements, he could not be found, for he had left the fort to join the American settlement in the Willamette Valley and was well beyond the range of company reproof.[37]

In the face of all the complaints and ill-feeling, Sinclair counseled patience, for he knew that while the Red River people's contract with the company had not been fulfilled, they were in no wise suffering; and although it was difficult to show restraint when they wished to be about their own business as Sinclair did, he assured them of Dr. McLoughlin's true merits and genuine kindliness, and was certain they would ultimately receive fair treatment and be placed on land to their liking. Nevertheless, a number of the settlers that he had brought across the mountains had become thoroughly infected with the discontent engendered by the American sympathizers, and Sinclair knew this might well lead to most serious consequences for the Hudson's Bay Company and British interests in the Oregon.

After many weeks of waiting about the fort, some of the Red River folk were placed on farms at the Cowlitz and a few others at Nisqually, under conditions that proved disheartening and displeased them greatly. All in all, it was not a reassuring end to the trials these people had endured in making their long journey to establish new homes across the mountains in the Oregon.

PART III: RETURN TO RED RIVER

7. RESUMPTION OF THE PRIVATE TRADE

I

After the unsatisfactory placing of the Red River people on the land at Cowlitz and Nisqually, Sinclair did not wait longer than necessary at Fort Vancouver. Simpson and McLoughlin had left together for San Francisco on a company ship. There their paths would separate, McLoughlin to return to Fort Vancouver and Simpson to proceed to the Sandwich Islands on another company vessel. It was Sinclair's intention to return as quickly as possible to Red River and resume his partnership with McDermot in the private trade. He left Fort Vancouver in the middle of December, 1841, and reached Fort Colvile with the intent to join a company packet for Fort Edmonton. This proved impossible because the exceptional depth of snow that winter would not permit crossing the mountains from the Boat Encampment to Jasper's House over Athabaska Pass by dog team without grave risk. He was therefore compelled to remain at Fort Colvile for the winter, making himself as useful as possible to his friend, Chief Trader McDonald, and learning what he could of conditions and business in this country. It proved to be so much to his liking that he was convinced the time was not wasted and he would like to return someday to enter the business of trading, ranching, and lumbering.

As soon as spring opened in 1842 Sinclair joined the first company brigade of bateaux bound upstream from Fort Colvile for the Boat Encampment. There he joined a company pack train to cross the mountains to Colin Fraser's Jasper's House, where he renewed his earlier friendship with Simpson's jolly piper turned trader. Other friendships were renewed some weeks later at Edmonton House, including that with the Cree chief and guide, Mackipictoon, who had conducted the party across the mountains the autumn before. Then Sinclair joined the earliest York boat brigade bound for Fort Garry, traveling down the North Saskatchewan River and Lake Winnipeg to rejoin his family and resume his trading.

II

When Sinclair returned to Red River from the Oregon in the summer of 1842 he found that his family had been safely cared for during his absence by his good friends Alexander Ross and Andrew McDermot. He found the settlement doing well—no further unpleasant incidents having taken place with the *Métis* since Duncan Finlayson had been temporarily placed in charge at Fort Garry, although Sinclair soon discovered that for some reason Finlayson was not so generously disposed toward the private trade as he had appeared to be when Sinclair had left with the party for the Oregon.

Sinclair also soon learned that a reorganization was under way in the American Fur Company. The able, aggressive trader, Henry Hastings Sibley, had been placed at the head of Astor's old company, and this might very well mean an attempt to revive the trade with the Red River *Métis*. Certainly there would be more Yankee gold in Red River if ever Sibley's agents brought much American goods to the region.

As for Sinclair himself and his renewed enterprise with McDermot, he was sent in the late summer of 1842 to accompany the Irish merchant's fleet of York boats to York Factory, carrying north a cargo of country produce consisting mainly of buffalo tallow secured from the *Métis,* and bringing back the trade goods McDermot had ordered the year before from London for his shops. This was in accordance with his agreement with Governor Simpson to the effect that if a Red River petty merchant imported goods from Britain to be brought out on the company's annual ship, either the importer or his officially delegated representative (in this case Sinclair) should claim the goods at York Factory and conduct them back to Fort Garry.

III

It could not have been long after the New Year of 1843 that Chief Factor Duncan Finlayson summoned Sinclair to Fort Garry to reveal to him some disturbing news just received concerning the Red River settlers Sinclair had conducted to the Oregon in the summer of 1841. A letter sent by swift packet from the company's London governor and committee via New York and Montreal also contained a copy of a dispatch sent to the London headquarters by Dr. John McLoughlin from Fort Vancouver. These documents stated that while the company's governor and committee had seriously considered sending Sinclair to conduct another Red River party across the Rockies in the summer of 1843, such a prospect now seemed most unlikely. The official communication read: "The views with which we recommended this experiment having been completely frustrated by the subsequent migration of these people from the Cowlitz and Nisqually to the Wallamet, we do not think it advisable to burden the fur trade with the expense of translating any more to the same quarter." [1]

Chief Factor Finlayson disclosed to Sinclair that after he had left Fort Vancouver in December, 1841, the Red River people had given Dr. McLoughlin considerable [2] cause for concern, for his disgruntled letter said: "From the first moment I saw them after their arrival from Red River, from their manner of speaking, I felt convinced they were desirous of going to the Wallamette . . . a finer country for tillage than Nisqually." [3]

It also appeared that the Red River people had some justifiable grievance. After their crops at Nisqually had failed in the summer of 1842, this group of settlers had demanded from McLoughlin a larger share of the increase of the livestock. McLoughlin had evidently not felt at liberty to change the terms of the company's earlier agreement in this regard, but he did consent to release these people from the contract entirely if they cared to remove to the Willamette Valley and become independent farmers there, thus removing them from any further obligation to the Hudson's Bay Company. Of this matter he wrote: "At Nisqually they would be a constant bill of expense to the Company, and would never after all be satisfied. By going to the Wallamet they had no further claim on the Company and would exert themselves, as they would have to look after their own support there." [4]

Sinclair left Finlayson feeling that a very real injustice had been done the people he had conducted to the Oregon, whom he had come to know well and who had followed him courageously and obediently across the mountains.

IV

The return to petty trading with McDermot provided Sinclair, for a while at least, with more time to be with his family in Red River, and he enjoyed genuine domestic happiness with his beloved wife, Elizabeth, and the children that had been spared to them. He took particular pride in his eldest child, Harriet,[5] who had grown to be very like him in temperament, and who by the year 1843 was an intelligent girl of eleven.

Harriet Sinclair, as was markedly evident through her exceedingly long life, had a great capacity for making and holding friends. McDermot was particularly fond of her, and she was playmate to his large family, who were like brothers and sisters to her. Alexander Ross also made young Harriet Sinclair feel as one with his neighboring family.[6] But it was old Thomas Bunn who held a particular place in Harriet's affection, with his delightful store of naive stories, many of which he had told Sinclair himself as a child at Oxford House.[7] Harriet was also a favorite with her uncle, Thomas Sinclair, at whose fine house at St. Andrew's Rapids she often visited, for Thomas had become prosperous in recent years with his brigade of York boats traversing the northern waterways to York Factory, and was a highly respected citizen of Red River. The devotion Harriet felt for her aging grandmother, Nahovway, was another thing again and was almost pathetic in its sincerity of feeling. The child often went to see the old lady at her little cottage near Seven Oaks,[8] where she lived with her aged, mild-mannered second husband, not far from the home of her daughter, Mary.

It was a source of joy to Sinclair to teach his children the old Orkney folk songs he had learned in his youth on the Isle of Pomona. Harriet was particularly apt at learning these,[9] for she loved all tuneful music. It was in this regard that Sinclair received something of a shock upon his return from the Oregon. A peculiar friendship had been established between young Harriet and a haughty Red River matron—the former schoolmistress, Mrs. Lowman—now the child's stepgrandmother since her marriage as second wife to the wealthy, aged chief factor, James Curtis Bird. Madam Bird was now of such affluence and generosity she could afford to shower young Harriet with fine gifts, including a piano,[10] especially imported for her by Andrew McDermot from Britain during the time Sinclair was in the Oregon.

But Sinclair's pleasure with his family was once more marred by a serious epidemic that struck the settlement, similar to the one that had taken two of his children some years before. This time the plague took the form of a virulent influenza, followed by a depleting type of dysentery. The disease seriously impaired the health of Sinclair's wife, who had recently given birth to a child; and within two weeks two of Sinclair's children were taken—first the infant daughter Emma, dying on May 22, 1843,[11] then his small daughter Louisa, two weeks later, at the age of two and a half years, on June 2.[12]

8. REBELLION THREATENS

I

By late 1843 conditions were beginning to run seriously against Sinclair, especially in regard to his petty trading with Andrew McDermot. Chief Factor Finlayson now gave unmistakable evidence that he felt Sinclair and the Irish merchant had become too sure of their somewhat preferred position in the past, and were taking advantage of it to their own profit and to the loss of the Hudson's Bay Company. Finlayson therefore refused to renew McDermot's and Sinclair's freight contracts and would not permit them to ship tallow from York Factory.

By the summer of 1844 certain natural events could be called to witness as also partially responsible for Sinclair's change of fortune. A gigantic prairie fire had swept across the plains below Red River and into American territory when the grass was tinder dry. The devastation wrought by this conflagration was almost beyond estimate. It not only destroyed any possibility of much profit from the annual buffalo hunts that year but the herds were scattered far and wide beyond their usual autumn grazing grounds on the plains of the Souris, so that the concentrated *Métis* hunts could not take place to bring in the customary amounts of pemmican and number of robes both to the Hudson's Bay Company and the private traders. This catastrophe also brought untold loss to the *Métis* and Indians directly in the quantity of food returned for their own winter needs. As a consequence of this, Sinclair not only had reason to fear for his own and McDermot's private trade, but there was grave danger that actual starvation the coming winter might confront the entire settlement.

In the face of all this, but particularly in evident retaliation against the restraints that Finlayson had placed upon the private Red River trade, and especially upon McDermot and Sinclair—who well may have been instrumental in what now occurred—an enterprising American trader reopened the old trading post at Pembina. Quebec-born Norman W. Kittson—a former British subject but latterly an ardent American citizen—seems to have felt the moment was ripe, in September, 1844, to resume trade in opposition to the Hudson's Bay Company for the reorganized American Fur Company. This was obviously a bold effort on the part of the Americans, under the guidance of the able Henry Hastings Sibley, to attract still more of the valuable *Métis* trade away from the Old Company at Fort Garry. Such an aggressive trader as Kittson was likely to cause the company serious loss.

With McDermot and Sinclair, as well as other Red River petty traders, now only too anxious to cooperate with Kittson in retaliation against Finlayson's opposition to any trade outside of the legitimate company channels, this was the beginning of the only free trade worth mentioning in the Red River region up to this time. Granted, there had been a "petty trade" of sorts—limited and comparatively tolerable to certain company officials—but with Kittson as agent for the American Fur Company in the Northern Minnesota region, by the end of 1844 serious competition to the Hudson's Bay Company had begun. As inducement to trade, Kittson offered increased prices and American gold for prime furs; in response to this all the fur was no longer likely to reach the Old Company's warehouses, and defiance of the company's chartered rights was bound to increase perceptibly.

It appears quite evident that Sinclair was not immune to the temptation Kittson offered, especially since he must support himself and his family in the face of the only real alternative the country offered to rejoining the Old Company. This he evidently could not bring himself to do, in view of the injustice he felt had been dealt his father by the company and the treatment his Red River party had received in the Oregon—not to mention his own personal grievance from the lack of reward or recognition he had expected for bringing the Red River party safely across the mountains. Nevertheless, Sinclair was not so dull that he did not see the stand the company was now compelled to take in the face of the very real threat a widespread free trade presented to it with Kittson's arrival. Such a situation could not be overlooked or tolerated, and the swiftly growing, illegal trade in furs now being carried on extensively by the *Métis* with the Americans must be checked if the company's monopoly were to be maintained and its license to trade remain valid. Unquestionably, the company had received its rights from the British crown, and it could do no less than defend them with every means at its command.

II

When Chief Factor Alexander Christie returned to Fort Garry in 1844 to replace Finlayson he inherited his increased quarrel with the free traders; and he lost no time in pursuing it diligently with the aid of his friend and legal adviser, the irritatingly pedantic Recorder Adam Thom, who quickly brought Christie up-to-date on what had occurred in his absence. From the moment of his arrival back in Red River, Christie made it only too apparent he meant to uphold the Old Company's charter and monopoly of trade at all costs and meant to eliminate all free trade, licensed or otherwise. This intent was publicly proclaimed when, in December, 1844, he posted the first of a series of sharply worded proclamations at Fort Garry, which served as fair warning that the day of the privileged petty traders, was over, and that the illicit traffic in furs that the *Métis* had been enjoying with Kittson and other American traders would not be tolerated. Sinclair found that his sympathies were now solidly on the side of the Red River half-breeds, and henceforth he intended to do what he could to bring them greater liberty of action, even if this meant challenging the chartered privileges of the Old Company.

The first of Governor Christie's proclamations demanded that all free traders must commit themselves in a written statement to the effect that they had either been guilty or not guilty of trafficking illicitly in furs. Unless such a self-indicting document were submitted to Christie at Fort Garry, the privileges a trader had previously enjoyed—in exporting the produce of the country, such as tallow from York Factory, or the right to import trade goods from Britain on the company's annual ship to York Factory—would in future be denied him. If another similar declaration, admitting or denying guilt of trafficking in furs, were not submitted to Christie before the following August, an importer of trade goods ordered the previous year and to be brought to York Factory on the company's ship this season would either have his goods detained for a year at York as a test of the importer's good faith in resisting further illicit trade in furs, or be paid by the company—should it deem it advisable—the initial cost of the goods purchased in Britain.

Naturally, this appeared to Sinclair and his associates as an endeavor on Christie's part to incriminate all free traders in written statements so they might be deprived of all previous privileges granted by the company, and as set forth in Simpson's special licenses to trade given McDermot and Sinclair. It was also felt that Christie was seeking to force petty traders to renounce the right to ship the produce of the country, such as tallow, at rates formerly acceptable to Simpson, or to bring back goods from Britain necessary for carrying on their private trade, which were secured from Britain with "good bills of exchange," and previously carried on the company's ships to York Factory at rates considered agreeable to Simpson. It, therefore, appeared that Christie now sought to abrogate Simpson's former benefits to petty traders, thus eliminating them from competitive business to the Old Company. McDermot and Sinclair were reluctant to sign such incriminating documents as Christie now demanded from them.

Certainly, Christie's carefully worded proclamations appeared to be directed against such successful petty traders as McDermot and Sinclair, who for some years past had been making large shipments of Buffalo tallow for some twenty of their *Métis* associates—carrying the tallow to York Factory in McDermot's brigade of York boats, from which place it was consigned to Britain in the company ships. Withdrawing such privileges was therefore sure to cause considerable hardship to the *Métis*, as well as seriously reducing McDermot's and Sinclair's credits in London, secured from the disposal of tallow, with which they were accustomed to purchase their supplies of trade goods. Thus, it seemed a cleverly thought-out scheme—undoubtedly framed by the astute legal mind of Recorder Adam Thom—to destroy with one stroke the petty traders' lucrative business both in and out of Red River.

Just two weeks after Christie's first proclamation, a second was posted at Fort Garry, equally shrewd and far-reaching. It was another restrictive edict that virtually gave notice of censorship by the Hudson's Bay Company of all written communications reaching and emanating from Red River. This appeared further designed to incriminate anyone who might be engaged in either licensed or unlicensed free trade. This second proclamation sought to compel an importer of goods from Britain, carried on the company ships to York Factory, to submit all written orders addressed to their respective purchasing agents in Britain for examination first by company officers at Fort Garry. These requisitions must also be accompanied by another incriminating document to the effect that the importer was *not* engaged in any private traffic in furs. All such documents were to bear the sender's name, clearly written in his own handwriting, on the outside left-hand corner of the envelope, so that it might be readily recognized by the examining officers at Fort Garry. If this ruling were not complied with, neither would the letter ordering the goods be delivered to the agents in Britain, nor would the goods sent for be brought back to York Factory on the company's ships.

Such a regulation could hardly be recognized by McDermot and Sinclair as anything but a serious breach of contract on the company's part, for it had previously been understood that the Hudson's Bay Company in Rupert's Land was bound to provide means of transportation for all settlers' communications, of whatsoever nature, at fair terms. It was also felt by the petty traders that if the British authorities should uphold the company's new stand on this matter, there were ways and means of overcoming the difficulty, for American traders such as Kittson, Joseph Rolette, and Joseph Renville—to mention but a few—would be only too glad to carry Red River communications with them south of the border if brought to them by wandering *Métis*. After this, facilities would be readily found, through St. Louis or by Michilimackinac, to have such mail reach its destination almost anywhere on earth.

III

By the closing months of 1844 it was apparent that many of the Red River people were prepared to resist a number of Governor Christie's more drastic regulations, and that the illicit traffic in company furs was flourishing with the Americans as never before. Even the settlers who had previously remained aloof from such trafficking in furs and *Métis*' quarrels with the company at last let it be known that they felt there should be greater liberty of action in the land. For his part, Sinclair was close enough to the half-breeds to see that serious trouble was brewing if greater restrictions were placed upon them.

It was also about this time that Sinclair experienced another great personal loss, which may well have seriously influenced his actions and inclined him to take a more active part in the illicit behavior against the authorized law of the land as vested in the Hudson's Bay Company and in Governor Christie. In February, 1845, Sinclair's beloved wife, Elizabeth, was taken,[1] leaving him with several small children.[2] The circumstances of his bereavement forced him to close his house and place three of his children in boarding school—his two young daughters, Harriet and Maria, and his eldest son being sent to the Anglican schools in Red River—and the infant child was in the care of relatives.

By May 4, 1845, conditions had become so alarming in Red River that Governor Simpson was compelled to write the company's London committee:

> At Red River settlement a second quarrel has taken place between the hunters frequenting the plains to the southward of Pembina and the Sioux tribes which has led to bloodshed on both sides. This might deter the Red River half breeds from prosecuting their usual summer hunts on the plains and be productive of some inconvenience by depriving the Company of the supply of pemmican from that quarter . . . but . . . as the population is now so numerous that those Indians, although exceedingly daring, are not likely to carry hostilities beyond the outskirts where they may from time to time pick up a few stragglers.[3]

It was also about this time that Simpson's attitude changed considerably toward Andrew McDermot, for he wrote the company's London headquarters:

> Two of the most influential settlers, McDermot and Sinclair, who are ambitious to become leaders in order to forward their private ends, have lately evinced a disposition to traffic in furs, encouraging traders from the United States to settle on the frontier, receiving through these Americans produce at a cheap rate and supplying them with British goods with a view of carrying on this clandestine traffic which if not checked, may be productive of serious loss and inconvenience to this concern. . . . By Mr. Christie's communications he suggested that, as a means of putting down this illicit trade, no goods should be taken to York by the Company's ships for McDermot and Sinclair . . . and I strongly recommend that this suggestion be favourably considered, as if the Company afford facilities to these people to import their supplies from England, they will have it in their power to injure the interests of the fur trade to a very serious extent.[4]

Again, on June 20, 1845, Simpson wrote the company authorities concerning McDermot and Sinclair:

> Such an infringement of the Honourable Company's rights, though it had not actually been carried to any serious extent, had yet arisen from causes which threatened a rapid and systematic growth of the evil. The recent rise in the value of furs had induced an American trader to plant himself at Pembina, who held out great temptations to the Indians and offered considerable facilities to some of our private dealers with respect to the importation of trading goods from the United States. In connection with this individual, and under the influence of some prospects of high profits which had brought him to the neighbourhood, Mr. Andrew McDermott and Mr. James Sinclair had trafficked largely in furs, and though they surrendered them to the Company at somewhat higher rates than those of the regular traffic, yet they unhesitatingly avowed their determination to prosecute their illicit traffic without regard to the Company's chartered privileges in any such way as might be most convenient and profitable to themselves. Over and above the direct results of their operations, the example of these two persons had proved to be peculiarly pernicious, inasmuch as their superior standing and comparative intelligence gave considerable weight to their opinions, while the contract for freighting the Company's property between Red River Settlement and York Factory, which they had long enjoyed had drawn a large proportion of the lower class within the sphere of their influence. . . .

The Governor went on to say that no time would be lost in endeavoring to "avert the blow thus aimed at the vitals of the Company's trade and power." [5]

Governor Christie began to issue his own licenses to trade, granting them only to those he considered worthy to receive them. The licenses read:

> On behalf of the Hudson's Bay Company, I hereby licence [name] to trade, and also ratify his having traded in English goods within the limits of the Red River Settlement; this ratification and this licence to be null and void from the beginning in the event of his hereafter trafficking in furs, or generally of his usurping any whatsoever of all the privileges of the Hudson's Bay Company.[6]

On July 10, 1845, Christie also sought to enforce the drastic terms of the far-reaching land regulations, which would completely end the Red River trading of those not found entitled to receive his special license. A new land act was framed stating that anyone, before he could secure land from the company, must declare that he would not—without such a new license from Governor Christie—carry on or establish any trade or traffic in "any kind of skins, furs, peltry, or dressed leather." Neither would he aid or abet anyone in so doing "in any part of North America." Other demands in the new act were no less broad in scope. They stated that the owner of land received from the Hudson's Bay Company must also agree not to "infringe or violate the exclusive rights, powers, privileges, and immunities of commerce, trade and traffic of or belonging to the said Governor and Company." [7] It also demanded that anyone receiving land from the company must

> . . . give assurance that he would not at any time during the said term of one thousand years underlet, or assign, or otherwise alleviate or dispose of, or part with the actual possession of the land thereby devised in any part thereof for all or any part of the said term, or any interest derived under the same, without the consent in writing of the said Governor and Company.[8]

From this it almost appeared that Christie had become overanxious, and that his well-meant actions might easily lead Red River into far reaching trouble and bloodshed, thereby damaging the very company interests he meant to preserve. More than this, the whole matter was resolving itself into the fact that Christie's and Thom's policy was actually but an extension of Simpson's broader policy of fighting fire with fire in an effort to control trade. However, the days of the company's monopoly in fur and trade seemed to be about over. It also appeared that Simpson's other policy of trying to prevent the American fur trade from invading what had always been conceived as British territory was failing—particularly west of the mountains—and had only succeeded in keeping it out of Red River or below the already established boundary line east of the Rocky Mountains.

As for Sinclair's personal efforts on behalf of the Hudson's Bay Company through McDermot, in which he purportedly endeavored to keep the *Métis* fur from falling into the hands of the Americans, the arrival of Norman Kittson at Pembina put a stop to this period of his career; and there seemed little left for him to do but serve the *Métis* cause henceforth as best he could. And, in all fairness to Sinclair, he appears to have sought for them normal freedom of life and work, as well as fair recognition as British subjects under British law.

This state of affairs had come about largely through the fact that on more than one occasion *Métis* leaders had come to Sinclair for advice as to their rights—if any—as descendants of those who had originally owned the land. In order to try to answer their questions with any degree of accuracy, he had decided to frame a petition for these *Métis*, placing his name at the head of a list of inquirers, as to what specific rights they did possess in Rupert's Land, and present it directly to Governor Christie for reply. This was done after careful consideration in consort with the leading Red River half-breeds; and on August 29, 1845,[9] the petition, worded as follows, was presented at Fort Garry:

> Sir: Having at this moment a very strong belief that we as natives of this country and as Halfbreeds have the right to hunt furs in the Hudson's Bay Company's territories whenever we think proper, and again sell those furs to the highest bidder; likewise having a doubt that natives of this country can be prevented from trading and trafficking with one another, we would wish to have your opinion on the subject, but we should commit ourselves by doing anything in opposition either to the laws of England or to the Honourable Company's privileges, and, therefore, lay before you as Governor of the Red River Settlement, a few queries which we beg you will answer in due course:
> (1) Has a Halfbreed, a settler, the right to hunt furs in this country?
> (2) Has a native of this country, not an Indian, a right to hunt furs in this country?
> (3) If a Halfbreed has the right to hunt furs can he hire other Halfbreeds for the purpose of hunting furs?
> (4) Can a Halfbreed sell his furs to any person he pleases?
> (5) Is a Halfbreed obliged to sell his furs to the Hudson's Bay Company at whatever price the Company may think proper to give him?
> (6) Can a Halfbreed receive any furs as a present from an Indian a relative of his?
> (7) Can a Halfbreed hire any of his Indian relatives to hunt furs for him?
> (8) Can a Halfbreed trade furs from another Halfbreed in or out of the Settlement?
> (9) Can a Halfbreed trade furs from an Indian in or out of the Settlement?

(10) With regard to trading or hunting furs have the Halfbreed or natives of European origin any rights or privileges of Europeans?

(11) A settler having purchased lands from Lord Selkirk, or even from the Hudson's Bay Company, without any conditions attached to them or without having signed any bond, deed or instrument whatever whereby he might have willed away his right to trade in furs, can he be prevented from trading furs in the Settlement with settlers or even out of the Settlement?

(12) Are the limits of the Settlement defined by the municipal law, Selkirk grant or Indian sale?

(13) If a person cannot trade furs either in or out of the Settlement, can he purchase them for his own and family use, and in what quantity?

(14) Having never seen any official statement, nor know but by report the Hudson's Bay Company have peculiar privileges over British subjects, natives and Halfbreeds resident in the Settlement, we would wish to know what those privileges are, and the penalties attached to the infringement of the same?

We remain your humble servants,
James Sinclair

Baptiste la Roque
Thomas Logan
John Dease
Alexi Gaulat
Louis la Tendre de Batoche
William McMillan
Antoine Morran
Bat Wilkie
John Vincent
William Bird
Henry Cook
John Spence
John Anderson
Thoms McDermot
Adall Trottier
Charles Hole
Joseph Montman
Baptiste Farman
etc.

Sinclair had recognized the fact that petitioning Christie had demanded a great humbling of spirit on the part of the half-breeds, and that it should have received from the Governor an answer framed not only to command *Métis* respect but to offer them assurance he felt genuine sympathy for their problems and was prepared to deal with them fairly and tolerantly.

However, Christie's answer was framed to have a somewhat different interpretation. Dated as of Fort Garry, September 5, 1845, it read: [10]

Gentlemen: I received your letter of the 29th ultimo on the evening of the 3rd. instant, and I am sure that the solemn and important proceedings in which I was yesterday engaged will form a sufficient apology for having allowed a day to pass without noticing your communications. However unusual it may be for the ruler of any country to answer legal inquiries in any other way than through the judicial tribunals which can alone authoritatively decide any point of law, I shall on this particular occasion overlook all these considerations which might otherwise prompt me to decline, with all due courtesy, the discussion of your letter; and I am rather induced to adopt this course by your avowal of unwillingness to do anything in opposition to the Hudson's Bay Company's privileges.

Your first nine queries, as well as the body of your letter, are grounded on the supposition that the half breeds possess certain privileges over their fellow citizens who have not been born in this country. Now, as British subjects, the half breeds have clearly the same rights in Scotland or in England as any person born in Great Britain, and your own sense of justice will at once see how unreasonable it would be to place Englishmen and Scotsmen on a less favourable footing in Rupert's Land than yourself.

Your supposition further seems to draw a distinction between half breeds and persons born in the country of European parentage, and to men of your intelligence I need not say that this distinction is still more unreasonable than the other.

Your tenth question is fully answered in these observations on your first nine queries. Your eleventh query assumes that any purchaser of land would have the right to trade furs if he had not willed it away by assenting to any restrictive conditions. Such an assumption, of course, although admissable of itself, is inconsistent with your general views; the conditions of tenure which, by the bye, has always been well understood to prohibit any infraction of the Company's privileges, are intended not to bind the individual who is already bound by the fundamental law of the country, but merely to secure his land as a special guarantee for the due discharge of such, your essential obligation.

Your fourteenth query, which comprises your thirteenth, and, in fact, all the queries that you either have or could have proposed, requests me to enumerate the peculiar privileges of the Hudson's Bay Company, on the alleged grounds that you know them only through report. Considering that you have the means of seeing the Charter and the Land Deed, and such enactments of the Council of Rupert's Land as concern yourselves and your fellow citizens; and considering further that, in point of fact, some of you have seen them, I cannot admit that you require information to the extent that you profess; and even if you did require it, I do not think that I could offer you anything more clear than the documents themselves are, on which my enumeration of the Company's rights must be based. If, however, any individual among your fellow citizens should at any time feel himself embarrassed in any honest pursuit by legal doubt, I shall have much pleasure in affording him a personal interview.

I am, Gentlemen,
Your Most Obedient Servant,
ALEXANDER CHRISTIE,
Governor of Assiniboia

The "important and solemn proceedings" to which Christie referred were certainly serious enough. A band of Sioux warriors had arrived at Fort Garry to make a gesture of peace to the Hudson's Bay Company and had been given entry to the fort's square for parley with the Governor, when a brave of the Salteaux tribe, long friendly to the Red River settlers, had become excited at this Sioux visit and had shot one of the visiting enemy dancers. Pandemonium instantly broke out. Such an incident could easily have brought savage retaliation from the Sioux unless prompt action were instantly taken by Governor Christie to forestall it and prevent a possible general massacre of settlers. In this emergency Christie acted with calmness and wisdom. The guilty, if friendly, Salteaux Indian was taken into custody at once by company officers, summarily tried and condemned to be hanged before the walls of Fort Garry—this hanging being the first such execution in the District of Assiniboia under authority vested in the governor and the Hudson's Bay Company by the British Crown. The action was intended to impress the Indians that white man's law prevailed in the land, and to serve as warning to the *Métis*, as well as all other citizens of Red River, that such crimes would not be condoned.

It was not long after this occurrence that Governor Simpson turned more pointedly against his former friend, McDermot, as he had against Sinclair for further transgressions in the free trade, upon the assumption that they were stirring up resentment and resistance to company authority among the *Métis*. It so happened that McDermot had tactlessly sent an irresponsible relation of his—a nephew named McLaughlin—to Lachine, Quebec, to demand from Governor Simpson personally repayment for what the Irish merchant considered underpayment to himself and Sinclair by the Hudson's Bay Company for their freighting contract. McLaughlin had taken it upon himself to badger Simpson at his residence at most inappropriate times, so thoroughly annoying the Governor that he had turned the matter over for settlement to his trusted secretary and brother-in-law, Chief Factor Duncan Finlayson, who was well informed on such matters from his former administrative duties at Fort Garry in Governor Christie's absence.

In his persistent annoyance of Simpson, McLaughlin had overplayed his hand. He had inadvertently revealed some most important information to the Governor, which was instantly conveyed for appropriate action to the company's governor and committee in London. Simpson's letter, dated August 26, 1845, reveals:

> The half breed hunters while on their annual buffalo hunting excursions this summer [1845], in the plains country situated between the Red and St. Peter's rivers fell in with a party of one hundred and ninety American cavalry. . . . the half breeds who from their volatile character . . . ever fascinated by novelty . . . flattered by the reception they met with and elated by the advantages they are led to believe would be derived from a more intimate connexion with the United States . . . a petition was sent round among the settlers for a signature, praying Congress to assist and protect them in the formation of a settlement at Pembina. . . . The petition seems to have been drawn up by McLaughlin, a British subject, who last year went to the Settlement from St. Louis where he has been for some time resident, and who, together with a relative of his, named McDermott, who has for many years been settled at Red River, and a partner of McDermott's, named James Sinclair, have been employed by some of the United States authorities as secret emissaries among our half breed settlers and the neighbouring Indians, with a view of sowing the seeds of disaffection as a preliminary measure to the overtures that have now been made, in which they appear to have been very successful . . . from the tone of discontent towards the Mother Country which has recently been evident among these people. McLaughlin . . . has been entrusted with this petition, which has been signed by 1250 half breeds and Canadian settlers, and is now on his way to Washington for the purpose of laying it before the authorities there.[11]

Whether or not Sinclair was actually guilty of the accusations made concerning him in this letter, there was sufficient evidence to make it necessary for Governor Simpson to ask the British government to send troops as soon as possible to Red River to prevent trouble and to maintain law and order there. The British government, although reluctant to send a garrison to remote Red River, was moved to do so by the American clamor for the Oregon Territory. The troops would arrive in the fall of 1846.

Several months later Andrew McDermot took it upon himself to write a series of somewhat extraordinary letters to Governor Christie personally, complaining of injustices done him. For example, on November 13, 1845, he wrote:

> If I have incurred your animosity because I have traded furs, I only did so with the sanction and encouragement of Sir George Simpson and yourself. Look at the prices you paid me for furs last year, being 100 per cent more in some skins than you paid to any other person with the exception of Mr. Sinclair. This alone speaks volumes. If I have traded furs from half breeds and the settlers you cannot bring forward a single instance, (though I have been suspected,) wherein I ever gave any to any other than the Hudson's Bay Company, though I had offers on much more liberal terms than those allowed me by the Company at the time. Neither have I supplied foreigners with cash, (which I might have done with a handsome percentage for the purpose of purchasing furs) . . . again, in no instance can you bring forward any instance in which I ever sent any goods to any part of the Hudson's Bay territories for the purpose of trading furs. You will know before you leave Red River that Mr. Sinclair and I have not been the worst in this matter. . . . Some years ago a Mr. D. Aikins established a trading post at Pembina. That same year Sir George Simpson wintered in the settlement but took no notice of such an opposition, but only by authorizing me to endeavour to procure as many furs from that neighbourhood as possible, and that he would not see me lose anything by it. I accordingly procured almost all the furs, but at a considerable loss, which has never been made up to me. Mr. Aikins never returned again. It was some years before he left Pembina the Government made the arrangement with him. During the winter Mr. Aikins visited the Settlement on several occasions, when Governor Simpson treated him in the kindest manner, and even drove him about in his carriole. How very different has been the reception Mr. Kittson has received lately from Fort Garry is so well known to the whole Settlement as needs no comment. Though I have known Mr. Kittson refuse to purchase furs in the Settlement, or to store them at Pembina for settlers merely from feelings of courtesy to the gentlemen of the Hudson's Bay Company, and particularly from the recollection of the gentlemanly treatment received from Governor Finlayson. . . . But this you will say is no business of mine!

My object is merely to tell you the line of policy pursued by Sir George Simpson under similar circumstances. . . . I acted openly with you. Neither have I done anything in an underhand manner. One thing, however, I regret is that I did not follow Mr. Thom's advice last winter. If you had acted in good faith last winter with respect to my signing the "Declaration" not to trade in furs, much annoyance and unpleasantness would have been avoided to all parties, but the conditions which you wished to impose on me and Mr. Sinclair were so different from that demanded from other importers that you could scarcely expect we could agree on it. Your demanding from Mr. Sinclair and I, in addition to signing the Declaration without any alterations which you had previously agreed to make that we would never import goods from the United States, that we would give up the American goods we had to the Hudson's Bay Company, which, by the bye, were only about 300 to 400 lbs tobacco in all, and to crown all this, a bond of £1000 from each for the due fulfilment of the above conditions. . . .

I shall look forward for the arrival of Sir George Simpson in the spring, when I am certain that some arrangement can be made equally to the interest of all parties concerned. In the meantime whatever may have taken place I shall regret the loss of your friendship.[12]

McDermot's letter brought a short explanation from Christie, concerning the impounding of Sinclair's and McDermot's trade goods from Britain at York Factory, with the added statement that the Governor had taken steps to see that no further goods would be carried for them in future to Rupert's Land from England. Christie's reply read in part:

In the face of the general prohibition, the Gentleman in charge at York was not likely to act otherwise than he did for it made no exception with respect to your goods. . . . But whatever inconvenience may have arisen from the detention of your property either at York or in England, or whatever embarrassment you may have felt from the steps which had been adopted for the suppression of illicit trafficking, I must be permitted again to remind you that you have yourself alone to blame; disregarding all intimations, public or private, you persisted in your course until a painful but imperative necessity compelled us to resort to the measures of which you now complain.[13]

Still dissatisfied, McDermot again wrote to Christie as follows:

In 1843 the Governor and Mr. Finlayson made an agreement with me in my own house, and written in the Governor's hand that he or the Company would pay me the following prices for all the furs I would take into Fort Garry, and I am convinced the Governor would settle all those little matters last spring had it not been for yourself and all the other Chief Factors. . . .[14]

To this accusation Christie replied a week later:

Now I must remind you once more that neither you nor any other individual whatever are at any time entitled either to trade in furs or import or even sell goods without a license from the Company to that effect, and unless you take this essential principle for the foundation of your proposals, it is impossible that they can ever be such as I will agree to. . . . I have just now been informed on what I consider the best authority that thirty martens, more or less, were secretly traded on the limits of the Hudson's Bay Company's territories. Now under the promise made in your letter I call upon you immediately to admit or deny the accuracy of this information.[15]

Within two days McDermot sent two more letters of explanation to Christie—one expressing his belief that he had dealt with a personal servant whom he did not regard as an Indian because he was baptized; [16] and the other seeking to excuse his son for some dealings with Kittson,[17] the American trader at Pembina. In a curt reply on January 12, 1846,[18] Christie rejected McDermot's explanations entirely, and so ended this acrimonious correspondence.

IV

The people of Red River were to experience a year of uneasy peace until the British troops arrived at Fort Garry to maintain law. Tension rose to a fever pitch when Christie took further action to repress the free trade, and warrants were given his officers to search and arrest anyone suspected of illicit trafficking in furs. Enforcement of the company regulations was carried to the point where *Métis* cart trains were stopped on the trails and half-breed encampments were searched for the possession of company furs. Even some settlers' houses were examined—in some instances without much consideration for the feelings of the occupants, guilty or otherwise. Fireplaces and chimneys were prodded, and a number of citizens became indignant when their explanations were unaccepted while their premises were investigated. At this juncture, the half-breeds began to look to their arms; there was genuine cause for alarm lest insurrection break out at any minute in the land. The climax came when a *Métis*, named Registé Larant, was subjected to particularly harsh treatment and detained on suspicion that he carried contraband furs to the Americans. About the same time, an English half-breed, known as Hallett, was angered by some of Christie's men when he was accused of illicit trafficking. Hallett was so incensed by his treatment that he roused his people to join the *Métis* cause. This was a singularly ominous sign, for the English half-breeds had heretofore for the most part refrained from entering the *Métis* quarrel.

At this moment of increasing tension, another terrible epidemic struck Red River; so grievous did it become that any immediate threat of rebellion was indefinitely postponed. Scarcely a household in the settlement was exempt from this new plague taking the form of virulent influenza, which immobilized many of the people from February to August of this year. An aftermath of shocking lassitude was in evidence everywhere, leaving little inclination to carry forward the *Métis* quarrel with the company for some time. During this period of uneasy peace Sinclair conceived the idea of writing a personal letter to Governor Simpson to await his arrival at Fort Garry on his annual tour of inspection. On June 4, 1846, Sinclair wrote as follows:

> I beg permission to address you in writing in the hope that I may by a simple narrative of facts convince you that I have not from choice been placed in my present attitude as regards the supreme authority of this country, and also to assure you of my desire for a return to more amicable relations. It is needless to remind you how I with your sanction entered into the business of trafficking in furs, nor how amicably and satisfactorily the business was conducted during the government of Mr. Finlayson; yet while pursuing the same course in the following season, I found myself by an official Proclamation subjected to serious penalties unless I signed a declaration "neither to trade in furs nor sell goods on credit nor advance money to such as might generally be suspected of trading in furs, etc."
>
> Now as I had on the faith of former sanction, (and this still unrecalled), given goods on credit to a considerable amount to persons who might hunt or traffic or otherwise obtain furs, I was thus subjected either to the loss of my property so embarked or of losing my privilege

of obtaining goods from London placed in a dilemma so pressing I suggested to Mr. Christie an amendment which might enable me with safety to sign the required declaration, viz. "that I would not give or sell goods on credit or advance money to any person for the purpose of trading furs." This alteration appeared so satisfactory to Mr. Christie that he appointed an hour the following day to receive the signature of Mr. McDermot and myself, but this arrangement was frustrated by Mr. Thom who, to my no small amazement, addressed us in tone and terms which might have suited a despot addressing his slaves but was little likely to influence parties equally independent. Amidst much that was offensive and irrelevant, he informed us that no goods should be shipped to London for us unless we complied with the following conditions:

(1) That we should sign the declaration as first draughted.
(2) That we should cease to carry on any commerce with the United States.
(3) That we should deliver up to the Hudson's Bay Company all American goods in our possession, and
(4) That we should sign a bond of £1000 each as security for the due fulfillment of the above conditions.

I must say that to such extravagant demands there could be but one reply. These conditions, sufficiently objectionable in themselves, became more so from Thom's personality; no such demands being made on any other importers.

Now, if we were held so amenable because we traded furs, I submit that Mr. Christie could not be ignorant that it was with the knowledge and sanction of Your Excellency, and which sanction he practically affirmed by receiving our furs at the same standards theretofore allowed by his predecessors, yet, while smarting under the injustice of one who participated and punished my offence, I made frequent overtures to sign the amended declaration, provided I was indemnified for my outstanding fur debts, (and to this I think I had an unquestionable right, seeing I had risked my property on the security of which I still deem a valid sanction), but no terms would be listened to except unqualified submission to Mr. Thom's first demands. To this I can never agree. My freedom of action and my life are my own, and no one has a right without injustice to demand their alienation.

I have, I acknowledge, urged by feelings of bitterness, continued a course which I know has been injurious to the Company's interests, but I am desirous of reconciliation. The work is profitable but it is distasteful. Yet I would not be guilty of affectation while addressing a man of business of proposing to sacrifice all without indemnity.

I would respectfully reiterate to your Excellency the proposal I have often made; viz: let me be secured for loss of my outstanding fur debts and I will sign the amended declaration. Nay, could I realize on my property here, (and it is not much), I would next year leave the country entirely. By remaining here and pursuing a course I am most anxious to terminate, I can in a short time profitably dispose of all I have, and believe me, Sir, such a course must be expensive to the Company and profitable to myself. It may be pursued with perfect safety so that no vigilance can detect it, nor any authority reach it. I can have active, zealous, and gratuitous agents while the Company pays high for luke-warm service.

Let me implore you not to understand this as using the language of threat. I candidly state my temptations and my wishes, indulging in the hope of a favourable reply from your Excellency. I remain respectfully,

Your obedient servant,
JAMES SINCLAIR [19]

An unusually prompt reply was sent by Simpson on June 8, 1846, from Fort Garry:

Dear Sir: I have to acknowledge receipt of your letter of the 4th instant but regret the pressure of business at the present moment prevents me replying at any length. I shall, however, as soon as I am a little more at leisure communicate with you further on the subject, and trust the result of such communications may prove satisfactory by terminating the unfortunate difficulties which have recently existed between yourself and officers of the Hudson's Bay Company in this colony.

I remain, Your obedient servant,
GEORGE SIMPSON [20]

As far as there is any known record, Governor Simpson does not appear to have pursued the correspondence with Sinclair at this time. It is believed that Simpson reached some sort of understanding with McDermot, but refrained from having any conciliation with Sinclair at this stage. Curiously enough, however, a change of attitude at Fort Garry became evident toward McDermot and Sinclair in their dealings there. It seems that their furs were once more taken on terms formerly acceptable to Simpson, despite the fact that there appears to have been little if any direct communication between Governor Christie, Recorder Adam Thom, and Sinclair. Even the privileges of export and import on company ships through York Factory, which McDermot and Sinclair had previously enjoyed under Simpson's patronage, was revived for a time. It is hard to tell the cause for these comparatively restored amicable relations—whether it was the impending arrival of the British troops in Red River, which gave some assurance to the company's London authorities that so long as the soldiers were in the settlement the free traders would not do too much harm; or that the more bland and flexible policy of the London committee prevailed over Christie's worried narrowness and Thom's pedantic sharpness. Certainly, things were generally better for a while for McDermot and Sinclair. Even the *Métis* seemed more peacefully inclined for a time, with the easing of Christie's and Thom's restrictive legislation against free trading; and with the promise once more of exceedingly good buffalo hunts, the threat of outright rebellion in Red River was postponed for a while at least.

9. SINCLAIR IN LONDON

I

In the spring of 1846, the Red River *Métis* leaders came to Sinclair with a proposal that he should go to London to represent them, and there place their case before the British government so they might ascertain once and for all what rights they possessed in Rupert's Land. Sinclair agreed to go, feeling that the half-breeds might now receive a more favorable hearing in London than would have been possible earlier. The Reform Bill of 1832 and the abolition of the Corn Laws in 1846 had awakened public consciousness to the importance of free institutions and free trade, which had become the leading topics of the day in Great Britain. More liberal legislation was being passed to aid the so-called downtrodden and underprivileged minorities throughout the empire. Sinclair was therefore prepared to spend the winter of 1846–47 abroad in an effort to further the *Métis* cause, with the understanding that the half-breeds were to meet the cost of this effort through the sale of some of their best furs to the Americans.

Sinclair also had considerable confidence through the assurance that his good friend and compatriot in London, the brilliant Alexander Kennedy Isbister, who had formerly lived in Rupert's Land, was prepared to plead the case. Isbister and Sinclair came of similar Orkney stock, and both were graduates of Edinburgh University, although Isbister had attended the university somewhat later than Sinclair, being considerably younger. Isbister was achieving success in London in the practice of law and was therefore in a position to place the *Métis* case before the proper British authorities. Despite the fact that he had lived abroad for some time and would continue to do so, Isbister's heart and thought were still largely in Red River; and although he never saw his native land again, he left large endowments for the education of his people. While Isbister was most loyal to the crown, his sympathies were also with the *Métis*, whom he felt had received unjust treatment in Rupert's Land. At the same time, he was in the peculiar position of being related through some family connections by marriage with Governor Alexander Christie. Nevertheless, Isbister was prepared to do all in his power to present the *Métis* cause fairly.

Traveling to Britain by New York, Sinclair took the familiar route south from Fort Garry to St. Louis, and from that place down the Ohio River and the new Alleghany railway to the Atlantic seaboard. In the year 1846 New York was a queer amalgam of many nations settling quickly into a solid mold of strong national feeling, although this swiftly growing metropolis still gave evidence of earlier Dutch and British colonial periods. When Sinclair reached New York the populace was talking about the new Trinity Church near Wall Street and the new public library, which John Jacob Astor and Washington Irving had planned together. Reservoir Square was already preparing for a great exposition, and some of the fine old Dutch mansions that had once been residences on farms in the Bowery were hidden strangely among the swiftly encroaching business establishments coming into being with the new prosperity.

It did not take Sinclair long to find the magnificent mansion where the aged John Jacob Astor lived, and to present the letter of introduction he carried from Henry Hastings Sibley, still commanding the American Fur Company in St. Peter's. But Astor was now so far gone with sickness and general decrepitude that he could not see Sinclair. The old fur genius had numbered days, and the thirty million dollars he had accumulated in the North American fur trade [1] could not prevent approaching death from claiming him.

When Sinclair was ready to sail for Britain, the New York waterfront was reflecting this unprecedented era of expansion in many ways. Here could be found craft of many kinds from all parts of the world, for its unique position made it one of nature's most favored sites in all North America where land met sea. When Sinclair took passage on a swift packet bound for London, similar ships crossed the Atlantic twice weekly. His ship was of some fifteen hundred tons burden, two hundred feet in length, New York built, and was boasted one of the finest in the American fleet, said to be quickly inheriting the world's seaways. The accommodation was considered exceptionally good, if somewhat expensive, with the best of food provided and good company to be found for the crossing. With favorable winds the Atlantic might be crossed in the incredibly short period for those days of five weeks, instead of the eleven weeks it had taken Sinclair to cross to York Factory from Stromness some twenty years before.

II

Sinclair reached London anticipating success on this unusual mission. He readily found his old friend Isbister, but was somewhat astonished at the change wrought in him since their last meeting in Rupert's Land some years before. Isbister had become very elegant, beautifully spoken, and quite *soigné*. He was exceedingly handsome, six feet three inches tall, and combined a natural grace of manner with acquired aristocratic bearing.

A most kindly welcome awaited Sinclair at the lawyer's home within the environs of the Temple at Bolt Court. Here Isbister lived the life of a confirmed bachelor, but with a good home provided for him by his widowed mother and spinster sister, whom he had brought out from Rupert's Land a little while before. In this charming home Sinclair was provided with an atmosphere of comfort, with amenities singularly remote and foreign to what he had experienced as the best in Red River.

London in the winter of 1846–47 proved to be a fascinating place for Sinclair in many ways, and certainly quite different from what he remembered during his short stay in 1818 as a child, when he had been the unwanted guest of the preoccupied and distraught Alexander Lean in the grim offices at Fenchurch Street. As Isbister's welcome guest he found every day filled with new interest, for when not engaged with his practice, Isbister shared with Sinclair the sights and pleasures of London, which the lawyer had come to enjoy almost inordinately. There were the theatres, and the clubs that Isbister's success and prestige brought him, as well as the famous restaurants, art galleries, and salons he found congenial in the circles of London's literary and legal worlds.

As a matter of fact, Alexander Isbister could never tear himself for long away from the actual environs of the Temple and the enchantment of the strange house in which he now chanced to live. The great Dr. Johnson had once lived there, and for a time his famous scribe, Boswell. As if to make it all the more pungently real, the former Red River lawyer would quote portions of Boswell's prose with relish. He was especially fond of the description of the fabulous Johnson's appearance and character —his leonine head, his drooping mouth, shrewd eyes, strange fits of stormy wisdom, and childishly affectionate prattle; his "brown suit of clothes, very rusty; his little old shrivelled, powdered wig, too small for his head; his shirt neck and knees of his breeches left loose; his black worsted stockings ill drawn up, and his pair of unbuckled shoes by way of slippers; his peculiarities forgotten when he began to talk." On hearing such renditions in Isbister's exquisitely intoned words, Sinclair marveled at his friend's versatile brilliance.

In contrast to Isbister's suave profundity, Sinclair sometimes found it a genuine relief to visit Mrs. Isbister and her daughter in their drawing room, where they managed to make London more tangibly comfortable for him—bringing him back to simpler ways with their bits of chitchat about Red River, where they had lived from 1833 to 1842. They, too, were hungry for scraps of news concerning mutual friends, such as the Inksters, the Kennedys, and Prudens, and even the good cleric, Cockran, but especially the family of Chief Factor Donald Ross of Norway House. Such people were all well known to Sinclair—especially the Rosses—for quite frequently his trips from Fort Garry to York Factory with McDermot's cargoes of trade goods and country produce took him that way. However, Sinclair was not a little surprised to learn from Mrs. Isbister that Chief Factor Ross's daughter, Jane—whom Sinclair remembered casually as a gangling girl when he had last seen her at her father's post—had recently been in London at finishing school. He gathered from Mrs. Isbister's remarks that she was especially fond of Miss Jane Ross and would not have been at all displeased to have had her become her daughter-in-law. Miss Jane was evidently a charming girl—unspoiled, gifted, pleasant, and intelligent. But Sinclair soon discovered that Isbister himself had no serious interest in this lass from Rupert's Land, nor in any other lady, for that matter; his interests were too deeply engrossed with his world of law, letters, and London generally. Indeed, sometimes this association with the literary-minded lawyer laid rather heavily upon Sinclair, although he also wished he might have continued with his own studies of law at Edinburgh for his own future's sake. He especially appreciated this when Isbister revealed he would soon be exchanging his gown of "stuff" for the silk of the Queen's Counsellor, and would enjoy to the full the honor and prestige this dignity would afford him.

With some difficulty Sinclair would draw Isbister back from his absorption in the past to the more relevant environment of the present. Even here this remarkable man was not found wanting. His volatile mind and wide interests embraced many of the more pregnant facts of current economics and social life in the broadening sphere of the Victorian era. He made it plain that he believed no war of any proportion endangered the moment. Great minds were at work in church and state, in letters, and in many of the fine arts. Parliament in Britain was busied with constructive and far-reaching legislation. Dr. Arnold of Rugby had become a force in British thought—as had Thomas Carlyle, with his remarkable essays; Ruskin, in the field of criticism; Turner, in painting; and Lyell, in the world of science. Periodicals, such as the *Edinburgh Review* and the *Quarterly Review*, were influencing public affairs widely both at home and abroad. The middle classes were enjoying unprecedented prosperity. Huge building projects were afoot for the improved housing of the poor. Vast developments in industry were taking place. There were, however, some dangers, Isbister conceded, especially in the unscrupulous exploitation of the public—for example, by the so-called railway king, George Hudson; and for such men Isbister held the most scathing contempt. There was also, he felt, the danger that overspeculation might bring ruin to many if fortunes to a few. But solid industry had become a colossal and constructive manifestation of the nation's best minds, which would bring great benefit and opportunity to all.

As examples of what was occurring in Great Britain in that fortuitous year of 1846, Isbister informed Sinclair that already five thousand miles of railway had been laid and were in use in Britain. Transportation had completely changed since Sinclair's school days in Scotland. Large railway terminals with grand hotels of unprecedented size, comfort, and luxury now served the traveling public. Gone forever were the lumbering stagecoaches and quaint wayside inns scattered along the highroads. In the city, the landau and smart hansom cab were to be seen. Magnetic telegraph was another wonder of the day, with nearly two thousand miles of wire already in use to relay messages quickly within Britain; and one day Isbister expected this great invention to span the Atlantic—overcoming, as if by miracle, the limitations of time and space. How much further such fantastic inventions would go one could scarcely imagine, for phenomenal discoveries appeared to be endless. Indeed, even far-off, benighted Red River could scarcely escape the wonders this fine new world of British industry and finance and human ingenuity was conceiving! Certainly, Isbister concluded, the irritating problems of backward peoples such as the *Métis* must sooner or later find satisfactory solutions, but this might take a little time to accomplish.

The London lawyer warned Sinclair that the processes of British law were often despairingly slow, if thorough and uncompromising. And although he would personally make every effort and use every possible approach to pursue the half-breed cause to the best advantage in London, Isbister was not too sure an early opportunity could be found to present the *Métis* petition to parliament. Sinclair realized after a few months in London that it was useless for him to remain there longer, so it seemed advisable to return as quickly as possible to Red River, for he knew the half-breeds would be growing impatient, and he dreaded the consequences should the British authorities delay their verdict too long. But before his return to Rupert's Land, knowing that Simpson had reached some sort of an understanding with McDermot to re-establish their former friendship, but without any show of conciliation to himself, Sinclair, with a certain amount of impudent bravado, attended the senior officers of the Hudson's Bay Company in London. He succeeded in getting to the presence of the governor, Sir John Pelly, with Isbister's assistance, and for his daring was read a lecture from Sir John that he would not likely soon forget. However, his efforts were rewarded to a certain extent by the company's committee ordering that he be paid £100 in settlement of the underpayment for freight carriage that he and McDermot had claimed previously. McDermot was given a reimbursement of the same amount. This task accomplished, Sinclair prepared to return to Red River.

III

Sinclair reached Fort Garry early in the spring of 1847 via New York and Pembina. He found his friend, Norman Kittson, the American trader, still in business at this post; and their former association was renewed, on somewhat better terms to Sinclair, who had been able to make certain rather advantageous financial arrangements in London through the good offices of his friend Isbister. Prospects, therefore, seemed brighter for him in the free trade for a time. Sinclair also learned from Kittson that word had recently come from Red River, through the popular priest of the *Métis*, Father Belcourt, that in the future relations between the Americans and the Hudson's Bay Company were also likely to be somewhat more amicable. This appeared to mean that Governor Simpson was once more exercising a more tolerant influence over Christie's anxious and rigid restrictions upon the free trade, as well as over the edicts of Adam Thom.

Sinclair was relieved to find his children safe and well at Fort Garry. He was disturbed, however, to discover that there had been some suffering among the settlers generally through the failure of the past year's grain and hay crops. A serious drought had also adversely affected the returns in pemmican, since the shortage of prairie grass for the grazing buffalo herds had meant a disappointing hunt. Apart from this, Red River had not fared too badly during the time Sinclair had been abroad, and things had seemed especially peaceful since the arrival of the British troops.

In the autumn of 1846, a party of the British Sixth Regiment of Foot (the Warwickshires), had arrived at Fort Garry accompanied by a detachment of artillery and royal engineers under the command of Lieutenant-Colonel John Ffolliott Crofton. These troops had left Cork, Ireland, under special orders from the Duke of Wellington and had reached York Factory on August 7, 1846. They were brought inland by York boat brigade via the fur-trade route through Oxford House and Norway House, then down Lake Winnipeg and up the Red

River to Simpson's Lower Fort Garry, where part of the soldiers were stationed and the remainder sent on to Governor Christie's Upper Fort Garry at the Forks.

The presence of these British soldiers served to ease the tension in Red River. For the time being, a number of the more disgruntled *Métis* moved with their relatives up the Assiniboine and Qu'Appelle rivers, leaving the amenable and cautious half-breeds to carry on the restricted free trade to the south of Fort Garry.

The troops were also providing such Red River merchants as McDermot with a lucrative new market, and at the same time affording a certain fillip to the colony's social life. Admittedly, there was some eyebrow-lifting and jealousy as the dashing officers became the *raison d'être* of many gay parties in the homes of the well-to-do retired company people, such as the social leader, Chief Factor James Curtis Bird. The noncommissioned men, in turn, were made heartily welcome to many other Red River homes.

Sinclair was also somewhat astonished to find himself suddenly made welcome to the social affairs of the Red River "elite" upon his return from abroad, which seemed to add a certain luster to his already desirable position as an eligible and comparatively well-to-do widower. Indeed, it took some clever maneuvering on his part to avoid the advances made by Madam Bird and several other ladies who sought to lionize him embarrassingly, and to avoid the obvious pitfalls laid by some scheming Red River mammas with marriageable daughters. As the most promising prospect of escape, Sinclair soon found it advisable to pay marked attention to one particular lady—Miss Jane Ross, approved by his London friends, the Isbisters.

It so chanced that Jane Ross was staying at this time in Red River with some mutual friends—the Prudens—whose charming daughter, Caroline, was a close friend of Sinclair's own daughter, Harriet, now swiftly growing to charming young womanhood herself. To Sinclair's astonishment, when he presented his respects at the Pruden home bearing the good wishes from the Isbisters, he found Miss Jane not the coltish girl he had seen some years before at her father's post, but a poised young lady. Jane had striking good looks, spontaneous good humor, and seemed genuinely glad to greet him. In temperament she proved to be very like her genial, quick-witted, capable father, the estimable Chief Factor Donald Ross, whom Sinclair had long known and admired.

Sinclair found it possible to see Miss Jane a number of times during her Red River visit, and before the day arrived for her to return to her father's post at Norway House, Sinclair had made up his mind to ask for her hand in marriage, despite the discouraging gossip that was then current in Red River concerning her unbridled extravagance.[2] On February 6, 1848, he wrote to Chief Factor Ross for his permission to marry Jane, enclosing his proposal to the girl herself. To the father he wrote:

> Dear Sir: Some few and not uneventful years have passed since our intercourse has ceased, and though circumstance may not infrequently have brought my name before you with perhaps no welcome odour, yet I assure you no feeling of interest or passion ever prevented my cherishing a warm recollection of the many favours and kindnesses I have received from you. From the address of the enclosed you will at once divine the object, and I trust you know nothing of my character or of my prospects in life to induce you to withhold your concurrence should I be so fortunate as to acquire a place in the favour of Miss Ross.
>
> It is, of course, the first consideration of every parent to secure the happiness of his child, and one essential ingredient is security against any doubt of the accustomed comfort and elegance of life. I shall add that my income ranges from £200 to £400 per annum, but this depends so much on the nature of my transactions for the time being. However, I am at this moment worth better than £3000.
>
> I am, dear Sir,
> Yours sincerely,
> JAMES SINCLAIR[3]

Sinclair's proposal to Miss Jane read:

> My dear Miss Ross: You will perhaps be surprised to be advised by me, a comparative stranger, but I would venture to indulge a hope that surprise will not be mixed with displeasure, even though I presume to declare that the sentiment of esteem for your person, and the admiration for your varied accomplishments impressed on my mind

during a short and fitful acquaintance have by time and circumstance become matured into a feeling of a more tender nature. Though it would be unpardonable to suppose that your recollection of our acquaintance at all assimilates with mine, but I would indulge in the pleasing hope that no hostile reminiscences will oppose my solicitation for permission to prosecute in person my progress to a place in your esteem; a permission I will embrace with alacrity, commensurate with the value I place upon those qualities of mind and person which I feel to be essential to my happiness. I am, my dear Miss, with every sentiment of esteem,

Yours sincerely,
JAMES SINCLAIR[4]

Sinclair's reply came with surprising swiftness by return company packet from Norway House. Chief Factor Ross's answer, dated February 18, 1848—with no accompanying letter from Jane—read:

My dear Sir: On the arrival of Mr. Clouston here the other day, I had the pleasure of receiving your favour of the 6th instant, together with the enclosure addressed to my daughter, Jane, and as Mr. Lane is now preparing to start for the Settlement, I embrace the opportunity of writing to you in reply. As Jane is under a solemn obligation shortly to become the wife of another gentleman [name scored out] before your application came to hand, which certainly, indeed, was the first information we ever received of your views and wishes in regard to her. Little more need now be said on the subject than my returning you my most sincere thanks in my own name by her special desire; and in that of my daughter, also, for the offer you have just made, in which, under other circumstances, might have led to a different termination.

I can assure you that, notwithstanding the events to which you allude, no personal feelings towards yourself, either of a hostile or unpleasant nature have ever rested in my mind, and should it hereafter be in my power to render you any kindness or service, I shall have pleasure in doing so. With best wishes, believe me to be,

DONALD ROSS[5]

This letter from Chief Factor Ross was written in all honesty, for Jane was betrothed to the Reverend John Hunter, an Anglican missionary stationed at Cumberland House, whose wife had died some time before, leaving him with an infant son. Miss Jane was to be married to Hunter at her father's house, after which she would accompany her husband to his home in the wilderness and help with his ministrations to the Indians near the Pas. To this end Jane had diligently applied herself by learning the Cree syllabics to translate the scriptures for the native charges.

Obviously hurt by the rebuff, however involuntary, he had received from Ross, Sinclair nevertheless was not slow to seek the hand of another Red River girl, Mary Campbell—the daughter of Chief Trader Colin Campbell of Fort Dunvegan in the distant Athabaska country.[6] Campbell was the son of Alexander Campbell and Magdalena Van Slice of River Beaudette, Lake St. Francis, in Glengarry, eastern Canada, who had been born in the year 1787. These people were of sound United Empire Loyalist stock—Campbell's father representing Cornwall in the first legislative assembly of upper Canada. At the age of seventeen, Colin Campbell had joined the North West Company and was soon sent to the Athabaska region. At the time of the Hudson's Bay Company's union with the North West Company in 1821, Colin Campbell was retained by the reorganized company and placed in charge of Fort Dunvegan where he remained for thirty years. No company man appears to have ever endured any greater hardships than did Campbell, according to the evidence to be found in his own journals.[7]

Early in his career, Colin Campbell had married Elizabeth McGillvray, daughter of the Honorable John McGillvray, one of the North West Company's senior wintering partners—those officers who remained in the interior at the posts. McGillvray had come from Inverness, Scotland, where he was heir to a fortune and valuable estates. He was in charge of Fort Dunvegan when Campbell was sent to that post as a junior trader. This was how it had come about that Colin had married McGillvray's daughter. Eleven children were born to this union—two sons and nine daughters. One of these daughters, Mary, who had been sent with her sisters from Edmonton House to attend boarding school in Red River, was married to James Sinclair in March, 1848.[8]

Upon his marriage, Sinclair evidently looked forward eagerly to the reopening of his fine house, situated between the dwellings of Alexander Ross and Andrew McDermot, near the gates of Upper Fort Garry. He anticipated bringing his children together again here under a mother's care. But this did not prove to be such a fortunate arrangement. Jealousies soon became evident, for Mary Campbell showed little desire to have Sinclair's children by his former wife live with them. At the same time, Sinclair's eldest daughter, Harriet—now a girl of seventeen—found it equally difficult to accept her father's new wife into the home her mother had established. Another source of jealousy was Sinclair's deep affection for his family. Harriet was singularly like her father in temperament; she enjoyed the same things as he did—such as music, dancing, and happy entertainment in the home—which the new wife apparently resented from the start. Sinclair also felt a deep protective devotion for his delicate daughter, Maria—now thirteen years of age and very like her late mother. As for his two young sons, Mary could tolerate them better. She was prepared to have the youngest—aged five—remain in the home, but Alexander, the eldest boy, was to be placed in the Red River boarding school.

Recognizing this unhappy situation as unreconcilable from the outset, Sinclair prepared to place his two daughters in a good boarding school at Galena, Illinois. But before their departure in the summer of 1848, Sinclair wished to formally present Harriet to Red River society at the most pretentious ball ever held in the settlement in honor of the British troops about to leave for the homeland. By the year 1846, the boundary dispute that had long caused tension between the United States and Great Britain—especially where it concerned deciding the border west of the mountains—had at last been more or less amicably settled. With the easing of this inflammable issue the regular British troops were to be replaced by a body of pensioners from Chelsea, London, who were to serve as a constabulary.

For his daughter's presentation at the military ball for the retiring troops, Sinclair had purchased for her a beautiful imported frock from New York and a pair of white kid gloves, said to have been the first of their kind ever worn in Red River.[9] Sinclair had also, as a special surprise for his daughter, tried to master during his travels the intricate steps of the polka, then fashionable in ball rooms both in New York and St. Louis. He proposed to introduce this dance to the colony as partner of his daughter and her young friends.

Surely no father was ever more proud than Sinclair when Harriet became the belle of that Red River ball. There were actually three belles at this affair, all bound to Sinclair with bonds of affection and relationships of one kind or another. There were, besides Harriet, the beautiful Caroline Pruden—Harriet's dearest friend, and already betrothed to Sinclair's prosperous younger brother, Thomas—and Sinclair's niece, Margaret—daughter of his oldest brother, William,who had become the second chief factor of that name in the company's service.

This Red River ball was the last of such affairs Sinclair would be privileged to enjoy for some time, for almost immediately after he and his two daughters set out for the United States. He again left his home and the remainder of his family in the care of his friends Ross and McDermot, as well as his brother-in-law, John Inkster.[10] It is likely that Sinclair anticipated being away from Red River for some time, with the unhappy domestic situation resulting from his second marriage and the increasing difficulties that now confronted him in the Red River free trade, added to the responsibilities he had assumed on behalf of the *Métis,* who, now the British troops were withdrawing, might again become a serious problem in Red River. It therefore seemed the part of wisdom for Sinclair to retire from the settlement, and, if possible, seek some way to make a new life for himself and his family, perhaps in the distant Oregon.

IV

It was early in July, 1848, that Sinclair and his daughters set forth from Fort Garry for Illinois.[11] The trip was a memorably happy one for the little family group, and Sinclair made traveling as comfortable as possible for his daughters in the Red River cart train, made up of three carts drawn by *Métis* ponies, and accompanied by six well-armed men to assist them and to act as guards through the dangerous Sioux country to the south of the forks. The rough, swaying, squalling carts in which the girls rode were padded with plenty of buffalo robes and blankets for comfort, and while Sinclair permitted the girls to walk sometimes beside him on the plains when riding in the carts grew wearisome, he was reluctant to let them ride the high-spirited buffalo runners as they would like to have done. It took the party some three weeks to cross the distance between Fort Garry and St. Paul, Minnesota, and the trip proved interesting enough in many respects.

The party was unexpectedly joined by a small cart train from the Oregon. It seemed a singularly out-of-the-way route for a party from the Far West, but the presence of the new Roman Catholic bishop of the Columbia River Diocese, recently consecrated west of the mountains, explained why he and his attendants were in this vicinity. This dignitary was on his way to visit a mission in Minnesota; and Sinclair was only too glad to meet this interesting stranger [12] who was able to give him a first-hand account of conditions in the Oregon. The bishop told him of Dr. John McLoughlin's recent retirement from the Hudson's Bay Company since the settlement of the boundary dispute, and that he had gone to live in the seclusion of the beautiful Willamette Valley. The extraordinary old chief factor had become an unhappy, disillusioned man, embittered by the ingratitude and treatment dealt him by British and Americans alike as poor reward for all he had tried to do on their respective behalfs.

On the way to St. Paul the Sinclair party also met two desperate and starving deserters from the American army.[13] The cleric assumed the authority of his high position to give the deserters sanctuary with his party until they could reach the mission to which he was traveling at Red Lake, where he was prepared to hand them over to the United States authorities on the understanding that the miscreants be given fair treatment.

According to Harriet Sinclair's recollections, these were several of the most unusual episodes on this trip with her father.

They managed to travel safely through the increasingly dangerous Sioux country to reach St. Paul, which proved fascinating to the two young girls. This settlement took the form of a crazy-pattern town in 1848, consisting of some one hundred and forty buildings—hotels, boardinghouses, printing shops, saloons, gambling spots, brothels, and cheap new dwellings—all hastily put together in a period of unprecedented pioneer boom. Here was a starkly bare, treeless, and rather uninviting community, but Sinclair and his daughters were compelled to stay here until the steamboat arrived from St. Louis to carry them down the Mississippi River as far as a settlement known as Oquaki. From here they took a stagecoach overland to Galesboro—a prim little Illinois town, where Sinclair was relieved to find in Knox college a pleasant environment for his daughters' next few years of schooling. Secure in his mind for their welfare, Sinclair then continued on to St. Louis to make plans for his anticipated move to the Oregon at the earliest possible moment.

V

St. Louis in 1848 was an interesting city whose source of wealth was turning from the fabulous fur trade to the more prosaic settlement that was extending ever westward. People were pouring into this place from many parts of the United States as the urge to migrate beyond the Mississippi accelerated. Sinclair was given cause to wonder if all these folk were as fearless as they seemed or merely ignorant of what lay before them as they prepared to face the very real dangers of the Oregon, Santa Fé, and California trails, bedeviled by thirst, starvation on the desert, or threatened by attack of hostile Indians in the mountains on their march westward.

While in St. Louis—still raw, boisterous, and violent, although alluring to any visitor—Sinclair was somewhat astonished to discover that a smart and delightfully smug and exclusive social set had come into being, most certainly different from the old fur aristocracy of the Chouteau, Ashley, and Sublette days. Into this new, polished clique Sinclair unexpectedly found himself graciously accepted.

Quite by chance Sinclair had struck up a friendship with a promising young American army Lieutenant, named Ulysses S. Grant,[14] who, apart from his somewhat arduous and confining regimental duties, was having some financial difficulties and was also deeply in love with one of St. Louis' most desirable and fashionable belles. It so happened that Sinclair was in a position to give some assistance to Grant, both with money and in his courtship of the beautiful young Julia Dent.[15] She was the daughter of an affluent Kentucky colonel who lived in the most exclusive quarter of the city, where Sinclair was made most welcome upon Grant's introduction. In return for the kindness shown him, Sinclair did everything within his power to further this delightful romance[16] in the short time at his disposal, and was pleased to find himself an honored guest at Grant's wedding on August 22, 1848.[17] This interesting little St. Louis episode was to prove of value to Sinclair for the rest of his life, for Grant's friendship stood the test of time, and many years later he was able to assist Sinclair's widow in a most unexpected and worthwhile manner.

10. THE SAYER TRIAL AND THE MÉTIS FREEDOMS

I

Sinclair appears to have remained south of the border for most of the winter of 1848–49. No further communication came from Governor Simpson to conduct another party of Red River settlers to the Oregon; and Sinclair, evidently disappointed that there were poor prospects for him in that quarter, took steps to become an American citizen, although he gave no intimation of this at the time to his friends and relations in Red River. For a while he seems to have continued his free trade quite openly with the Americans, especially with Kittson at Pembina, and aiding his *Métis* friends in the sale of their furs to the best advantage.

When still south of the border, word was sent Sinclair from Red River with comparative regularity—carried by the wandering *Métis*, and delivered to him by his good friend, Joseph Renville. It was from this source that he learned of the increasing uneasiness of the half-breeds, growing impatient that no further word had come from Isbister in London, although he still continued to press their cause upon the proper British authorities. It was also through this means of communication that Sinclair must have learned that a child born to a girl of native blood had been baptized with his name in Red River, on November 29, 1848 [1]—such progeny not an unusual occurrence in the Rupert's Land of that day.

With reference to less personal matters, but having certain bearing upon his affairs at a later date, Sinclair was also informed that Alexander Christie had retired as governor of Assiniboia on September 20, 1848, to be replaced by Major W. B. Caldwell, the officer commanding the first body of Chelsea pensioners brought to Red River to take over the policing duties of the regular British troops. Caldwell held a commission as governor of Assiniboia from the Hudson's Bay Company on the recommendation of Earl Grey,[2] the British colonial secretary. He was also empowered to make a complete investigation and report on the conditions then evident in Red River, with special reference to the *Métis* petition as formally presented to the British government by A. K. Isbister, with allegations against the Hudson's Bay Company for maladministration and harsh treatment of the half-breeds. These charges were either to be established or disproved. Caldwell was also instructed to look into the alleged embarrassment occasioned the people of Red River through lack of adequate medium of monetary exchange, except for the promissory notes payable on London by such recognized licensed petty traders as McDermot and Sinclair had once been.

Unhappily, the people of Red River—particularly the half-breeds—were not slow to show their dissatisfaction with the new administration of Assiniboia and the body of pensioners, who do not appear to have been either feared or respected to the same extent the British troops had been. The disgruntled *Métis* once more threatened serious trouble by the winter of 1848. At the same time as conditions were deteriorating in Red River, Isbister in London was experiencing disappointment in his representations to the British government on behalf of the Red River half-breeds. He was compelled to report regretfully that legal opinion

"Half Breeds Travelling," by Paul Kane. The equipment shown here is identical with ıat of Sinclair's 1841 party (*Courtesy Royal Ontario Museum*)

North side of Bow Valley looking toward Whiteman's Pass. (*Department of North-rn Affairs, National Parks Branch; courtesy Miss Gerry Fish, Calgary, Alberta*)

Red Rock Gorge—now Sinclair Canyon—over which Sinclair led his 1841 party (*Department of Northern Affairs, National Parks Branch; courtesy Miss Gerry Fish, Calgary, Alberta*)

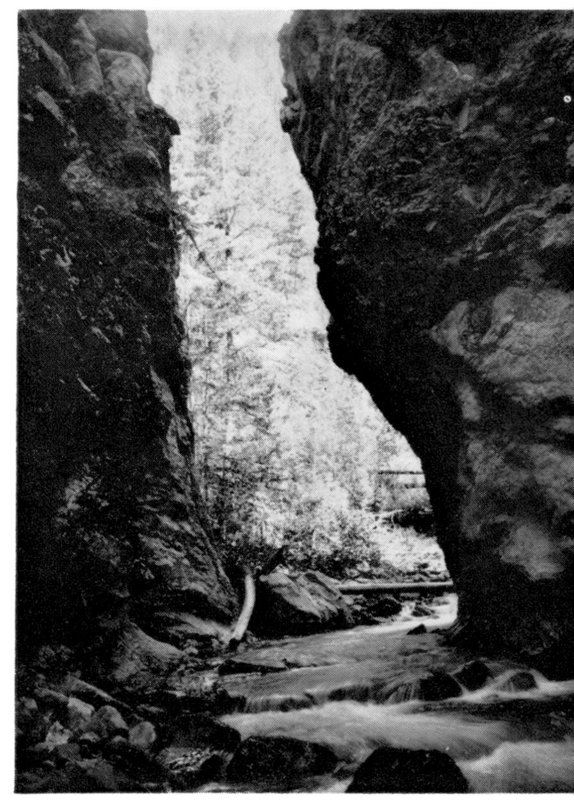

Fort Ellice, through which Sinclair and his parties traveled on their way west from Fort Garry (*Courtesy Manitoba Public Archives*)

in Britain was solidly in favor of the Hudson's Bay Company. The British authorities appeared to accept in its entirety the statement of Sir John H. Pelly, Governor of the Hudson's Bay Company, that the petitions Sinclair had carried to London for the *Métis* were completely without foundation in fact. Earl Grey had stated that after investigation it had been found that the Hudson's Bay Company's charter was valid as recognized by the British acts of Parliament, and that it was considered there were no grounds for making application to the British Parliament by the *Métis* for consideration of the claims that they had suffered oppression by the Hudson's Bay Company in Rupert's Land. The British colonial secretary had added that the Hudson's Bay Company was now in a position to willingly undertake consideration of any justifiable representations that might be made in future of any substantial grievances by either the *Métis* or any other settlers in Red River.[3] As a result of this, Sinclair and his confreres were forced to accept the fact that the *Métis* had received an adverse judgment in their petitions, but Isbister assured Sinclair that he would continue to press the *Métis* cause to the proper British authorities in the hope of securing for them in time the justice and freedom it was felt they deserved. However, the processes required to achieve such a desirable end were likely to be slow and demand much patience from all concerned.

It was soon discovered, however, that the Red River *Métis* were not inclined to wait for any British decision. Before Isbister's news arrived, developments in Red River were brought to a head unexpectedly. It so happened that Chief Factor John Ballenden, then in charge at Fort Garry, had suddenly instituted legal proceedings against a half-breed named Pierre Guillaume Sayer and three of his associates in the free trade—known as McGillis, Laronde, and Goullé—on evidence that Ballenden claimed to have against them for illicit trafficking in furs. The formal charge stated that these half-breeds had accepted furs from Indians in exchange for goods, contrary to the rules and regulations of the Hudson's Bay Company within the rights set forth in its original charter. The four had been arraigned before the magistrates of Assiniboia and were held on bail to stand trial on May 17, 1849.

Advised of all this, Sinclair stood ready to do all within his power to aid his *Métis* friends, for since 1844 he had been considered "chief" of the half-breeds, rivaled only by the aging Cuthbert Grant who had withdrawn to a considerable extent from his former activities on behalf of his people. Nevertheless, Sinclair, for reasons best known to himself—perhaps because he felt himself to be dignified as the son of a chief factor and better educated than most of his fellows, with ambitions somewhat above those of the average half-breed, sympathetic as he was to their cause—held himself still a little aloof, particularly in accepting the publicly recognized leadership of the half-breeds. Perhaps it was also a certain astute dramatic sense that allowed him to be the half-breeds' representative up to a point, while never completely accepting the role Cuthbert Grant had taken. However that may be, when the day of the Sayer trial finally arrived, Sinclair was prepared to act then for his people, but with reserve and discretion.

When he reached the little courthouse within the walls of Fort Garry on May 17, 1849, a restless mob, consisting mostly of half-breeds, milled about the building. A rumor had reached the crowd that Governor Caldwell was about to command a party of his pensioners to maintain order during the trial, and this had deeply offended the *Métis,* who were prepared to resist such control of their actions by a show of force if necessary. But as time wore on that day no pensioners appeared. With other delegates of the *Métis* council, Sinclair was given entry to the courthouse. Governor Caldwell and Recorder Adam Thom, who acted on this occasion in his official capacity as recorder of Assiniboia, had already taken their seats on the bench without any guard to protect them. Outside, the *Métis* were more quiet, although it was accepted among them that the accused men would not be condemned. Already several threatening volleys of musket fire had been discharged as warning of what might happen if things were not permitted to go in the *Métis*' favor.

While the preliminaries of the trial were getting under way, Sinclair stood quietly at the back of the courtroom, listening attentively to the court's demand that Sayer be formally called to answer to the charges laid against him. But Sayer apparently could not be found to answer, for he had been deliberately detained by his *Métis* friends outside the courthouse. Such tactics, Sinclair must have realized, were not likely to aid the *Métis* cause; but he did not dare go outside to demand Sayer's entrance in response to the court's demand for fear the aroused *Métis*, doubting his allegiance to them, might suddenly turn against him also.

At this strained moment Sheriff Alexander Ross calmly rose to advise the court that Sayer was delayed momentarily but would shortly be at hand, and that he would go himself in search of him. This was the cue Sinclair had waited for. At a prearranged signal, Sinclair and Peter Garrioch, a relative of his by marriage, and several other of Sinclair's friends presented themselves before Governor Caldwell and Adam Thom in place of the defendant Sayer as delegates of the *Métis* outside the courthouse, who were now yelling loudly that they wanted some immediate action. They were holding Sayer until some plan could be formulated to insure that the trial should be a test case, and until Sinclair as their representative was given a chance to speak on their behalf.

Recorder Thom, obviously irked by the unorthodox proceedings, questioned Sinclair as to the capacity in which he and his associates appeared before the court. Sinclair calmly replied "as delegate of the people." Thom then indignantly informed Sinclair that such was not acceptable to the court, and he launched into a lengthy diatribe against irregular procedure and gave a dissertation upon the majesty of the law. Outside, the ominous shouting, shooting, and threatening increased because of the delay. Thom's legal arguing could now scarcely be heard above the din, but he said his say and ended by suggesting that Sinclair—even without legal standing—be permitted to plead the case for the defendant.

Taking his time and carefully considering every move, Sinclair had stood quietly and respectfully beside his friends before Thom until this permission was granted him to speak for the *Métis*. (Evidently, a hasty consultation had taken place behind hands, in which Thom, Caldwell, and the other officers of the court had decided what should be done in the face of this unexpected turn of events.) When a decision was reached, Thom sent a messenger to the *Métis* leaders outside the court to appoint a man to act as their tribune who would be given the right to assist Sayer throughout his trial. Only a moment was needed for the crowd's unanimous selection of Sinclair; it was known that he had some knowledge of the processes of British law, gained both from his studies at Edinburgh and from his later association with Isbister in London, although he had never been called to the bar.

Sinclair was then permitted to withdraw from the courthouse for a few moments to consult with Sayer and his associates as to what he should plead on their behalf. When he returned to the courtroom, Thom instructed Sinclair to challenge the jury now to be empaneled, and then informed the assembly that in his official capacity as recorder of Assiniboia, all he wished to see was a fair and impartial trial. Following this, Sinclair and his associates then asked permission from Thom to withdraw again from the courtroom to consult further with the *Métis* leaders outside. Permission was granted for this, and Sinclair did not take undue advantage of such liberty, returning in a few moments to stand before Thom fully prepared for his next move. First, he objected to several of the jurymen selected on the grounds that they were likely to be prejudiced. To a further accompaniment of *Métis* shouts, jeers, and curses outside, the questionable jurors were dropped and replaced by those more satisfactory to Sinclair, and an acceptable panel—half English, half French—was finally selected.

With all necessary preliminaries completed, including the appointment of Chief Factor John Ballenden to act as prosecutor, Sayer was at last brought into the courtroom, and in accordance with his instructions admitted that he had traded in furs with the Indians. Upon such admission the jury brought in the verdict of "guilty" with recommendation of mercy.[4] Prosecutor Ballenden then stated that the Hudson's Bay Company was not so much concerned with the value of the furs involved but with the principles such transactions entailed, and this must now be taken to be upheld by the pronouncement of the Bench. But before anything more could be said, the entire case was suddenly lifted completely out of the hands of the court and placed in those of the insurgent mob of *Métis* outside the courthouse. Somehow or other word had circulated among the half-breeds that the verdict of the court was for them, and before any sentence could be pronounced on Sayer and his associates, a great shout of victory went up from the crowd: "Le commerce est libre! Le commerce est libre! Vive la liberté!"

This cry was emphasized by wild yells and whoops of joy and volleys of gunfire. A look of astonishment went around the courtroom, while Governor Caldwell and Adam Thom appeared bewildered by all that had occurred. The *Métis* seemed prepared to celebrate with an exuberance typical of them in such moments of jubilation. The crowd was now beginning to sift away—many of the half-breeds crossing over to St. Boniface as quickly as the old ferry and a number of small boats could carry them, with one last roaring cheer from all on the river bank and three more volleys of gunfire for "la liberté!"

There appeared no further need for the court to continue to sit. The grave farce was all but ended, and it surely could not matter now what Thom's pronouncement on Sayer or his fellows might be; it could not be carried out anyway. Sayer and his confreres by this time were safely away, under the protection of their jubilant compatriots, and well beyond the clutches of any law. Neither did it matter what the tardy processes Isbister was invoking in London might be. The *Métis* had won their case for the moment by their own means, and it was not likely the Old Company could ever again inforce the monopoly it had enjoyed by legal or any other means. Indeed, the *Métis* had won a temporary victory at least, and the methods of the free trade, which Sinclair had used for a time to assist Simpson to check the advances of the American fur trade, were now a thing of the past.

While the details of this curious trial were still fresh in his mind, Sheriff Alexander Ross wrote this summation of it:

> About 9 o'clock . . . on the morning of the 17th May, 1849 . . . half breeds and Canadians, all armed and from every quarter, began to assemble at Fort Garry, giving strong indication of a general revolutionary movement. Sometime previous several persons had been arrested for illicitly trafficking in furs with the natives. One man, by the name of Sayer, had been imprisoned and others held on bail to stand trial at the first Criminal Court.
>
> The immediate cause of this physical demonstration was to prevent the parties thus implicated in the trade in question from being either fined or imprisoned or in any way punished by the authorities. Judge Thom and myself were the chief objects of hatred—I for having issued the summonses against the fur traders. But the remote cause is more deeply rooted, and has arisen out of causes we shall hereafter explain. . . . The half breeds of the country, considering [*sic*] and always have considered that they have a right as natives of the soil to trade, traffic and barter furs among themselves and also from the Indians as a kind of circulating medium among a rude people. And what set the whole in a blaze was the report spread that the Pensioners were to be armed on the day of the Court, which report was first given by a pensioner named Cormelly to McGillvray on the Monday preceeding the Court.
>
> As the radical party mustered about 11 o'clock, boats and canoes were all in requisition crossing the river. The armed multitude as they arrived flocked about the Court House and bushes behind. At this time the members of the Court entered. Not intimidated by the threatened storm, the Court proceeded to business, but what business could be gone through under the threat of an armed rabble? Sayer, the person who had been imprisoned for trading but afterwards liberated on bail, was summoned to appear, but Sayer as well as McGillis, Laronde and Goulet, the other persons implicated, were held in custody outdoors by an armed force of their countrymen, and the police forced to approach, so that no Sayer was to be got. Nor did the Court, we shall suppose, consider it prudent to oppose force to force, to have

him brought forward. Neither did the Court call on Sayer's bail to answer for his appearance for reasons known to itself.

The Court then entered on some business of minor importance which occupied it till one o'clock. Sayer was then called for again, but no Sayer. On this occasion Mr. McLaughlin attempted to interfere, but was abruptly ordered off. It was then intimated to the half breeds that they might appoint a leader and send in a deputation to assist Sayer during his trial, and state what they had to say. After some little time Mr. Sinclair and ten others of his class took up a position in the Court Room as a deputation from the half breeds. Sayer then entered upon their protection, and after some preliminary remarks, a Jury was empanelled and Mr. Sinclair, Chief of the half breeds, challenged nine out of the twelve jurors, and as a further concession was allowed to pick out and place the jurors. The case then went on. But as Sayer confessed he had traded there was little for a jury to do, and his confession was backed by a declaration that Mr. Harriott had given permission to trade and his permission confirmed by Alexis Goulet's oath, Sayer was allowed to go off Scott-free, having got one fox skin he had trapped, and some in a present from Pembina either to confirm or rebut Sayer or Goulet's statements.

During the mock trial—for under all circumstances we can give it no better name—what was the state of feeling outdoors? The arms of the deputation were put under a strong guard to be ready at a moment's warning. A sentinel was placed at the prison gate, another at the prison door so that had there been any punishment awarded Sayer the signal was to have been given, the arms of the deputation were to have been brought, and a general rush made to rescue Sayer by force, expell the Judge from the bench, and give him timely admonition to prepare to leave the country on the 5th June, and if resistance was made, Boucher, the steersman, and another were to have gone a short way to work, and myself warned from holding office any longer. Boucher then called out, "I will shoot such a one." Another, "I will ride down such a one with my horse." In this state two or three moves were made to commence mischief. So strong at one time was their feeling to effect their object that had it not been for the calm conduct of Mr. Sinclair and the influence of Mr. McCallum and Pascal Borland the rush would have been made.

Lewis Bruce and Ariel were sent in to urge Sinclair and others out, although they kept pulling Sinclair's coat, visible from the bench, Sinclair would not move and all was safe. The lives of many having been risked as to a hair for more than two hours. It was when Sinclair would not move that Lewis Bruce said to the Judge, loud enough to be distinctly heard on the bench, "you speak too much! We don't understand you." During this ferment outdoors the half breeds might have been seen in the Court Room with their powder horns on and their shot pouches also, and gun covers dangling from their belts. But that was not all. Men sat in the jury box with their powder horns and pouches on. . . . Ducharme was one.

After the Sayer case, their being no motion made to bring forward McGillis, Laronde, and Goulet, this was the half breeds' triumph. "Vive la liberté" was echoed from a hundred voices out doors. "Le commerce libre" followed, and from that moment the armed party endulged the hope of free trade because it was not explained to them otherwise, and if this is doubted, let the attempt be made!

Sgd. ALEXANDER ROSS, Sheriff [5]

Not long after this, word came to Red River from Isbister in London that things had not gone well for the *Métis* case there. Earl Grey had asked the Hudson's Bay Company for an ex parte statement of their claims.[6] The company's carefully worded reports had been laid before the renowned British legal experts, Sir John Lewis and Sir John Romilly, who, after examining these documents, had given their opinion that the claims made by the Hudson's Bay Company concerning their monopoly of trade in the jurisdiction granted them under their original charter must be upheld. But Lewis and Romilly in their final analysis conceded that these questions might justifiably be referred for ultimate decision to the Judicial Committee of the Privy Council by means of a formal petition to the crown setting forth specific charges of the *Métis* against the Hudson's Bay Company. Advising Isbister of this decision, Earl Grey had asked him if he were prepared to act as the party of the prosecution. Isbister did not feel in a position to do this and was compelled to decline; he recognized the fact that under such conditions he would be expected to defray the costs of such a suit, and this neither he nor the *Métis* could undertake. So there the *Métis* case stood abroad, but it had been settled by force at home.

Following this unusual testing of the law by the *Métis* themselves in the Sayer trial, the Hudson's Bay Company appeared to change its attitude toward the free trade considerably, evidently realizing that the Red River half-breeds fully intended to buy and sell whatever and wherever they pleased at competitive prices without any undue interference from anyone. The Hudson's Bay Company, already keenly competitive with Kittson at Pembina, now turned its resources to compete with its own unruly subjects. It drew on its old prestige and liberal supplies of fine British merchandise to outbid the Americans, and again drew trade back to Fort Garry from the Americans south of the border. Indeed, a Hudson's Bay Company post was placed near Pembina north of the boundary line, and experienced traders roving the frontier in winter now held the line for the Old Company. They pressed Kittson hard and made the free trade, so hardly won, a minor victory for the *Métis* and a defeat not too costly for the Old Company. But never again were the Hudson's Bay Company's legal rights under its original charter and its license from the British crown to be invoked against the Red River free traders.

II

As for Sinclair himself after the Sayer trial, 1849 became literally a lost year where he was concerned in the eyes of Red River people. He remained away much of the time from the settlement, possibly to lessen his influence among the *Métis* now that victory was theirs, and to attempt to carve out a new career for himself in some other place than where there had been experiences he was glad to forget.

It was also about this time that the fever of the great California gold rush suddenly gripped the imagination of the entire North American continent, and, typically enough, Sinclair could not refrain from participation in adventure of this kind. When word of the famous strike at Sutter's Mill was made known, by a man named James Marshall, on January 24, 1848, it did not take long to reach St. Louis where Sinclair chanced to be at the time. Like many another anxious to seek a fortune in the fabulous gold fields, he set off as quickly as possible in July, 1849, up the Missouri River in company with seven Yankee miners,[7] crossing the Rockies by the hazardous California trail. It would appear that Sinclair was well in the vanguard of the gold rush in 1849. When he reached Sutter's Fort he found it to be much like any other American frontier post—a jumble of poor huts, adobe in this instance, clustered within a crude stockade, in the center of which was a flagpole where the "Yankee duster" now flew instead of the Spanish ensign of earlier days. Sacramento City had not yet been laid out, and San Francisco had yet to become the rip-roaring, wide-open metropolis it would be in a few months' time. When Sinclair arrived it was "first in, first win," and he was lucky enough to find some gold. For a while he appears to have been something of a force in the earliest of the California gold fields, possessing a voice in the miners' councils, especially against the would-be shysters at Sutter's camp. However, Sinclair was wise enough for once to take what gold his claim gave and return to St. Louis well before many another adventurer entered the big rush of 1849. He set about making his plans to go west again, but to try what he now believed would be sounder ventures in the Oregon.

News traveled fast concerning Sinclair's luck in the California gold fields, and by the time Sinclair returned to Red River, word of his reported good fortune had preceded him. An example of this was contained in a letter to Fort Garry from an officer at Fort Edmonton, John Lee Lewes, who said that "Sinclair in California washed out 22 lbs weight of gold near Sutter's property worth £1300 sterling!" This was sufficient to inspire any number of rumors, increased with each telling, which proved hard to deny. Characteristically enough, Sinclair let those who would believe what they would and held his peace, leaving few letters of his own either to confirm or deny what was said of him throughout his entire career.

PART IV: SINCLAIR GOES WEST OF THE MOUNTAINS

11. PREPARATION FOR THE TRIP TO THE OREGON

I

Although Red River's tempestuous days seemed over for a time—with the rights of his *Métis* friends recognized to a certain extent, permission to carry on the free trade assured, but apparently with little desire on his part to be considered "chief" of the half-breeds in Red River any longer—Sinclair wished to move with his family to the Oregon and there attempt to make a new start. It was necessary first for him to sell what property he could in Red River [1] to finance the shipment of his most prized household goods to the west coast, including his daughter Harriet's piano.[2] (Such things were expensive to ship around the Horn, but it was considered worth the effort, for they were most difficult to procure there.) Such matters cared for, Sinclair went to Illinois to bring back his daughters from boarding school so they might accompany the other members of his family on the long trip across the plains and Rockies.

Harriet Sinclair was now a young woman of eighteen; and the delicate Maria, fifteen. While the girls were eager to join their father to make a new home in that distant land, the plan seemed doomed to disappointment in the year 1850. After Sinclair and his daughters had traveled by stagecoach from Galesboro, Illinois, to Galena, then up the Mississippi to St. Paul by steamboat, they found that the rest of their journey back to Red River promised to be difficult. Water was especially high this season in the rivers to the north, and much of the country that had to be crossed was like one vast lake. There was also serious danger of Indian attack in the Sioux country, where these Indians were once more on the warpath.

In view of these problems, Sinclair organized a small cart train at St. Paul, and because of the flood conditions on the plains, prepared to follow the Crow Wing Trail to the north, since it was believed to offer greater protection from the Sioux. However, even the Crow Wing was threatened by high water in many of the eastern tributaries of the Red River that had to be crossed, and several times the carts had to be converted into crude rafts to cross the swollen streams. Fortunately, at one of the more dangerous crossings the party met an old friend of Sinclair's, James MacKay,[3] who continued on with them to the north. MacKay was one of the great frontiersmen of his day—a most delightful and interesting man, possessing some native blood like Sinclair. He was handsome and well mannered, delighting in a well-groomed appearance, with well-trimmed beard, and colorful attire, favoring finely tailored broadcloth trousers, plaid flannel shirt, gaudy *ceinture flèché* sash, and beautifully beaded moccasins even when on the trail. He could dance a jig or gavotte with equal charm and dexterity at *Métis* encampment or in the most sophisticated ballroom. Naturally, such gifts pleased the Sinclair girls, as they later did the Earl of Southesk and his lady in their travels.

At the crossing of the Red Lake River, MacKay performed a feat surely designed to impress these girlish hearts; at this flooded ford when the cart carrying Sinclair's daughters bogged down in midstream,[4] the dashing frontiersman plunged into the muddy stream in his fine attire, unhitched the horses, and placing himself between the shafts, with startling show of strength dragged the gleeful Harriet and Maria to safety. From this point on, MacKay, for added protection to the party, continued with them until they reached Kittson's Pembina post. It was well he did, because for several days and nights, in fear of the warlike Sioux, the party dared not light campfires and had to live off the dried, uncooked pemmican rations Sinclair had secured at St. Paul for just such an emergency.[5]

When Pembina was reached it was found that the waters of the flooding Red River extended more than two miles each side from the hill where Kittson had built a new house for his recent bride, a short distance from his trading post. Here Sinclair and his daughters stayed four days, until York boats were readied to carry them the rest of the way to the forks. At some places north of Pembina the Red was as much as eight miles wide, and the party was compelled to spend the nights on the way north in the York boats tied to tree trunks, lest they be swept helplessly down stream by the surging water. It took four days to make the journey from Pembina to Fort Garry.

II

It was now only too obvious that it would be impossible for Sinclair to take his family overland to the Oregon by his 1841 route because of the flooded condition of the plains in 1850. Too late a start would have to be made to safely cross the mountains before the autumn snowfall. Furthermore, when Sinclair reached Fort Garry he found a letter waiting for him from Governor Simpson that changed his prospects considerably.[6] The Governor's letter disclosed that several of the company's forts in the Oregon—especially Walla Walla—had fallen into poor condition since the settling of the boundary dispute, as well as from the inability of those who had succeeded Pierre Pambrum to handle the difficult Indians of the region. Simpson therefore wished Sinclair to go to the Oregon to discover if some practical means could be found to re-establish these posts on a paying basis. Under the circumstances, Simpson's offer was most acceptable to Sinclair, and as soon as he was able to get his personal affairs in order he set out from Fort Garry with a cart train of company men traveling with trade goods to Fort Edmonton, leaving his family once more in the care of his friends at Red River until he could formulate new plans for his future.

At Fort Edmonton Sinclair found his old Cree guide, Mackipictoon, once more available to conduct him as quickly as possible across the mountains with a few men and a light pack train, using the same route over which the Indian had taken him in 1841, by Whiteman and Red Rock passes. Once more the Cree Indian proved reliable as a guide, and Sinclair appears to have crossed the Rockies again with little trouble, reaching Fort Colvile well before snowfall, unencumbered as he was with only a small party. However, at Colvile he was disappointed to find his old friend Chief Trader Archibald McDonald gone, having been elevated to a chief factorship a short time before. The Cree guide again left Sinclair at Colvile to return across the Rockies to the plains, leaving him to go on to Fort Vancouver via Fort Walla Walla with some company men. At Walla Walla, Sinclair was shocked at the condition into which Pierre Pambrum's fine post had fallen. His semi-Spanish fort had been almost completely destroyed by fire and had been replaced by a crude, log trading post, armed to the teeth by inmates who were in deadly fear of Indian attack. Here Sinclair heard something of the terrible fate that had befallen Dr. Marcus Whitman, his wife, and a number of his followers a few years before. More particulars of this tragic affair were later told him at Fort Vancouver by his friend Chief Factor Duncan MacTavish, jointly in charge there with Chief Factor Peter Skene Ogden, who had arranged for the rescue of Whitman's survivors.

Duncan MacTavish and Peter Skene Ogden had been placed in charge of Fort Vancouver upon the retirement of Dr. John McLoughlin to the Willamette. While they were able administrators, Sinclair could see at a glance that Fort Vancouver had greatly changed, and not for the better, since his last visit nine years before. McLoughlin's dynamic personality was lacking, and obviously the once large volume of business had shrunken unbelievably. The company's old monopoly of trade in the Columbia River region, as well as its administrative role, had been taken over almost completely by the self-governing American settlers, with their headquarters moved to Oregon City in the Willamette Valley. Indeed, the company's business west of the mountains was now largely carried on from New Caledonia to the north, transacted chiefly from the company's headquarters on Vancouver Island at Fort Victoria, where one of Dr. McLoughlin's most able assistants, Chief Factor James Douglas, was now in charge.

Sinclair also discovered that as the great company had withdrawn to the north of the Columbia River, the incoming settlers to the Oregon had roused the Indian tribes to resist the inroads of the white man, and already the American Oregon was beginning to know the terrible horror of Indian war. When the Whitmans tragically perished in 1847 only a desperate effort on the part of a few American volunteer troops had beat the warlike tribes into a temporary submission; and this was possible only because in 1848 the Oregon had been organized as a territory of the United States, and a government in accordance with this new status effectually set up.

Although things appeared deceptively quiet on the surface when Sinclair reached Fort Vancouver, he was told by Chief Factor MacTavish that the whole Columbia River country was dangerously insecure, with constant threat of Indian attack. The formation of the new American territory had not come a moment too soon to offer some sort of protection to the two thousand-odd settlers now living in the Oregon. Sinclair was also told that members of his 1841 party could be largely thanked for deciding the fate of the Oregon in favor of the Americans. Most of these people had moved to the Willamette from Cowlitz and Nisqually, disgruntled at the treatment they had received from the Hudson's Bay Company, and had helped to hand over the valuable country south of the forty-ninth parallel of latitude to the United States. Despite all this, Sinclair was assured that the country under the American flag had a great future, and that ultimately the Indian troubles would be controlled, once sufficient American troops were brought in to maintain order.

III

Sinclair spent several months this time in the Oregon making his investigations for Simpson. He then took ship from Fort Vancouver to San Francisco and found it highly disappointing after his earlier visit, for now the first flush of the exciting gold rush had passed and a serious recession started to set in. However, while in San Francisco, Sinclair learned to his great surprise that a Captain Colin Sinclair, who had become well known in California,[7] said to be an Englishman owning his own clipper ship, had been in port for more than a year. This Captain Sinclair, curiously enough, had exerted considerable influence during the height of the gold rush, representing the miners' interests at Sutter's camp after Sinclair himself had left that place. This sea captain, Sinclair now had reason to believe, was his own brother whom he had not seen since childhood at Oxford House, but unhappily he had left California before they could meet.

Apparently Colin Sinclair had made himself well liked for his fairness and good sense. Realizing that the best of the gold rush was past, Colin had husbanded his takings well, bought another good sailing ship, manned it with reliable men, and set sail for England by way of the Pacific—picking up a profitable cargo of sandalwood in the South Sea Islands, which he planned to dispose of for valuable China tea and other oriental goods in Shanghai—returning to London a much richer man than he had left to go to California. All this was the first news Sinclair had of his brother Colin in many years, and although he had inquired in London while visiting Isbister in 1846, he had only gathered that through the good auspices of Governor George Simpson, Colin had been trained as a sailor. Being a conscientious lad, Colin had worked his way up until he had owned his own ship. Now the news Sinclair received of Colin in San Francisco in 1850, even if it brought word of his success, filled him with regret at not seeing again the child he remembered from over thirty years before in 1818.[8]

While in San Francisco, Sinclair was also able to gather other news to send back to Red River. Before he had set out on this trip, Andrew McDermot had asked Sinclair to discover what he could concerning his daughter, Mary, who in 1848 had become the wife of a promising but erratic company man named Richard Lane. Lane had been well known in the company's service, especially for carrying dispatches between Fort Garry and Norway House, before going to the Oregon shortly after marrying McDermot's daughter, whom he had taken with him across the mountains. Lane had been employed for a time in McLoughlin's service at Fort Vancouver, and after the doctor's retirement to Oregon City, Lane had followed him there, earning a precarious living at whatever he could find to do. Learning of this, McDermot had grown concerned for his daughter, now in ill health and mother of several young children.

Recognizing McDermot's worry, Sinclair had assured him he would do all in his power to find his daughter, and help her if necessary. In this he was as good as his word, for on March 19, 1851, Sinclair wrote from his hotel in San Francisco to McDermot, sending his letter via the Panama Isthmus, St. Louis, and Kittson's Pembina Post, and saying:

> I scarcely have any courage to write any more letters to Red River as I have written so often without receiving any in reply. Still I shall write this time again in the hope of receiving some word from Red River in a day or so. The mail is every moment expected from Panama. I have not heard one single word from Red River since I left. You may judge of my anxiety. Still I hope to find letters in Oregon when I get up. I leave here either tomorrow or the day after, and in four or five days at the farthest I hope to be at Oregon City. I have been detained down here three weeks longer than I expected in consequence of the steamer that ran between this and Oregon having been withdrawn.
>
> I shall not attempt to give any description of California further than to say that the change respecting mercantile matters has altered wonderfully against importers in particular. Indeed, business is so overdone that goods are sold every day at ruinous rates below New

York prices. What do you think of boots being sold at $1.35? Flour, $3.25 per 100 pounds; cooking stoves at less than freight; houses at one quarter of the cost; brown sugar at 4 to 4¼ cents a pound; clothing 30 per cent below New York prices; coal, $7.00 per ton? Tea below Canton prices? Still in the face of all this ships are arriving daily from every corner of the world. Property (landed) has fallen 75 per cent from last year's prices except in the best business locations. I have sent you some newspapers. . . . Prices mentioned in them cannot always be obtained. Few men are making money now. Mining is the safest.

Oregon is equally glutted with all kinds of goods; everything you can imagine, and money is very scarce. This is particularly the case since two months ago. Almost every house in Portland and Oregon City is a shop. The first town contains a population of 900 souls, and the other 1400.

You will naturally expect me to give you information of what Mr. Lane is doing. All I know is that he was to be in business on his own account at Oregon City on 1st. March in partnership with a young man, Chase. From what I saw of him he appeared to be a gentlemanly young man, but I doubt whether he has any capital. They also have an agency in one of the Hudson's Bay Company's shops, situated about 20 mile above Oregon City. In this business they get 7 per cent on the amount they sell. Lane is a great favourite from his obliging disposition. He has been rather unwell but was much better when I left. As for Mary [9] she is little altered, only a little thinner. She was so glad to see me, and I have been so kindly treated by them that I felt quite at home. She has two of the best brought up and best behaved Red River children I ever saw. You could be proud to see them. Tell all the girls in Red River they ought to be proud to hear that there is one Hudson's Bay girl who knows and keeps her children neat, clean and in good order. Tell Mrs. McDermot the little girl, Maria, is very like her.

I have just heard that three-quarters of the people in Oregon are preparing to leave for the Klamath Mines. Indeed, the rush for that quarter is now the rage. Vessels are leaving this daily for Trinidad and Humbold Bay as being the nearest points to the new mining regions. I shall start for the same quarter as soon as I get back and add a few Indians to my party.

I think Oregon offers better and certainly more safe opportunities for business operations than California. I shall try the gold digging this summer till fall, and by that time I shall understand or know better what to do. Not hearing from my family for such a length of time keeps me uneasy and unsettled. You can write me by every opportunity, either by way of St. Peter's or Sault Ste. Marie, in care of Messrs. Allan, McKinley and Company, or to Mr. R. Lane, Oregon City, Oregon.

After all, I am very sorry I left my family. What do you think of my returning to Red River and doing business there? I am uncertain when I may be able to see my family. If my feelings and wishes were consulted, I would be off tomorrow!

The season has been beautiful here; the hills are covered with flowers, and the wild oats about 15 to 18 inches long. Very little sickness prevails, though the cholera was very fatal here in October and November.

I hear McLoughlin[10] has sued the Hudson's Bay Company for damages—£2000 for their prosecution against him last year, and that he is likely to recover it. Isbister is well provided for in a lucrative position in King's College, London. This I presume you have already heard.

I have been blamed more in all the above affair than I deserved. I might have done much, but you know how little I cared about the free trade provided I was let alone and fairly treated! But enough of this.

Mr. Ogden[11] has been kind to me. He is about one of the best men in the Hudson's Bay Company service.

How did the Foss and Pelly[12] affair end? I hear Ballenden[13] is off after all. If Black[14] only plays his cards well he will be able to retain Fort Garry, as he is certainly one of the most talented men in the service. I expect to hear that you have retired altogether from business and fixed yourself forever at Sturgeon Creek.[15] My best regards to Mrs. McDermot and the young ladies; and to Grant,[16] Ross[17] and T. Truthwaite.[18] He could do well here.

Excuse this incoherent letter, I am in haste, Yours ever sincerely,

JAMES SINCLAIR

P.S. I depend on you to see my wife and family comfortable. Mary[19] will consult you personally regarding her wants. J.S.

P.S.2. The safest way for letters to reach me is to enclose them to some respectable house in New York, say to Messrs. Maitland, Phelps and Company, but pay the postage to here, and with a request to mail them at New York. Tell Mrs. Sinclair this. J.S.[20]

IV

Sinclair set out from San Francisco after the New Year, 1852, having spent more time in Oregon City and tasting fresh disappointment in trying his luck at the Klamath mines. He took ship to Panama City, but before leaving San Francisco he learned that his prized possessions—including Harriet's piano—which had been shipped the year before from St. Louis via New Orleans and around the Horn to San Francisco had been lost at sea.

From Panama City, Sinclair traveled across the Isthmus of Panama on mule back over a treacherous, muddy trail slashed by natives with machetes through the tropical jungle to the colorful port of Chagrés. Here he took a steamer for Cuba, where he remained until another could take him to New York. From there he traveled the old Ohio route back to St. Louis, and up the familiar trail to Fort Garry past Kittson's Pembina post.

Sinclair's absence seems to have done something for his domestic life, for there appears to have been a genuine reconciliation upon his return with his wife, Mary. He was also pleased to learn that his beloved daughter, Harriet, was betrothed to a young Scottish physician, Dr. William Cowan,[21] who had come to Red River to serve as surgeon to the Chelsea pensioners. Cowan was a man of fine character and sound medical training, who, upon his graduation from a Scottish university, had contracted the dread Asiatic cholera, then rampant on both sides of the Atlantic, before he could set up practice in Glasgow. Cowan's only chance of recovery was said to be to come to the New World, and the post offered with the Chelsea pensioners in Red River provided the opportunity. It also so happened that in Cowan, Sinclair now found a close and sympathetic friend as well as a son-in-law.

V

Despite brighter prospects in Red River than had obtained in the past, Sinclair was determined to leave and settle in the Oregon. But before he could carry out these plans, another catastrophe struck the settlement. This time it was another terrible flood, in the year 1852. Sinclair had noticed with growing alarm the soggy condition of the country when he had brought his daughters back from boarding school in 1850, and again when he had returned from San Francisco in 1851. Now the entire country between St. Paul and Fort Garry seemed to have become completely water-logged. Added to this, an excessive snowfall in the winter of 1851–52, with an abnormally late runoff in the spring of 1852, brought about a flood climax.[22] By April the Red and Assiniboine rivers rose to overflow their banks. Everything of value in old Fort Garry at the forks was removed to the upper stories of the strongest buildings—the water reaching a depth of fourteen feet within the walls of the fort. All of the fort's personnel, except Harriet's fiancé, Dr. Cowan, and his friend, Chief Trader John Black, who were left in charge, were taken to Lower Fort Garry.

Once more the Red River Settlement became a place of destruction and desolation as it had been twenty-six years before in 1826. The Sinclair, Ross, and McDermot families were more fortunate than many other folk—although reluctant to again leave their homes and possessions to the destruction of the swirling water—for McDermot had provided a place of refuge and safety at his property, high and dry at Sturgeon Creek. Here they camped out until all danger was over and they could return, like other Red River people, to undertake the dismal task of salvaging and cleaning what was left. Once more there was surprisingly little loss of life, but property and livestock loss was heavy, and again the settlement was faced with the harsh task of rebuilding homes, herds, and financial resources. However, things were not actually as bad as they had been in the previous great flood. There was much to be thankful for, as well as the same Red River courage and fellow-feeling in common danger to rehabilitate the settlement.

When these unpleasant days were past, Harriet Sinclair and Dr. Cowan were married at St. John's parish church by the Right Reverend David Anderson,[23] the first Anglican Bishop of Rupert's Land, who had come out from Britain on the same ship as Dr. Cowan and had become a close friend of the Sinclair family. As a special token of his affection for Harriet, the Bishop presented her with a beautifully bound, white kid prayer book to carry on her wedding day. As his special tribute to his daughter, apart from her finely arranged wedding, Sinclair gave Harriet an exquisite white silk embroidered Chinese shawl he had secured in San Francisco for just such a happy day as this. Indeed, Sinclair's wedding for his daughter was almost his social farewell to the Red River Settlement.

12. GOVERNOR SIMPSON'S ROLE

I

While Governor Simpson was in residence at Fort Garry in the summer of 1853 he sent for Sinclair to propose that he conduct another party of Red River people across the Rockies to settle in the Oregon, giving him the opportunity to join the company as a commissioned officer. As reward for another safe conduct of people across the mountains, Sinclair was to be granted a timber limit and some breeding stock with which to set himself up in the private business of lumbering and ranching once his assignment with the company was finished. The astute Governor's real intent may well have been to diminish the population of Red River of further dissenting elements, at the same time ridding it of a free trader whose future dealings might have been detrimental if his popularity and influence became too evident in the settlement.

Apparently pleased enough with Simpson's offer, Sinclair, on August 28, 1853, wrote the Governor with considerable confidence and candor:

Nothing of importance has transpired since your departure from hence. All goes on quietly. The crops were never better. Respecting the Oregon emigrating scheme, I did not say a word on the subject for some considerable time after your departure. I have lately spoken to a few individuals on the advantages that Oregon has over Red River, and that it is my intention to cross the plains next spring with my family, and to evince the same I am purchasing a few cattle so as to remove any doubts any of them may have. I shall begin soon to take the names of those intending to go, and have them enter into a bond, to forfeit the same on their declining to go in the spring. Of my progress in this I shall acquaint you as opportunity may offer.

I have much pleasure in saying that I have every reason to think that Chief Trader, Mr. John Black, and I will get on well together. I am, at the same time, actuated with a desire to serve the Company honourably and faithfully, and trust you will never regret the arrangement entered into with me.[1]

The following day Sinclair added this postscript to his letter:

During my last interview with you I felt reluctant to annoy you unnecessarily so that I did not enquire what allowance you intend to grant me. I trust you will not deem my request extravagant by expecting the same allowance as that of a Chief Trader—Walla Walla being on the route for all the U.S. emigrants proceeding to the Oregon. I will be so situated that I cannot well avoid extending the hospitalities of the establishment to the more respectable class whose necessities may induce them to visit Walla Walla.

I am not aware exactly of the nature of the business carried on by the Company at Walla Walla, but it strikes me by the time the emigrants reach thereabouts they must be in want of many things, and by having a general supply of such as may be most required a good deal of ready cash might be picked up. However, I shall be better able to judge of these matters after I have been on the spot for a few days.

P.S. I am thinking of a project to induce the U.S. Government to purchase the H.B.Co.'s possessory rights to the Oregon, presuming the Company are desirous of effecting the sale. In my next I shall enclose it for your perusal.[2]

Simpson replied promptly from Lachine on October 8, 1853:

I have to acknowledge receipt of your letter of 28th and 29th August. Your course in reference to the Oregon party was, I think, the most prudent and cautious. [Chief Trader] Mr. John Black will be ready to assist in the necessary preparations, and I will give you letters to the posts on route to obtain supplies, but the less you have to do with our people in Red River and elsewhere the better. I think you will find the prospects in the Oregon very promising. Trade is brisk, and the population increasing. I expect a good outfit will be sent in this season in time to meet the demand of the emigrants.

I have already written to [Chief Factor] Mr. Peter Skene Ogden about the 200 head of cattle. They will, no doubt, be forthcoming.

I intend to send this letter enclosed to Mr. Black to St. Paul in the care of Mr. J. W. Simpson, to be forwarded by the first opportunity that may offer; and not feeling very sure it may not fall into other hands, I have written briefly and obscurely. I fear I shall not see you next year as you will have left before I can reach the Settlement. Let me, therefore, hear that you will write me from time to time.[3]

This correspondence continued between Simpson and Sinclair for the next few months—some of it apparently of such a nature as to have been discreetly destroyed. From what has remained, we find that Sinclair wrote to Simpson on November 1, 1853:

The Oregon Emigrating Scheme is attracting the attention of several old settlers so that I intend to call a meeting at an early date of those favourable to it. But I fear the party will not be large. In the meantime it will be necessary to be provided with a letter from you to the gentlemen in charge of the posts en route to afford us assistance in the shape of provisions, horses, etc., by paying for the same either on the spot or on my arrival at Vancouver. I should like to get the service of La Grace for as far as the Crossing Place on the Kootanei River. I think he is now at Carlton. He knows the route well and will act as interpreter should we meet any Blackfeet.[4]

Simpson again replied quickly, writing from Lachine on December 22, 1853:

I have to thank you for your letter of the 1st, and two of the 4th. November,[5] which convey much interesting intelligence. I hope your arrangements for the party to cross the plains next spring are proceeding favourably, although I am sorry to observe you expect the number will be small. I feel sure, however, you are doing your best to carry out the scheme, and a small party well managed on the journey so that no particular discomfort is experienced, and successful in reaching their destination, may excite an interest in the emigration movement which may lead to more extensive movements in succeeding years. I enclose a letter to the officers in charge of posts on the route from Red River to render your party assistance and to sell you horses and provisions should you be in need of them. I also sent a letter to Mr. Rowand, the officer in charge of Carlton, requesting that La Graisse may be attached to the party to act as guide as far as the Kootonais River crossing place.

I have carefully perused your scheme of operations in reference to the Company's possessory rights in Oregon, which is very bold and comprehensive, and I have no doubt the monopoly in the hands of the Company of all branches of business there, banking, steaming, importing, etc., would lead to a great hue and cry against us. At present I do not consider it necessary to change the course we are pursuing, but should arrangements now under consideration not take effect, we may consider in what way to turn to better account the advantages we possess in Oregon.

I am obliged to the details you give respecting the proceedings of the Red River people. I am glad to find the private traffic has received a check.

I have written to Mr. Ogden to make provisions for furnishing you with cattle next autumn, and have no doubt he will do his utmost to meet the demands.[6]

II

Preparations for the 1854 trip across the mountains went forward quietly from the autumn of 1853, to May, 1854. Sinclair tried to personally influence a number of settlers well known to himself to accompany his party, but many he might have wished to go with him were unable to do so. In accordance with Simpson's instructions, Sinclair was careful not to intimate that he was in any way employed by either Simpson or the Hudson's Bay Company, and deliberately spread it about the settlement that the project was purely on his own initiative, and that he intended to establish himself in private ranching and lumbering in the Columbia River country—preferably in the region around Fort Colvile or Walla Walla.

In February, 1854, Sinclair received another letter from Simpson that read:

I have had the pleasure to receive your favours of November 17, and December 11 and 27, and beg to return thanks for the varied information they convey, and for the amusing chit-chat of my old friend, your late father-in-law.[7] Although rather shaky and infirm when I last saw him, he looked like a man who was likely to last a number of years longer.

I hope your emigrant party is gaining numbers, and that as the scheme becomes known it may be more popular. The withdrawal of a few hundred across the mountains, I believe, would be beneficial to those who go and to those left behind. I have already ordered the letters of introduction to the Company's officers in the Saskatchewan, etc., which you applied for. With the long journey before you, you cannot, I think, make too early a start. And I would recommend your endeavouring to move off on the 1st. May if possible.

I learn from Mr. Ogden that the 200 head of cattle will be forthcoming at the appointed date; the greater part in the vicinity of Walla Walla. The result of Governor Steven's [8] explorations, I understand, is to cross the Columbia River and pursue a route already explored and found practical to the Puget Sound. When this railway is constructed, Walla Walla will undoubtedly become a place of importance —in time, I hope, to make you a fortune.[9]

III

Sinclair discovered that the plans for the 1854 trip were infinitely more complicated than had been those for the 1841 crossing of the plains and mountains with his first party largely made up of *Métis*. This time most of the emigrants were of a different type—many leaving good properties and homes of their own in Red River, which, in some instances, had been disposed of at considerable loss to themselves, in order to undertake a largely speculative venture in establishing new lives in the Oregon. However, the equipment required was largely the same as for the 1841 expedition, except in this instance most of the settlers' carts were drawn by oxen instead of *Métis* ponies. Oxen, while they traveled more slowly, had certain advantages over horses for such a long overland trek as this. They possessed greater endurance in drawing the heavy loads day in and day out over great distances. They could work more effectively and keep in consistently better condition on the grazing to be found along the way. Oxen's hooves were more adaptable to the rough and muddy terrain, and the beasts could be used as pack animals if the carts had to be abandoned when crossing the mountains. If starvation threatened, oxen could be butchered for meat. Lastly, oxen, when broken, were likely to prove less fractious for women and girls to drive, for once again the men and older boys in the party would ride horseback, taking their turns to guard the lumbering cavalcade, to reconnoitre, hunt game, and herd the wandering stock along the way.

Each leader of groups in the party was instructed to bring only enough carts to carry their belongings and serve as shelter at the camps. But Sinclair's 1854 party was compelled to accept a troublesome addition. One member of the party, related to some of Red River's most influential families, insisted that he be allowed to bring a flock of some three hundred sheep with him. Sinclair knew these animals would prove a most serious drag and source of worry on the trail, but he dared not refuse this settler's demand, for fear of engendering ill will that would cause others to refuse to go, thus spoiling the entire venture—including Sinclair's own prospect of settling in the Oregon and obtaining the advantages Simpson offered.

Other than the regrettable factor of the sheep, the demands made upon Sinclair's 1854 party were largely the same as those in 1841. The one noticeable difference was the sort of firearms carried. Sinclair had requested that wherever possible his men should replace their old flintlock trade guns with the American Sharp breech-loading rifles, both for protecting the party and securing game. He also carried one of the greatly improved Colt revolvers,[10] placed on the American market not so long before.

Even with Sinclair's best efforts to get the party under way by the date Simpson had set of May 1, 1854, it proved impossible to set forth before the end of May. A total of some one hundred persons were at last ready to leave[11] including twenty-eight adult males, eleven of these heads of families. There were thirteen men of fifty years and over—four between thirty-five and forty, six between twenty and twenty-five, three youths between fifteen and twenty, and two boys below fifteen years of age. There were also eleven married women and several unmarried girls, besides many children and some infants.[12] Most members of the party were from Red River families well known to Sinclair throughout the years, including Gibsons, Birds, Sutherlands, and Whitfords. George Taylor, belonging to the old York Factory family who had been well known to Sinclair's people there, proved to be his right-hand man on the trip, and so remained until the end of Sinclair's life.

The members of Sinclair's family accompanying him included his wife, Mary, and the two children born to them—one an infant in arms—as well as three children by Sinclair's first wife. These were the delicate girl, Maria, now almost nineteen years of age, and his two sons by the first marriage—one a lad of sixteen and the other nine. In this party was also Mrs. Sinclair's unmarried sister, Margaret Campbell, and a married sister accompanying her husband, John Moar, to settle in the Oregon. There was also Mrs. Sinclair's young brother, John Campbell, aged twenty-two, not long out of the Red River boarding school. Upon him Sinclair placed the responsibility of keeping a log of the entire journey.[13]

It was not until the eve of the party's departure, on May 24, 1854, that Sinclair confided to anyone the terms under which he had taken this latest assignment for Simpson. He placed his confidence in his son-in-law, Dr. William Cowan, who in the past few years had become Sinclair's greatest friend. He now told him that he had received from Simpson the recognized rank and salary of a chief trader in the Hudson's Bay Company, amounting to some £150 a year,[14] with the additional and somewhat unusual privilege under such peculiar circumstances of being permitted to raise stock for his own advantage near the post of Walla Walla of which he was to assume charge. This he was to do, however, only after he had paid back to the Hudson's Bay Company the initial cost of a herd advanced to him, at the rate of fourteen dollars per head for some two hundred cattle,[15] to be delivered to him after he had given safe conduct to the Red River party as far as Fort Vancouver.

13. THE DEPARTURE OF THE 1854 PARTY

I

By prearrangement—as had been the case with his 1841 party—Sinclair assembled his expedition in 1854 at a rendezvous some seven miles out of Fort Garry on the Portage trail. He remained behind as long as possible in the settlement to see that all arrangements were completed, and to say good-bye to his friend Norman Kittson,[1] the American trader, who was coming up from his post at Pembina to settle some outstanding business and see the party get away on friendly terms.

Some days prior to the date of departure Sinclair had moved his family from their old home to a temporary camp on the Hudson's Bay Company's reserve near the main gate of Fort Garry. Dr. Cowan [2] came to spend the last hours there with them before they moved off to join the rest of the party at the rendezvous. Harriet had not felt equal to coming with her husband to say good-bye to her beloved father and sister Maria. Cowan, according to his own written testimony, stood beside Sinclair as they watched Margaret Campbell, Sinclair's sister-in-law—a strong, capable young woman—drive the Red River cart, which carried Sinclair's wife and children, drawn by a well-broken black ox,[3] as she would drive it like a veteran all the way to the Oregon.

Indeed, it must have been quite a leave-taking for Sinclair. There was a kind of finality about this move for him across the mountains, and about his farewell with his closest friends—Alexander Ross, Andrew McDermot, John Inkster, and Chief Trader Black. Realizing this, Dr. Cowan tactfully suggested that he and Sinclair get off to the rendezvous without further delay, since he must return to tend his patients in the settlement before nightfall.[4] He also knew that Sinclair was eager to get the party started without further delay, since there was little enough time with this late start for the crossing of the plains and mountains before snowfall overtook them at the height-of-land.

When he reached the rendezvous Sinclair was annoyed to find that despite his warnings not all the members of the party had arrived there as promised. Some of the stragglers had sent word that they would catch up with the others at Lane's post some twenty-five miles farther out beyond White Horse Plain. Here they were as good as their word, and the entire party was assembled and ready to leave this post on May 26, making a train more than a mile in length, with wandering stock—including Sutherland's three hundred sheep—ranged for more than a half a mile each side.

The party had scarcely started when a strangely ominous heavenly phenomenon took place that greatly disturbed some of the more superstitious members of the party. A complete eclipse of the sun [5] darkened the face of the earth for a few terrifying moments before the party again moved on its way.

As in the case of his 1841 party, Sinclair laid down some rigid laws for marching and camping. His word as leader was to be regarded as final, after careful consultation on more important matters with the most reliable members of the party. This precaution was necessary for the safety and comfort of all con-

Hudson's Bay Company establishment at Moose Factory, 1854 (*Courtesy Hudson's Bay Company*)

Hudson's Bay Company establishment at York Factory in 1853 (*Courtesy Hudson's Bay Company*)

Front view of Fort Nez Percés—Pierre Pambrum's "old" Fort Walla Walla—as remembered by Alexander Ross and as it may have appeared to travelers on the Oregon Trail (*Courtesy British Columbia Provincial Archives*)

Fort Walla Walla as Sinclair knew it when in charge there from 1854 to 1856, after Pambrum's establishment had been burned (*Courtesy British Columbia Provincial Archives*)

cerned. No tardiness was to be tolerated, and Sinclair held the right to start each day with the old cry of the trail—"Every man to his ox!" This order was quickly passed around the entire camp each morning at dawn, as a signal for everything to get instantly under way for the day. Animals were immediately to be brought in; oxen harnessed to carts; tarpaulins, buffalo robes, and other equipment loaded into exact place; and each group to take its allotted place in the line for the day. Thus began each morning's spell of travel.

However, it soon proved not to be as simple to get everything in order on this trip as it had been in 1841. Carts drawn by oxen were not so readily handled at first as those drawn by *Métis* ponies. Indeed, there were some extraordinary scenes before the oxen were properly broken to their task. The great brutes pulled some of their drivers in all directions, especially at harnessing up. Some reared and turned, throwing off tackle and smashing carts or harness to right and left. On more than one occasion they gave a terrifying performance in unison, and it was difficult to get them in hand again. These antics were as dangerous as they were amusing, and only gradually did they become more tractable and broken to the trail.

Sinclair's premonition that Sutherland's sheep would prove a source of continual annoyance and delay was only too true. They were inclined to dawdle and browse and required constant herding and prodding. But Sinclair could do little about it unless he took the unpleasant responsibility of ordering the sheep slaughtered, which would have split the party into factions—one group supporting the owner's right to bring sheep, the others indignant that he had been permitted to do so. In such matters Sinclair tried to be fair and impartial. For example, he permitted no special privilege in taking the desirable first place in the line, where there was less dust and danger of bogging down in deepening ruts as the train moved forward, also insuring first choice of a camp site. However, the rule held that from the first day on the trail the largest family group had original precedence, the next in size following in order until all had their turn at the head in fair rotation, and the order repeated as the days wore on.

In case of an accident or breakdown on the trail, the unfortunate cart must turn out to let the others pass until temporary repairs could be made. The unfortunate group then took its place at the rear of the train for the rest of the spell; when the next camp was reached it resumed its rightful place so no unfair advantage could be taken.

Sinclair sought to maintain an average rate of two and one-half miles an hour when traveling under normal conditions. With Roderick Sutherland's sheep in the wake it was difficult to keep this pace, but it must be striven for if they were to cross the Rockies in safety.

II

Between Fort Garry and Fort Carlton travel was not so rough or uncertain as it had been in 1841. With more cart brigades on the Saskatchewan trail its "spells" and camp sites were better known. Once more the party's first important stop was at Portage la Prairie, where there was noticeable improvement since the first party's visit. In the summer of 1853, Sinclair's old friend, Archdeacon Cockran, had brought a number of people here who were anxious to escape the recurring floods along the Red River, and where more land could be secured for new homesteads. Among these settlers were a number of friends and relations of people in Sinclair's party, who made them welcome at a pleasant encampment for several days. It was near Portage that Sinclair, on June 1, 1854, wrote a letter to his daughter Harriet, sending it back to the settlement with a friend, and saying:

> I give Mrs. John Garrioch a beautiful black otter for you. She goes down in a day or two. You need not be afraid to use it. I got it from my brother William.[6] We are now fairly on the way. All well so far. Our cattle give us little trouble but still enough to keep us on the move. I have not all my cattle here, but I will write Mr. McDermot about them, and on these matters tell him so. Our cattle are improving very much. All desire their love and yours.
>
> Affectionately,
> JAMES SINCLAIR

P.S. I will be obliged to send McLeod back.[7] I found him useless and careless. I paid him for a month's wages. I was told by Smith and Inkster and others that he would not answer well. We can do very well without him. J.S.[8]

The same discomfort from bulldog flies, mosquitoes, and the danger from pilfering Indians [9] was experienced in this region between Portage and Fort Ellice in the Bad Woods as had been endured by the 1841 party. Fort Ellice was found to have changed but little, and again Sinclair was relieved to find the Indians in this country away up the Qu'Appelle River on their annual hunt. After replenishing supplies at Ellice and moving some distance beyond, a serious accident was narrowly averted. It happened that young John Campbell, Sinclair's brother-in-law, was painfully hurt at the hazardous crossing of the Qu'Appelle. Of this experience the young man wrote:

The banks on either side of the stream were very long and steep made slippery by rain, with big round boulders. Several accidents occurred, one nearly fatal. An ox became unmanageable and ran downhill dragging a driver. I remember that for I hurt my back very bad. There was no way to fasten a brake to those carts, so we just had to tie a rope around the oxens' horns and hold them back from running down hill. I recollect it had been raining and the boulders were wet and slippery. I was walking along the side of a youngster I had in the cart and was holding him back when I slipped and fell, and away went the steer down the rest of the way, and the cart ran across my back, and I had to crawl out of the road for there was another cart coming down, and it just grazed my toes. After everybody else had got to camp some parties came back and carried me down.[10]

By 1854, the Hudson's Bay Company had installed a crude ferry across the Qu'Appelle, over which animals, carts, and people were carried at a charge of two shillings for each trip, placed to the company's credit. Each scow-load took across two oxen and two carts—the sheep and the people being transported in the same manner.

The trip through the beautiful Touchwood hills was enjoyable, and not too much difficulty was experienced in crossing the bit of desolate plain after the descent from the hills to reach the South Saskatchewan River. Again, the crossing of this stream must be faced with the added worry of Sutherland's sheep. Of this experience Campbell wrote:

> Because of the sheep requiring constant herding along the way we were about three weeks or longer in making the South Saskatchewan than would have been normally required for a party to reach this place from Fort Ellice. . . . The South Saskatchewan was 80 yards wide at the crossing . . . flowing at the bottom of a deep trough cut several hundred feet below the level of the plains, running a strong current of muddy water. . . . At the crossing a Hudson's Bay Company batteau was found. A man swam across to get it. Animals were unharnessed, wheels taken off the carts from which the loads were removed, and the business of ferrying began. . . . Six carts and six loads were taken across on each trip. . . . The cattle and horses were made to swim the river, driving into the stream the more refractory animals. . . . The sheep had to be taken in groups in the batteau, requiring a number of additional trips. Some ten hours were needed to carry the party, their belongings and stock across the stream. Once over, it took us about three days to get another start for the next stream—the Northern Branch of the Saskatchewan.[11]

There was now very real danger of Blackfoot attack, for the feud between the Blackfeet and the Crees had increased in savagery in the years between the Sinclair expeditions. Of this young Campbell said: "Evidence of Blackfoot scouts had been seen in the form of ominous smoke signals. We had to keep out of the way of hostile Indians. We were obliged to stand guard nights from here on." [12]

However, the party came through safely to Carlton House. Except for stronger defenses this important company post had changed but little since Sinclair's last visit. Guards were now constantly posted in each of the square bastion towers at the four corners of the twenty-five foot stockade; some formidable three-pounders showed at regular intervals in the heavily reinforced palisade. A warm welcome awaited Sinclair's people, and although he wished to push on as quickly as possible he was unable to do so: "The river was very high—almost overflowing its banks so that it was impossible for the cattle to effect a landing on the other side." [13]

Because of the danger from Blackfoot attack, the party was forced to take the trail to the north of the Saskatchewan despite the delay involved in crossing the many small streams between Carlton and Edmonton House. At Carlton, Sinclair secured the guide that he had especially requested and who was to lead them to Edmonton. This was a shrewd, dried-up little *Métis,* known as "Le Graisse." He knew the trail well but demanded a high price in advance for conducting the party.

The flooding Saskatchewan receded enough in a few days to let the party make the crossing. Carts were ferried over; horses and oxen compelled to swim; and sheep taken over in company bateaux, with—happily—no serious incident or loss so the party could move on again. Of this crossing Campbell relates:

> We had to make rafts from the carts and row and tow them as well with boats which were loaned us by the trader at the post. It was a hard stream to cross. The water was very high with a swift current. We came very near losing our rafts of carts. Our canoes were very light, and we could not tow the rafts across fast enough and were carried a long way down the river. We happened to land on a long point on the river, and by snubbing the raft to some trees on the bank we managed to save the carts, but it was a close shave. Our canoes were made of a frame of willow tied with ropes and oil cloth stretched over the frames. They would carry four or five persons. It took us all of a week to get a start from here. We had a good deal of trouble to get our carts out from the high point. We had to make two rafts of our carts as we had quite a load of them. After getting straight again we kept on the north side of the river . . . towards the next trading post called Fort Pitt.[14]

Between Carlton and Pitt the same difficulty was experienced, as with the 1841 party, of crossing streams and building bridges as the party plodded doggedly onward, racing at slow pace against time. Unfortunately, there was increased evidence that greater vigilance must be kept against the possibility of Blackfoot attack. Signal fires were spotted on the horizon to the southwest, signifying that the party had not gone unnoticed by watchful Blackfoot scouts. The expedition passed Fort Pitt's large horse guard, maintained by the company twelve miles outside this post for the wintering and conditioning of horses, where the party's worn-out mounts were exchanged for fresh ones.

As they neared Fort Pitt the deafening row of barking sleigh dogs was heard, serving as warning to the inmates that an approaching cart train or Indian war party was near, and soon a salute of musketry went up from the fort. Once certain that Sinclair's group was genuine, the gates were opened and a rousing welcome assured. The post was dangerously undermanned. Many of the *Métis* usually to be found at this place were away after buffalo, and the summer brigades of York boats had already passed downstream and would not return with trade goods until the autumn.

Fort Pitt, in the summer of 1854, was in a state of exceptional nervousness. Some hundred tepees of Cree had recently pitched outside the stockade, offering special inducement for daring Blackfoot parties eager to steal horses, squaws, and scalps if circumstances offered. If this occurred it was certain the Indians would fire the fort and try to plunder the company's usual large supplies of trade goods and firearms. An additional cause for alarm came from the fact that the famous and powerful chief factor of Edmonton, John Rowand, had recently died at this post. Due for retirement, he had come to pay a visit to his son, who was in charge of Fort Pitt. While here, he had been angered by the impudence of an Indian, which had resulted in his being stricken with a paralytic stroke and dying almost instantly where he fell.

Rowand's death at Fort Pitt had created a somewhat alarming situation throughout the entire Saskatchewan River country, for he had ruled it with a firm hand. He had been feared and respected by both Cree and Blackfeet, with whom he dealt. Now that he was gone anything might happen, and every white and *Métis* in the district was in danger of attack unless an equally capable and firm successor could be appointed at Fort Edmonton. Indeed, so nervous had become the inmates at Fort Pitt under these circumstances that by the time the Sinclair party arrived all business with the Indians was being done through a small aperture in the fort's walls—as had been done at Walla Walla. This was offending the Indians who were growing increasingly antagonistic. On the first night of the Sinclair visit the ominous sound of the tom-tom and the chanting of war songs could be heard incessantly. The Cree were warming up to retaliate against recent Blackfoot attacks on their encampments, with the time ripe for retribution. Furthermore, it was this very night that a savage orgy of bloodletting also took place when the hundreds of ravenous sleigh dogs broke loose, killing all of Sutherland's sheep. Of this young Campbell wrote:

> Here we were in the heart of the buffalo country. The Company kept a great many train dogs at Fort Pitt. There must have been 300 to 400 dogs here at the time. They had plenty to feed them, being in the big game country. There was one of our party that was bringing 300 head of sheep along with his cattle. The dogs cleaned them out the first night here, so that Sutherland's sheep were no more! [15]

To add to the party's concern, a son was born this terrifying night to one of the women in the group.[16]

The only relief provided at this tense moment was the unexpected return of a number of *Métis* from the buffalo hunts; they brought word that the party could now move on with some semblance of assurance to Fort Edmonton, since fairly reliable word had come that the main body of Blackfeet were still far to the south hunting and trading with the Americans along the Missouri. If the party were to get away at once it was likely that they would reach Edmonton without too much chance of Indian attack, except perhaps for a few little skirmishes if some isolated Blackfoot war parties should be encountered. However, as a precaution, Sinclair ordered that his men keep their guns constantly ready, and had the entire cart train divided into four sections—each placed under a competent lieutenant—for added mobility and security. Experience had taught Sinclair that if a party were too compact in the line when traveling, it became too ready a target for Indian attack, becoming confused and disorganized, and enabling the attacking Indians to cut off isolated portions without sufficient general defense. Unfortunately, at Pitt, also, Sinclair lost one of his most able men, Thomas Hudson, who decided to "hire out to the Hudson's Bay Company . . . rather than proceed to the Oregon"; [17] so the party was short one competent man in an emergency.

The train again set out on July 17, 1854, and had not gone

far before it was met unexpectedly—or so it seemed—by Sinclair's old Cree friend and guide, Chief Mackipictoon and his band, who immediately offered to accompany the party the rest of the way to Edmonton. The wily chief pretended the meeting was quite by accident, but it appeared that he had learned of the party's approach by the Indians' curious means of communication. Sinclair quickly turned the meeting to advantage and secured the Cree chief to serve as guide, grateful for his band's additional protection against possible Blackfoot attack. Of this coincidental meeting Campbell wrote:

> I had forgot to say that we came on a band of Cree Indians. This party of Crees travelled along with us until we came to Fort Edmonton from Pitt. We hired the Chief of this band of Crees, whose name was Mackipictoon or Broken Arm, to act as guide. These Cree Indians were very friendly to our party. They used to accompany some of our party when they went out to hunt the buffalo, and kept all the party supplied with fresh meat. . . . There must have been very near 100 of these Crees. They acted as an escort to our party, stood guard at night, and kept with us. . . . I am very near forgetting to tell about the buffalo being very plentiful in the country between Forts Pitt and Edmonton. Very frequently we went hunting them and charged them with our fastest horses. Sometimes our horses were too fast and we would outrun the buffalo. It was very dangerous to get ahead of them as one could not see the many badger holes on account of the clouds of dust. Our horses were apt to step into one of these holes and fall down and get trampled on by the band of buffalo. One has to take big chances but as it happened we were very fortunate and nobody ever got thrown down. The last day that we saw the buffalo was on a Sunday. We were travelling along as usual, and we could see a black mass moving towards us. These were the buffalo travelling towards the north and we had to stop to let them by. When they came up to us they separated; some going ahead of our carts and the others behind. We had to stop and let them by and go around our loose cattle and horses as they wanted to follow the band of buffalo. We were obliged to remain at that place for over two hours to let them go by us. Just as far as the eye could see there was nothing but a black mass of them and they were going on a small lope. One cannot think how they came to be gathered, as it were, into one band and started travelling north. . . . The young men of our party were very eager to take a shot at them but the oldest people would not allow that as it would have been very dangerous to have shot them. They would have stampeded our whole outfit and killed all the women and children.[18]

Certainly, the presence of the Crees made traveling easier, since they helped to make and break camp, herd the wandering stock, and hunt game. Even the building of bridges over the many swollen streams was made simpler by the Indians' aid. Occasionally, quite strong bridges had to be constructed over deep ravines to bear the weight of the heavily laden carts and oxen. It was estimated that after leaving Fort Pitt the Sinclair party had to construct no less than eight such bridges over streams too deep or steep to ford—the shortest forty feet long, the longest one hundred feet in length.

Thirteen miles east of Fort Edmonton the company's horse guard was reached at Sturgeon Creek. They were at last on the edge of a bit of human habitation, having come through the portion of dangerous Blackfoot country unscathed. Once they had left Edmonton House, however, largely untrodden paths lay ahead, for the Cree guide had persuaded Sinclair he could lead them over another still untraveled pass across the Rockies to the Oregon.

III

A peculiar reception awaited the party at Fort Edmonton, that latter part of July, 1854. Young Campbell wrote: "We found everything very quiet. The gates of the fort were closed and not a movement was to be seen." [19] (Knowing something of this post, and appreciating that Chief Factor Rowand was but recently dead, Sinclair immediately sensed some sort of tension engulfing the place, which he took to signify fear of an impending Blackfoot attack. It was possible that the fort's sentries had seen the dust caused by the approach of the party, and, noticing that it was accompanied by a large band of Indians, may well have believed it had been taken by Blackfeet who were holding its members as hostages.) Sinclair at once "hoisted the white flag as a salute of gunfire was made." [20] A few of the most reliable men were sent ahead on horseback to announce what the party was. The challenge was accepted, and soon the large, oddly decorated main gate was flung wide for the party—the heavily laden carts passing through with general rejoicing and offers of generous hospitality by the resident company people.

When Sinclair presented his credentials at Rowand's impressive great house to the acting commanding officer—no official successor to Rowand having yet been appointed—he was informed that Edmonton had been recently threatened by a large party of Blackfeet who had defeated a big band of Cree with much loss to them but a short time before. The Blackfeet were still heady with victory and had come "chopping" with arrogant threats to secure goods at the fort gates. When word had gone around the place that a large party of white men with carts was surrounded by mounted Indians, the inmates instantly feared the worst, as Sinclair had suspected, thinking that the party members had been taken prisoner and that the fort was about to be besieged and fired. That there was very real danger was only too obvious, for Edmonton was badly undermanned. The post's regular complement of men was seriously depleted at this season by the numbers gone with the company's boat brigades to York Factory and Red River, as well as with the pack trains for Athabaska and the Boat Encampment.

While there were still competent officers at Fort Edmonton, there was actually no one there at the moment with sufficient prestige to impress the Blackfeet as either Chief Factor Bird or Rowand had done in the past. Nevertheless, business went on as usual. Fortunately, through the years he had been in charge, Rowand had organized the establishment with diligent discipline and efficiency, and it was fully realized by all within the fort that the outlying posts were dependent upon it. It was not only essential to safeguard the personnel of the fort but to secure the large stocks of goods upon which so many depended for their existence. In order to protect these interests since Rowand's death, "the Indians were never now allowed to enter the fort as formerly. They traded for what they wanted through the aperture in the gates." [21] As at Fort Pitt, this annoyed the Indians, and both Blackfeet and Cree had become churlish when they came to trade.

Several of the best members of Sinclair's party expressed the desire to remain at Edmonton. They were prepared to forfeit their bond, given in good faith at Fort Garry, rather than continue farther. They would work at Edmonton until they could earn their passage back to Red River with the first York boat brigade the following spring. It took all of Sinclair's powers of persuasion and reassurance to make them continue across the mountains, for more dangerous Blackfoot country must be crossed to reach the base of the Rockies.[22] However, nearly all the original members of the party agreed to remain with him and were soon ready to follow the Cree guide over the new pass.

Mackipictoon had assured Sinclair that he believed the ox-drawn carts could be taken the entire way across the mountains. Of this Sinclair had his misgivings, but was willing to take them as far as possible for the comfort of his people. He also realized that while pack trains had proved the best means of travel for crossing the mountains, it was difficult for settlers with so many women and children along to adapt themselves to this means of transport. Therefore, while appearing to accede to the Cree's suggestion they continue cart travel beyond Edmonton House, he took every precaution to see that the party would be able to revert quickly to pack train if necessary. As an added safeguard, he had his most able men learn the most efficient means of packing, which had become something of a fine art at Edmonton. The "diamond hitch" was mastered by a few of his followers as well as the use of the cross-tree packsaddle with crupper, breeching, and thick pads—packs held in place by bellybands drawn tight with lash ropes to the animals' backs. Double blankets were used under each saddle, and loads equally balanced on each side of the pack animals, enabling them to carry from 150 to 200 pounds each. Teaching the men to pack oxen was another matter again. The animals had never borne a pack before, and they cut some queer capers at the first experiment—one or two of them turning fierce and not permitting their owners to come near them for days, until they were gradually and patiently broken back to cart harness. Sinclair also had several of his best men learn how to construct useful ox saddles, in case the women and children should be required to ride ox-back if not enough ponies could be found to carry them with their belongings across the mountains. Sinclair saw to it that his right-hand man, George Taylor, was supplied with enough hand-forged nails to meet such an exigency.

Sinclair also had some difficulty in persuading his people to travel light from this point on. He urged them to leave behind all nonessentials as gifts to those who had befriended them at Edmonton, or to have those goods acceptable to the company credited to their accounts when they reached Fort Vancouver.

Summer was already beginning to wane when the party was finally ready to leave Edmonton. Knowing the nights would be cold when crossing the mountains, Sinclair directed the people to bring sufficient, if not excessive, warm garments and enough blankets and buffalo robes to serve as shelter if the carts were abandoned. He also saw to it that enough pemmican was carried, as well as sufficient arms and ammunition to secure any game that might be encountered in the mountains.

IV

While the party was at Edmonton, Sinclair heard of several interesting crossings of the mountains made since he and Simpson had discovered their respective new passes in 1841. In 1845, shortly before the boundary dispute west of the mountains had been settled, two brilliant British officers—Lieutenant Henry J. Warre of the fourteenth British Regiment and Lieutenant M. Vavasour of the Royal Engineers—had come through Edmonton House on their way to the Oregon. Not then disclosing their military status, they presented themselves as sportsmen, artists, and explorers of independent means. The whole business had been carried out with mystery, the party conducted personally by Chief Factor Peter Skene Ogden and using Whiteman Pass and Red Rock Pass, which Sinclair himself had earlier discovered but for which he had been given no recognition. It now appeared that the expedition had been undertaken by Simpson in conjunction with Sir Richard Jackson, Commander of the British Imperial Forces in Canada, for the sake of military information to be used in case of war if the boundary dispute were not settled by diplomatic means.

Sinclair also learned at Edmonton that in the same eventful year still another crossing of the Rockies had been made—this time from west to east by an Oregon priest, Father de Smet, who had acted as Dr. John McLoughlin's spiritual adviser and confidant before the doctor's retirement. This crossing had been made as a genuine missionary endeavor among the Indians, and was not in any sense a competitive undertaking of personal, military, or governmental significance.

14. THE DISCOVERY OF KANANASKIS PASS

I

When the Sinclair party set forth from Edmonton House it was already mid-August of 1854. The ox-drawn cart line struck out in the same single file as from Fort Garry, with the wandering stock—now increased by the extra horses to be used for packing—spread out along each side of the train. Mackipictoon once more rode at the head of the train beside Sinclair directing the way. The party traveled in a general southwesterly direction, following for a time the same path over which the Indian had led Sinclair and his people in 1841. Of the beginning of this part of the journey, Campbell wrote: "After leaving Edmonton we went to the north bank of the Red Deer River and kept on it for several days when we forded the stream which happened to be quite shallow with a fine gravely [*sic*] bottom. From here we could see the first sight of the Rocky Mountains." [1]

Beyond the Red Deer Crossing, the Cree guide took another course. Instead of striking directly for Devil's Gap—his previous entry to the Rockies—he took the party past the Spruces,[2] a landmark consisting of a prominent grove of evergreens, the way then leading more directly south through rolling foothills. Another landmark was soon reached called Minne-Hay-Gwak-Pas-Waksut,[3] so named from a solitary evergreen that marked the way they would take. Here the trail once more turned south-southwest, heading for a place today known as the Dogpound,[4] and from this point the way led directly to the broad valley of the Bow River.[5] Their entrance to this valley was farther to the east than the point where Sinclair's 1841 party had come into it to enter Whiteman Pass.

In the wide and beautiful valley of the Bow River the party was threatened with attack by a band of Blackfeet:

> The Crees acted as escort to our party, stood guard at night, and kept with us until we came to a camp of Stony Indians on the Bow River. There was something I missed telling you. When we were encamped at the Bow River . . . we were followed by Indians for eight days. . . . Although we did not see them, we knew that they were near. One terrible night was spent in momentary expectation of attack. All waited in suspense. But the night passed without any disturbance till towards day break when some of the cattle came running with poisoned arrows sticking in their bodies. . . . That was how we happened to find out about the Indians being around.[6] . . . As soon as it was light some of our party started right out on some horses that were kept staked out in case something like this happened. . . . Mr. Sinclair and some of the men ascended the high hill, but the renegades got away with three horses. I suppose that they could not catch any of the others. . . . They could see no Indians. They, however, found they had killed two animals and carried off the meat.[7]

It was discovered shortly after by Mackipictoon's Cree scouts that the attack had apparently not been as serious as feared. It seemed that some "old men left behind the main body of Blackfeet as unfit to travel,"[8] had evidently wished to steal some horses in order to catch up with the rest of the tribe, and to secure fresh ox meat for food since hunting the buffalo was denied them. They appeared to have had no guns and resorted to the use of their old bows and arrows to kill the party's livestock.

Once this disturbance was past the Cree guide led the people westward for a time, up the Bow Valley through beautiful foothill country of benchland—the landscape broken by groups of spruce scattered among the yellowing birch and poplar along the river; the country gradually becoming more rugged as they approached the foot of the Rockies.

At last they reached a stream that Mackipictoon called the "Strong Current River," [9] which flowed into the Bow—the latter he called the Minnee-znee-wap-tah, or Cold Water River—where it continued not far from the site of the Hudson's Bay Company's old Piegan Post.[10] This site had been abandoned in 1837, when the company had been compelled to move their trade back to Rocky Mountain House farther to the northwest because of the truculence of the Blackfeet in this region. Little evidence was left of this post, which had once been managed by Sinclair's Red River friend, Chief Factor J. E. Harriot; for the Indians, in retaliation, had burned the buildings to the ground after the traders had escaped unharmed from this dangerous country.

Mackipictoon proposed to take the party up the Strong Current River to the height-of-land at Kananaskis Pass,[11] named after a famous old Cree chief. There were actually two Kananaskis passes in close proximity to one another, the Indian said, and he would take them over the one that the women and children could negotiate with the least difficulty. But before attempting the crossing they must encamp at the point where the Kananaskis River joined the Bow,[12] to reorganize their equipment to the best advantage.

It was here that the party met with further annoying delay. As Campbell wrote: "It was at this camp we remained another two weeks as another youngster was born to Mr. and Mrs. Robert Flett, but this little one did not live but a few days." [13] During this delay, Sinclair and his men reconnoitered some distance up the Swift Current River; they were somewhat disturbed at the nature of the country they must cross, for it appeared rougher than Whiteman Pass, and there was much deadfall timber. But he gave in to Mackipictoon's protestations that this would prove the better way, although he insisted that the carts be abandoned at this point and that the people make pack train their means of conveyance from this place on.

The decision to abandon the carts was not easily made, for it was opposed by a number of the people who believed that they could cross the mountains the entire way with them. But Sinclair was adamant, backed by the advice of his best men, and the party could not risk any further delay or be caught by snowfall at the heights. It was only too evident that the people would suffer some discomfort if not hardship from this point on, for they no longer had the shelter of the carts at night and only the barest necessities could be carried with them. It was decided that women with babes should carry them on their backs papoose-fashion, and that other small children should ride behind them on their mounts—the women to ride whatever horses or oxen could be spared from packing.

While the party was at the Bow camp and in the midst of breaking down the carts [14]—some of the men constructing crude saddles for the women and packing their belongings to the best advantage—a band of Stony Indians returning from a hunting trip in the mountains visited the encampment. Sinclair could speak quite intelligibly to them, for they used an Assiniboine dialect somewhat similar to what he had earlier used in trade south of Red River. From this band Sinclair gained considerable information concerning the way they would take across the mountains; he also bartered for some of the game these Indians had brought out and were carrying home, including carcasses of moose, elk, mountain sheep, and their peculiar delicacy, the siffleur—the dried flesh of the marmot. Of this encounter, Campbell relates:

> At this camp on the Bow River . . . we also hired two of the Stony Indians as guides over the mountains, as the route had not been travelled before, and the trail was full of fallen timber. We had also to go to work to break up our carts and use the timber to make pack saddles to carry all our traps. We were fortunate in getting nails and other necessities at Fort Edmonton to put the saddles together with. We had to make everything strong as some of the young steers were very frisky. In using carts we had used collars and breechings, and we

used these to fasten the packs on the steers. They were tied fore and after and around the middle, and would still sometimes break off. It was a grand sight to see their capers, and there were not but one or two in the whole outfit who knew anything about packing before we reached Edmonton. We had to stay in camp longer so as to get the young stock broken in to their job, but we had the time of our lives when we started travelling through the timber. On the narrow trail a steer would bump his pack into a tree and then he would take to bucking to get free and start to throw his pack off, then we would have a time catching him to put the pack on to him again. We had to go very slow to get the stock used to their work. Some of the women had to ride on the back of the old oxen as there were not enough horses, but these had to be led as they did not guide very well with just the halter lines."[15]

Adjusting to their new mode of travel as quickly and easily as possible, the party moved up the Strong Current River, the country becoming increasingly difficult to negotiate. Each day became harder—the people growing increasingly fatigued, and the stock footsore and weary. The trail took them over mountain shoulders and swamps. Sometimes the trail was perilously narrow and high, on a mountain shelf with a steep rock wall to one side and an abyss hundreds of feet deep on the other, where if ox, horse, or traveler had lost footing nothing could have saved them. Almost as if by miracle all the party came through unscathed and with surprisingly little loss of stock. Nevertheless, as time wore on Sinclair could see, with growing concern, that some of the people were showing signs of nervous strain; and he often cursed himself for letting the Cree guide bring them this new way across the mountains instead of again taking the Whiteman Pass he had crossed twice before with comparative ease. Now it was necessary to literally shove their way through burnt-out remnants of forest, which created an almost impenetrable mesh and through which the men had often to slash a path for the stock and people to pass. It was also necessary to have a party of men move ahead of the main group each morning in order to try to discover their best route for the day—these scouts carrying emergency rations and axes to slash their way through. The stock suffered severely: "Some days we did not make more than seven or eight miles as some of the stock was getting foot-sore . . . the long drives that they had been compelled to make over these difficult trails and without sufficient feed were daily wearing down the poor animals now failing rapidly." [16]

Furthermore, Sinclair was forced to carefully husband the supplies of food, for very little game had been met with while crossing the mountains, and the only recourse was to butcher some of the oxen if the pemmican supplies gave out. That some of the animals had to be destroyed for another reason is evident:

> About half of our route across the mountains one of my horses—the fastest of our buffalo runners—got tired, and we left him for a day. But as one of our Indian guides threatened to go back and take the horse with him, I was requested to go back and shoot the horse, but that was something that was hard to do—to kill my old friend! [17]

The Cree guide at last admitted that he had become lost in this difficult region and did not actually know his way across. Campbell writes: "The Cree guide now led us into an impassable defile through the mountains. There we wandered back and forwards, obliged to make wide detours to find a road through which the men could drive the cattle. Often the party was compelled to proceed entirely on foot." [18]

Sinclair was thus forced to act as guide as well as leader:

> We had to travel by compass. At one place we came to a place that had to be bridged; a most fearful spot. Small trees were thrown across a narrow chasm that seemed almost bottomless. . . . Mr. Sinclair said —"that is the Crow's Nest!" One of the people replied, "the Devil's Bridge would be a better name for it!" Over such gorges we had to construct bridges even stronger for cattle and horses, women and children, to cross these terrifying abysses.[19]

By this time most of the party was thoroughly weary and dispirited. Sinclair had to urge them on step by step, with the encouragement that surely the worst was past and they would soon reach their goal. The only compensation was the country's astonishing grandeur. They had reached a most impressive region—the Lower and Upper Kananaskis Lake country. They were now close to Mackipictoon's mysterious new pass. To add to the growing concern, a heavy storm threatened just as the party was about to cross the height-of-land. Supplies were running low, and they had to kill more of the oxen for meat, which added still more to the people's discomfort for it diminished the number of pack animals and each member had to carry heavier burdens.

Now the decision must be made as to which of the two Kananaskis passes they should take. As no white man had ever come this way before there was no precedent to follow. Presumably, the higher and therefore more difficult of the two passes was chosen [20]—by accident or design—and the terrain was so rough that none of the party, no matter how exhausted, was able to ride over the divide; all had to walk leading the pack animals. Men, women, and children alike stumbled over the rough masses of shale and boulders, made even more treacherous by a recent heavy fall of snow. Of this precarious crossing Campbell states simply: "We crossed the height-of-land walking through snow three feet deep in October, 1854."

And so the first crossing of Kananaskis Pass by white people was made over the mighty ridgebone of the North American continent—a crossing that has long been forgotten, and for which another man has been given credit instead of James Sinclair.[21]

With a kind of relieved finality Campbell writes of the crossing: "Our mountain guide took a new route across the mountains which took us thirty days whereas we could have gone by Mr. Sinclair's old route in ten days." [22]

II

The gravest danger over, a swifter descent was made down the western slope of the Rockies. The party now followed a swift-flowing mountain stream [23] to the valley of a larger river,[24] which led directly to the Kootenay country.[25] On the way down they passed several magnificent peaks,[26] then entered the Kootenay Valley at a point where another fine stream [27] joined the one that had brought them down from the height-of-land.

They then continued along the course of the Kootenay River, following the benches covered with good bunch grass to provide excellent fodder for the stock. The landscape was singularly attractive and parklike, open in the broad valley and framed on either side by the massive mountain walls of the Rockies they had left behind and the Selkirk Range before them. The country was now aglow with warm autumn coloring, the air clear and bracing, and travel comparatively easy and pleasant after what they had come through.

Having followed the south-southeast course of the Kootenay for a time, the trail they now took swept in an arc toward the southwest, taking them directly to the Canal Flats at the base of the beautiful Columbia Lakes. Here the Cree chief and the two Stony Indian guides announced that they were returning to their tribes across the mountains, confident they could reach them before winter trapped them at the heights.

Disgusted as Sinclair was with Mackipictoon for losing them in the mountains, he nevertheless entrusted a letter to him addressed to his son-in-law, Dr. William Cowan, at Fort Garry. Knowing the ways of the Indians he was confident it would reach its destination safely. Dated October 24, 1854, this letter reads:

> Kootenay River, (two miles from the lake, the source of the Columbia) Dear Doctor: As my guide, Broken Arm, returns from hence, I have merely time to say we are well. We have had a long time on our journey so far, but I expect to be at Walla Walla in twenty days hence. Our rascally guide took us by a pass over the mountains known only to himself, which he represented as the best and the shortest, but which took us thirty days, and this was hard work in cutting our way and hunting after cattle through a dense forest, windfall timber, deep ravines, steep side hills, following up one river—the Strong Current River—which falls into the Bow River near the Old Fort, to its source and following down another—the Kootenay—to this point where it is two hundred yards wide. Altogether it was the worst road I ever travelled. Had we taken the route by the Red Rock—our old route—We should now be near Walla Walla. Eight head of cattle were left or lost on the way, but none of mine, belonging to Moar and Sutherland. I am only surprised we were able to bring a single animal here. Had I seen this road before I should never have dreamt of driving

horned cattle by such a rascally route. Our guides have turned out a set of rascals from Beaver Creek near Fort Ellice to this place. To them we attribute the slow progress of our movements.

At Bow River the Blackfeet shot seven of our cattle with arrows. Two of them died on the spot. The others have since recovered. About forty men hovered about our camp the night before, but of this we were not aware until the following morning. I presume they saw we were on guard, and that it would not be safe to molest us. I still think the cattle were shot by a few young scamps, and that they were prevented by some others from molesting us. That same night they stole three horses; the owners of which took no trouble to take care of them. Neither the cattle nor horses belonged to me. Our animals are in pretty good order; even now some would be good beef. I have no apprehensions of any being left between this and Walla Walla.

Agnes Lucy thrives well,[28] and sucks her pemmican soup well as any others in the party. The whole party have been in pretty good health but all are tired of the journey. However, I feel we are now over the worst part of it. I will write by Panama, and enter into more details. In the meantime present our love to Harriet and her boy, in which all unite, Yours sincerely, JAMES SINCLAIR

P.S. Mrs. Sinclair and Meg [29] send their love to their mother.[30] Compliments to McDermot, and I will write to him via Panama. Thomas Bird [31] had his horse stolen, and one of his oxen was wounded by the Blackfeet, and his other ox was left a few weeks ago. Mrs. Flett had a young one some weeks ago, but he only lived for twenty-four hours. In the whole camp we have not two hundred weight of flour, two pounds of tea, two pounds of sugar, but plenty of animal food such as beef, pemmican, venison and dried fish.[32]

When an oxen was killed and the flesh not eaten at once, it was prepared by the women as pemmican, after the fashion of treating buffalo meat on the plains. The food supplies had been replenished when a band of Kootenay Indians was encountered and had exchanged the produce of its hunt for the party's heavy clothing, no longer needed on this side of the Rockies. They were able to secure such native delicacies as dried huckleberries and serviceberries pressed into hard cakes, dried skunk meat—unexpectedly tasty—as well as dried salmon.

Of the party's encampment at Canal Flats, Campbell wrote:

The Canal Flats are bounded by the lake on the north side and on the south by the Kootenay River, and on the east side by the Rocky Mountains and on the west side by the Selkirk Mountains. It is perhaps two miles across the flats from the base of the Rockies to the base of the Selkirks. From the lake to the Kootenay River the distance is three and one-half to four miles. The Flats have very open timber on them and plenty of fine bunch-grass. We stayed there two days and then our guide, the Cree Chief, Mackipictoon, and the two Stony Indians left us to go back across the Rocky Mountains to their own country on the east side. There were some Kootenay Indians at Canal Flats, and we hired a guide from them to continue on our route from there. . . . We turned south, forded the Kootenay River, and followed the base of the Rockies all the way down to Elk River. The route of the Sinclair party down the Kootenay River to the Spokane country followed the general course of the canoe route travelled by David Thompson on his trip to the Columbia in 1807. This became the regular route between the fur trading posts of Spokane and Fort Colvile, and those on the Kootenay.[33]

Sinclair acquired from the Kootenay Indians several fine horses in exchange for some of his cattle[34] that were in poor condition. He feared that they could travel no further, but would recover in the Indians' care if fed the good bunch grass of this region with time to rest.

Continuing his description of this part of the trip, Campbell says:

We followed the Kootenay River again to Kootenais Traverse and forded the stream. Then we kept on south to the Tobacco Plains through a rolling country. Then we crossed over to the American side of the International Boundary Line, at least where it would be marked, for it had not yet been surveyed when we crossed where Mr. Sinclair said it would be.[35]

We camped three days at Tobacco Plains and found here a Hudson's Bay Company trader by the name of John Linklater, a Scotsman, who was in charge of Fort Kootenay. He had come up country on his annual trip from Fort Colvile to do business with the Indians. Mr. Linklater's trading post was on the west side of the Kootenay River, and we were travelling down the east side. Mr. Linklater was the first white person we saw after leaving Fort Edmonton on the Saskatchewan River, and we were very happy to see some white people here. At this time Mr. Linklater was all alone in this country. There was not another white person nearer than three or four hundred miles from this station. He came across to our camp from the other side of the river by fording it. We had all got done unpacking our animals when he came over. He was so glad to hear that some white people were on the other side of the river that he did not take time to saddle his horse but jumped on it and rode over bareback to see us. While he was in our camp and all were eager to see him there was very near an

> accident. Mr. Sinclair's mount took fright at something and started to run among the other animals. His saddle got loose and under the horse's body. There was a Colt revolver in his holster tied on the saddle. It somehow started to shoot, and it was fortunate that none was hit. All the party had not reached camp. We travelled very slowly as our animals were very tender footed, and it took some of the party a long time to get into camp. There were a lot of Kootenay Indians standing around also, and wondering what kind of gun that was that could shoot so often. They had never seen one of these six-shooters before that time. It was a sight to see them standing around open-mouthed when they saw the pistol, and Mr. Linklater showed them how it was handled. At the time the only kind of guns they had used or ever saw were those flint-lock guns.
>
> After starting away from the Tobacco Plains, we followed the Kootenay River on the east side. The river was running more towards the west now. We travelled south for a week until we came to the Big Bow country about four days more. Then we crossed the Kootenay again, and left it to go south to the Pend d'Oreille River. There we crossed the river in canoes, swimming our horses and stock. We were obliged to leave camp on the south bank of the Pend d'Oreille in a hurry as there was not much feed there for our stock. From this camp we travelled south towards the Spokane country which we made in four days.[36]

This was easier country to cross, but they were now entering more dangerous Indian territory. Linklater had warned Sinclair to be extraordinarily careful in crossing this section, particularly near Walla Walla. Matters had grown much worse in that vicinity since Sinclair's last visit. The Cayuse tribe, which was popularly held responsible for the Whitman massacre, were again warming up for trouble. With regard to this part of the journey, Campbell's notes read as follows:

> Our cattle were getting very tired and footsore again by this time, and we had to crawl along very slowly. It took us nearly all of November to make out to the Spokane country. . . . All our party were getting tired also of the trip and were happy to find some white people there, Messrs. Owen and Gibson. . . . After visiting a few days most of the party continued on down towards Walla Walla.[37]

The party reached this post on December 16, 1854, almost seven months after leaving Red River, having expected to reach it not later than September.

III

With conditions as they were around Fort Walla Walla, Sinclair realized it would be foolish to range his cattle here, for the Cayuse Indians would now make short work of the stock either by theft or killing. Owen and Gibson proved agreeable to looking after the cattle, if Sinclair's brothers-in-law, Moar and Campbell, would remain with them for a time and take them down to Walla Walla later when things became more peaceful there.

Several other members of the party had decided to remain and settle at Fort Colvile, feeling that that country offered more promise and safety:

> One family, Mr. Thomas Brown and his brother Henry Brown, went up to the Colvile Valley and took what cattle and horses they wished with them to that country. Thomas Brown became one of the first white settlers there. Mr. John Moar, his family, and myself remained at Spokane. The rest of the party kept on the way down to Walla Walla. Mr. Moar and I were to stay there to winter the cattle in that country. . . . There were a couple of waggons made. The wheels were about seven to eight inches thick. The axles were fir, and holes were bored and gouged out of the wheels. There was no iron about them at all except the few nails used in making the bed for the waggon. Just two horses were used to draw them, and all the dunnage was piled on the waggons and a start was made.[38]

Sinclair's own family and several other people, including the Whitfords, were to remain at Walla Walla, while the rest of the party moved on down the Columbia by bateaux to make new homes along the way or near Fort Vancouver.

Walla Walla was found to be in a worse state than when Sinclair had last seen it in 1852. Dominic Pambrum was now its master—a relation of the former successful Chief Trader Pierre Pambrum, and a friend of Sinclair from earlier days. Dominic Pambrum had come to the Oregon as a member of Sinclair's 1841 party. He had been a Red River schoolteacher and had married a daughter of Sinclair's father's friend, Peter Fidler of Brandon House. Dominic was ill-fitted to manage such a difficult post as this, and he was only too pleased to have Sinclair take it over and to leave it to settle in the more peaceful Willamette Valley.

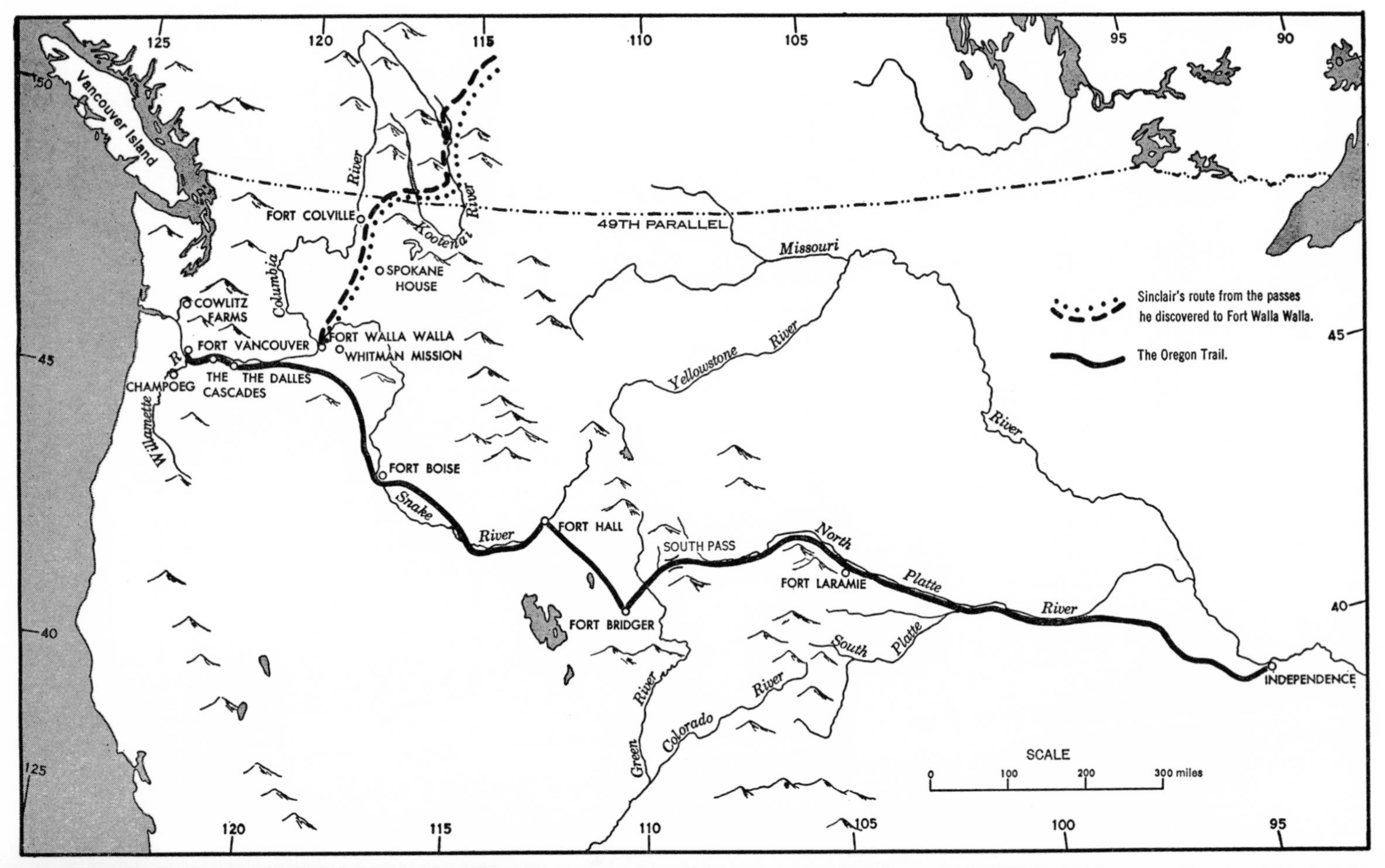
Sinclair's route from the passes he discovered to Fort Walla Walla.
The Oregon Trail.
Vancouver Island
49TH PARALLEL
FORT COLVILLE
SPOKANE HOUSE
COWLITZ FARMS
FORT VANCOUVER
FORT WALLA WALLA
WHITMAN MISSION
CHAMPOEG
THE CASCADES
THE DALLES
FORT BOISE
FORT HALL
SOUTH PASS
FORT BRIDGER
FORT LARAMIE
INDEPENDENCE
Columbia
River
Kootenai
River
Willamette
R.
Snake
River
Missouri
Yellowstone
River
River
North
Platte
River
South
Platte
Green
River
Colorado
River
SCALE
0
100
200
300 miles
125
120
115
110
105
95
90
50
45
40
125
120
115
110
105
100
95
45
40

With only a few days' rest at his new post, Sinclair continued with the party down the Columbia, in order to reach Fort Vancouver as soon as possible after informing the officers there of his party's safe arrival. On the way there, some of the party decided to stay at the Cascades and some at the Dalles. When Sinclair reached Fort Vancouver he found his friend, Chief Factor Dugald MacTavish, still in joint command of the post with Chief Factor Peter Skene Ogden, who was then away at the company's new headquarters at Fort Victoria on Vancouver Island. He was at once handed a letter from Governor Simpson, which had reached Vancouver some time earlier by the company's regular route via Edmonton and the Boat Encampment. This letter read:

> I had the pleasure to receive your letters of 10th and 21st January, February 14th, March 14th, April 23rd, May 2nd, and 15th June [39] reporting the organization of your party at Red River, and its progress as far as Fort Ellice which are satisfactory. I shall address this reply to Fort Vancouver so as to reach you upon your arrival at Walla Walla, after all the troubles and uncertainties of the march are over, so that I need not refer to your arrangements further than to say that you seem to have conducted them with success and secrecy, as there does not seem to be a suspicion when I was at Red River in June that the movement was anything but a purely spontaneous one on your part. I have written the Board of Management of the Oregon Department respecting your position at Walla Walla, and have requested that if either Mr. Ogden or Mr. MacTavish can spare the time from Vancouver they will proceed inland to meet you in order to arrange matters connected with your charge, and to make over to you the 200 head of cattle according to agreement. You will find the business at Walla Walla and the Snake Country, which is almost part and parcel of the same, greatly disorganized by bad management, and the Board will concert plans with you for a thorough reform with a view of putting matters on a proper footing.[40]

Simpson's authorization to Chief Factor MacTavish to see Sinclair settled as master of Fort Walla Walla stated that this place was to be

> . . . placed under the charge of Mr. James Sinclair, late of the Red River Settlement. This gentleman entered the service for a period of five years from June 1, 1853, on the understanding that he should have charge at Walla Walla, and that the Company should sell him 200 head of cattle, one year old and upwards at the price of $14 a head, deliverable at Nisqually, Thompson's River and Colvile. Mr. Sinclair's

object is to establish a stock farm at Walla Walla in which we are willing to assist him on the assurance that his proceedings shall in no way be allowed to interfere with the Company's possessory rights of that place. He left Red River in May last with a party of emigrants provided with horses and cattle who are under no engagement to the Company but remain with Mr. Sinclair or proceed elsewhere as they feel disposed. This party may be expected to reach their destination in the course of the month of October. I think it might be advisable that one of the members of the Board of Management proceed to Walla Walla to concert arrangements with Mr. Sinclair in reference to his charge, and to the delivery of the 200 head of cattle according to agreement. I have informed Mr. Sinclair that while in charge of Fort Walla Walla he will have a commissioned officer's allowance which you will be good enough to provide him.[41]

While staying at Fort Vancouver, Sinclair again wrote Dr. Cowan, on January 3, 1855, giving the following summation of his party's trip across the mountains:

I have merely time to say that we are well. I left Mrs. Sinclair and the rest of the family at Walla Walla. I arrived here on the night of the 30th ultimo with only one of my Red River party, G. Taylor. Some of the party went down to Colvile, others remained at Walla Walla, and the balance I left between Walla Walla and the Dalles, from whence I came in a small canoe to this place, not feeling inclined to wait for the steamer. The steamer went up to the Cascades today. Tomorrow I expect the whole party down. Generally we have all enjoyed excellent health and suffered few privations. We always had plenty to eat, and we had very little bad weather.

I left my cattle at Spokane, where I found two Americans herding their cattle which they had driven up from below. The grass was excellent. Those who had only a few horned cattle exchanged them for horses, one for one. A few animals have been left or lost on the road. Sutherland and Moar were the greatest sufferers. They had more than they could tend to, and the men they had were not the right sort. Consequently Sutherland lost nearly all his. I lost none. He also had too much baggage. I dropt you a few lines on the return of my Cree guide. I then expected to have reached Walla Walla by the 30th November, but I could not procure a guide to take me the short route. I had then no other recourse but to follow down the Kootonais River by the Tobacco Plains. This caused a delay of about twenty-five days, and to save our animals we were necessarily obliged to travel slow. All our cows were in prime order; the oxen, of course, were very thin from packing. Our long journey had been caused by various circumstances. In the first place our Fort Ellice guide lost himself. By this detention we lost eight days. At Carlton the river was full from bank to bank so the animals could not effect a landing on the opposite shore.

At this time Mrs. Brown had a son. This caused a further delay of fifteen days. Our mountain guide took a new route which took us thirty days whereas we could have gone by my old route in ten days. In following the Kootonais River by the Tobacco Plains we lost twenty days more. Again, before we reached Carlton the greatest number of our cattle had some sort of distemper in their feet. Three or four were left from this cause, and we could only move on slowly with the rest to enable us to save them. We ought to have been here about the end of September. However, here we are and well.

Business has changed very much since I left in '52—money scarce. Cows are worth still from forty to sixty dollars each. But from the small emigration this year must go up. Goods are abundant and cheap. Wheat one dollar, potatoes fifty cents a bushel. Beef twelve cents per pound. Labourers' wages from twenty-five to forty dollars per month. Mechanics three to four dollars per day. The Land Bill [42] has been extended to December, 1855.

Present our best regards to Mrs. Campbell and family. I expected to have heard from you and others. Not a line from anyone. Tell Harriet that Agnes was ready to crawl as soon as she got on a floor at Walla Walla. If you have no time to write she has plenty, and presuming you have, continue the U.S. mail to Crow Wing. I shall expect to hear often. In the meantime, I remain, Yours very affectionately,

JAMES SINCLAIR

P.S. Address your letters to this place. Mr. MacTavish will always have ways and means to forward them to me wherever I may be. Compliments to Ballenden. Say he owes me a sheet or two. Excuse haste. J.S.[43]

This separate enclosure was for his daughter Harriet:

Tell me what I can send you from here, either for yourself or the little boy? Remember me to Mr. McDermot. I shall write him a long screed. Lane [44] is doing nothing. Rather worse. The children are well.[45] I have not seen them but I shall today. Mary MacKay is married. Mr. MacTavish is everything I could wish. We get on very well, and Sir George is disposed to be liberal. Every effort shall be made to meet his approbation. However, much of this at another time. Before I leave here I shall write you a few lines after I look about. Mrs. Roderick Sutherland [46] expects to have a young one soon. She parted with her servant at Walla Walla. I do not know what Sutherland is to do. He is a poor devil—no head piece! I return in a few days hence to assume my charge at Walla Walla. Sir George writes me that I am to assume charge also of the Snake Country, Fort Hall and Fort Boise. These have all gone wrong—especially disorganized. Those who have been in charge have attended only to their own affairs. The Americans and the Snakes are at war, and in the opening of the spring lots of regulars and volunteers will move toward these regions. This will keep me in hot water. In the meantime no ammunition is sold to the Indians. What is to be the result of this time alone can tell.

J.S.

IV

Apparently satisfied with his reception at Fort Vancouver, Sinclair returned hopefully to his new charge at Fort Walla Walla despite the threat of Indian trouble there. He reached the post on January 16, 1855—relieved to find his family safe and well. The winter months, following his assumption of charge at Walla Walla, seem to have passed uneventfully enough. Sinclair tried—with the help of those in the party who had chosen to remain with him—to improve the place as much as possible, and sought to encourage trade with the Indians by peaceful means. However, he was increasingly annoyed that the cattle that Simpson had promised him had not been delivered as arranged for in the Governor's letters. Finally he wrote his complaint to Simpson, who promptly replied on March 1, 1855, from Lachine, stating that he had "written strongly to the Board of Management about non-delivery of your cattle." [47]

In the meantime Sinclair seems to have felt that things had become sufficiently safe at Walla Walla for his brothers-in-law, Moar and Campbell, to bring down his livestock from Spokane House to be cared for near the post:

> I remained with Mr. Sinclair at the Hudson's Bay Company's post at Walla Walla and looked after the cattle. Mr. Moar stayed some time in the valley before going on down to the Dalles. I stayed on tending stock along with another member of our party, George Taylor. . . . Mr. Sinclair building houses and barns, and also constructing a saw mill out of Walla Walla.[48]

V

In May, 1855, an important event took place at Fort Walla Walla bringing added concern, responsibility, and labor to Sinclair. The United States administrator for the new Washington Territory, Governor Stevens, arrived at the post with some fifty men, wishing to make Sinclair's fort his headquarters for a great Indian council to establish a peace settlement with the warlike tribes of this region. Sinclair was expected to afford these American officials every comfort and courtesy, and to assist generally with maintaining peace with the visiting tribes while the conference was in progress.

Stevens proved to be a man of unusual sense, ability, and tact, who was prepared to treat Sinclair fairly for his trouble and inconvenience. Immediately upon his arrival he told Sinclair that he was sending out messengers with formal announcements that the chiefs of the seventeen Columbia River tribes were to attend upon him here at Walla Walla, and hold parley with him not later than the end of May or early June, 1855. Sinclair and Stevens got on well together. The Governor was fearless and forthright. He took command of the situation with extraordinary mastery and adroitness. Soon some twenty-five bands of the various Columbia River tribes gathered about Sinclair's fort, and with every day that passed more warriors in barbaric display arrived to swell the numbers. A large party of Nez Percés came, led by their powerful chief, known as the "Lawyer"—an Indian of superior intelligence and integrity who was ready to assist the Governor in every way and act as intermediary and peacemaker with the various tribes.

After two days of serious deliberation everything was suddenly thrown into confusion by the arrival of three hundred of the treacherous Cayuse tribe, bent on creating dissension. The Cayuse leaders were impudent and aggressive, led by a peculiarly dangerous chief known as the "Five Crows"; one of the band was believed to have been responsible for slaying Dr. Marcus Whitman and his followers eight years before. Two days after the arrival of the Cayuse, two thousand more of the quarrelsome Yakima, Umatilla, and Walla Walla tribes arrived, led by two other dangerous chiefs—Kamiakin and Peu-peu-mox-mox, also called the "Yellow Serpent."

With the utmost patience and tact, Governor Stevens continued to hold meetings with the leading Indians through the remainder of May and well into June, 1855,[49] setting forth far reaching plans for creating reservations satisfactory to the various tribes. Upon hearing the Governor's terms the Indians held a great *waw-waw*, or powwow.[50] As a result of this, the tribes divided into two divergent groups—one favoring peace and acquiescence with the American terms, the other opposing all agreement with the whites and anxious to resume war against them throughout the Oregon. The amenable Indians were led by the astute Lawyer, the dissenters led by Chief Apashwayayikt, the "Looking Glass," of the Nez Percé tribe.

In an impassioned speech, framed to incite all the assembled Indians, the Looking Glass commanded them to reject the Governor's treaties and never agree to live on reservations, but return to their respective tribal lands, relinquishing neither them nor their freedoms to the white man. At that moment all Stevens' efforts seemed in vain, and serious trouble threatened, with enough Indians present, if they united, to wipe out the Governor's party and Sinclair's people as well. If this had occurred all the Oregon would have been set aflame. In a supreme effort to avert such a catastrophe the Governor and the Lawyer once more appealed to the Indians in prolonged council to maintain the peace. Strangely enough, they were listened to quietly and with respect. The influence of the treacherous Looking Glass seemed to have been overridden by the wise counsel of the Lawyer. It was agreed that the Oregon tribes should continue in peaceful relationship with all whites in the country, and that three great reservations should be set up by the American government as soon as possible—one to be situated on the Umatilla River, one in the Yakima Valley, and the third on the Clearwater and Snake rivers.

While the Indians appeared to acquiesce to Stevens' terms, some of the more deceptive natives were only feigning good will and were actually fomenting new trouble behind the scenes. However, obviously well satisfied with what they thought had been accomplished, Stevens and his staff prepared to withdraw from Walla Walla to proceed across the Rocky Mountains and try to make further peaceful negotiations with the warlike Blackfeet in their country.

Sinclair was deeply relieved when he saw the various tribes depart from his post, endeavoring to assure as many of them as possible that he would be prepared to deal fairly with them. Yet they had scarcely left Walla Walla before word was brought to Sinclair by his faithful half-breed interpreter, John MacBain—who, though little more than a lad, had been trained by his father before him when employed by Pierre Pambrum at this post—that more trouble was brewing with the Indians throughout the entire Columbia River region.

Despite these ominous warnings all was deceptively quiet at Walla Walla for a time. Pierre Pambrum's old irrigation canals were reopened and filled with clean water from the river. Gardens were planted anew, and the remains of the orchard pruned in readiness for crops that autumn. Indeed, Sinclair was almost prepared to feel that the future might hold real promise for him at this place, and threatened trouble might pass.

On July 4, 1855, Sinclair wrote to Dr. Cowan of family affairs and of prevailing conditions in the country:

> Yours of the 10th April met me at the Dalles on the 26th ultimo. I am glad to see you are well. I have much pleasure in saying that we are all pretty well. Mrs. Sinclair is improved very much but still complains of a pain in the chest extending towards her back. Her liver is seriously affected, as I understand from Dr. Suckley of the United States Army. Maria [51] has a bad cough and keeps very thin.
>
> The confounded gold discovery at Colvile is creating quite an excitement all over the country. As I expected, all our men at Colvile and Walla Walla have cut and run. I have only one man left, and this is a hard matter in times like these. No contract will bind men, and it is absurd to expect to get a man at the old scale of wages when others are paying four and five dollars per day, but few of them will work even at that rate. When the news extends to New Caledonia, the Company's people will desert, and then good-bye to the profits of the fur trade. The rush has commenced towards Colvile. Prices of everything have gone up. Beef is going up also. Sixty dollars has been paid for spring calves at Colvile. Older animals will command a proportionate rate. The stock of cattle in the country is not so great as has been supposed. There has been a constant drain from the Willamette Valley towards the mines in northern California, and there are few on the north side of the Columbia. The Company had about sixty-five hundred head at Nisqually in the spring of 1852. All have disappeared.
>
> The allied fleet is expected at Fort Victoria this summer, and to

supply these Dr. Tolmie has been obliged to purchase forty to fifty head from the settlers about him. Douglas [52] is building a hospital. They evidently expect another brush [53] and it is hoped they may be more successful than the disgraceful affair of last year.

Business here has been fair. But it is again gradually improving. So far I have done a good business in Walla Walla. I had Governor Stevens and his suite for nearly two months near here and hundreds of Indians. He has concluded treaties with them by which they have ceded all their lands as far as Okanagan and along the Spokane. He left on the 12th ultimo for Fort Benton to see the Blackfeet. He was afraid to go near Colvile for fear of his men deserting. The news had scarcely got out there. The largest bag of gold dust that I saw from Colvile was about the size of a half pint tumbler—beautiful thin flakes containing from thirteen hundred to fifteen hundred dollars, and this was the work of one man for about a month or rather less.

Please remember me to Mr. Ballenden. I received his of the 10th April to which I shall reply as soon as I have more time. In the meantime I thank him for your good wishes. This is the 4th of July. The garrison is firing away, and our folks are returning the national salute. My love to Harriet and her son. Yours sincerely,

JAMES SINCLAIR

P.S. Tell Mrs. Campbell that George Taylor and John Campbell are well. They are both with me, and John Moar is also near Walla Walla. Mary is growing fast, but Jane Margaret and Agnes,[54] particularly the latter, bids fair to be very intelligent and smart. I expect to see Emily tomorrow. I hear they are well. Maria Lane [55] is going to school. She promises to be very pretty and intelligent. I shall see Lane and endeavour to prevail on him to allow them to be sent to their grandfather at Red River. In the meantime they are supported by individuals none too well off. Affectionately to all,

JAMES SINCLAIR [56]

VI

During the summer of 1855 Sinclair did not hear directly from Governor Stevens again. He continued his endeavors to make peace with the Indians on both sides of the Rockies. But another ominous message came from Sinclair's half-breed interpreter, John MacBain: Stevens had succeeded in making treaties with the Flathead tribe of Coeur d'Alene and with the Pend d'Oreille Indians near the lake of that same name. He was then proceeding east of the Rockies to make his headquarters at Fort Benton with his escort of twenty-two men, and he was prepared to set about negotiating peace treaties with the truculent Blackfeet.

However, no sooner had Stevens left Fort Walla Walla than the treacherous Cayuse and Yakima Indians commenced new intrigue, with the aim of murdering Stevens and his party on their return west of the mountains in the autumn of 1855.

Hearing of this appalling prospect from MacBain, which he had gathered from trustworthy Indians, there was little Sinclair could do to forestall such a terrible incident. However, he was soon relieved to hear again from MacBain that Stevens had been warned of the threat upon his life by his good Indian friend, the Lawyer, who was able to help him escape the trap laid for him. The Lawyer had been able to get word in time to the American authorities at Oregon City, who had at once sent a famous express rider, named Pearson,[57] to convey word as quickly as possible to Stevens at Fort Benton of the trap prepared for him; as a result, the Governor was enabled to take another, safer way across the mountains to his home.

While this threat upon Stevens' life was serious enough, MacBain brought even more terrifying word to Sinclair concerning his own safety and that of his family early in October, 1855. At last the dreaded Indian war was almost ready to break out throughout the Oregon—the threat upon Stevens' life being the cleverly planned signal for general uprising against all the whites in the Columbia River country. Not long after MacBain's announcement of trouble, several scattered attacks had been made upon isolated settlers, with some loss of life at the Cascades, in the Yakima Valley, on the Grande Ronde, the Rogue River, and even at Puget Sound.

The only hope of saving Fort Walla Walla, next marked for attack, was the attempt being made to rally American volunteers and move them into the threatened area before trouble began, and this seemed most unlikely to happen. Sinclair, therefore, set about at once to prepare such defenses as he could—realizing his post was shockingly undermanned and quite unable to resist a long siege. Thoroughly alarmed at the immediacy of trouble, and worried for the safety of his family and those serving at the post, Sinclair sent word for aid on October 12, 1855, to both the

United States Army commander at the Dalles and to Chief Factor Dugald MacTavish at Fort Vancouver, intimating that there might be serious loss of company property as well as life if the Indians struck, and there was little he could do to prevent it. To MacTavish he wrote:

> I beg to represent to you the precarious state of the relations at present existing between the Indian tribes in this quarter and the white settlers around. No actual demonstration of evil intention has so far been made, but matters wear a very suspicious appearance. On the part of the Hudson's Bay Company which I represent at this place, and equally on account of the settlers in this vicinity, I venture to claim from you such protection as it may be in your power to afford.[58]

Sinclair also enclosed in his letter to MacTavish a copy of the appeal sent to the American Indian agent nearest to Walla Walla several days earlier, asking for his immediate assistance in attempting to control the Indians under his jurisdiction. This agent, Nathan Olney, had been having some serious trouble himself with the dangerous Chief Peu-peu-mox-mox—the Yellow Serpent. Peu-peu-mox-mox had sworn revenge upon all whites in the region for what he believed to have been the murder of his son by a white man. Olney had been instructed by his government to try to make a peace with this Indian with a gift of five hundred dollars in silver and some other presents, as tokens of good will in an effort to stave off a general attack upon white settlers. These gifts the vengeful Indian had sullenly rejected—his refusal being a virtual declaration of war upon all whites within reach of his followers. Alarmed with this turn of events, Agent Olney immediately warned all settlers of their danger in this area, informing them that they must accept his written order to evacuate the district immediately as a command from the American government.

When Sinclair received his copy of Olney's order to remove his family from Fort Walla Walla to a safer location, he realized the command could not be disregarded and prepared to obey it. Olney's order had read:

> Judging from the present appearances, I am induced to believe that a war with the tribes of Indians in your immediate vicinity is un-

avoidable. If such an unfortunate event should occur your own and the lives of your family and those you employ must necessarily be sacrificed unless you remove beyond the reach of danger. I, therefore, as Indian agent order you with your family and hands to leave the country without delay.[59]

Before Sinclair had time to obey, angry and aggressive Indians began to assemble about the fort, and so dangerous did the situation become that when Sinclair returned to the post, he found his wife Mary in a state of near collapse. While Sinclair had been tending his stock, an Indian in full regalia had stealthily entered the living quarters of the fort; before Mary could help it, her small daughter of three had run toward the warrior, eager to play with him. The Indian picked up the child and was about to make off with her when Mary seized the gun left for her protection, but before she could fire the Indian dropped the child and ran from the fort.[60]

Scarcely had Mary told Sinclair what had occurred when Olney arrived from his nearby quarters at Wallulu to see if his orders for evacuation were being carried out. He immediately ordered Sinclair, on this late afternoon of October 13, 1855, to take all the company's powder and balls stored at the fort and have them thrown by his servants into the Columbia River, with the explanation that if the Indians raided the place the ammunition would fall into their hands and be used against the whites. He even commanded Sinclair and his men to the river bank to see his orders were carried out at once. Somewhat angered at Olney's arbitrary attitude, but yielding quietly to the inevitable, Sinclair nevertheless insisted upon receiving from Olney a receipt for the property destroyed. He felt justified in this request in his capacity as an officer of the Hudson's Bay Company, and Olney wrote the following receipt for Sinclair to hand to the company officers at Fort Vancouver:

Received from James Sinclair, Agent for the Hudson's Bay Company at Walla Walla, a quantity of ammunition. Such ammunition has been destroyed by my authority, thrown into the Columbia River before proper witnesses to prevent it falling into the hands of the Indians under the critical circumstances now existing; 400 lbs. T.P.F. gunpowder, 1008 lbs. ball. Sgd. NATHAN OLNEY, Indian Agent[61]

Then, under the cloak of darkness that same evening, the Sinclair party abandoned Fort Walla Walla. They left everything behind except what they wore and the little they could carry, but abandoning much of their personal property, horses, and cattle, as well as the Hudson's Bay Company's valuable trade goods and livestock kept at the fort.[62]

Fortunately, some time before, Sinclair had sent his young brother-in-law, John Campbell, to the comparatively greater security of Fort Colvile with some twenty head of horses when he had first heard of impending serious danger at Walla Walla. Between the time of sending Campbell to Colvile and the evacuation of Walla Walla, Sinclair's interpreter, MacBain, had brought back reassuring word that Campbell had managed to reach Colvile in safety with Sinclair's stock.

It also happened that just as Sinclair, his family, and servants were about to leave Walla Walla, accompanied by Olney, in the company's bateau down the Columbia, George Taylor, upon whom he had placed such reliance both when crossing the mountains and since, stood up defiantly to Olney and flatly refused to leave the post. Taylor declared that he was a free British subject and that he stood on British soil until full compensation had been paid for it by the Americans for occupancy of the country. Taylor then intimated that he intended to remain at Walla Walla at his own risk to look after the company's property and Sinclair's stock as long as possible, and would find his own means of escape when the time came. Sinclair may well have wished to remain with Taylor, but, as was apparently then known to none but himself, he had committed himself to obey Olney: some time before, while at St. Paul, he had taken steps to become an American citizen. He had, therefore, no redress but to set out with Olney.

When Sinclair and the other members of the group from Walla Walla arrived at the Cascades of the Columbia, he was surprised to find Chief Factor Dugald MacTavish awaiting him there. He had come upstream in response to Sinclair's appeal.

But it now appeared useless to proceed farther in view of what Olney and Sinclair had to relate concerning the deterioration of conditions there. Of these matters MacTavish had made a report to company headquarters in London on October 23, 1855:

> Mr. James Sinclair writes me from Walla Walla on the 12th instant that the conduct of the Indians in this neighbourhood has of late become suspicious leading him to believe that some outbreak may take place there; more particularly as they have been very troublesome in consequence of his refusal to sell them ammunition. Mr. Olney, the Government Indian Agent, arrived at Walla Walla on the 12th instant, and the next day he destroyed all the ammunition in the fort to prevent the Indians taking it. I transmit a copy of Mr. Olney's receipt for the ammunition; likewise a copy of letters addressed by Mr. Sinclair under date 12th instant to Mr. Olney, and the officer commanding the United States troops at the Dalles. As Mr. Sinclair may be compelled to abandon Walla Walla either through pressure from the Indians or by authority of the Government Agent, I am anxious to know in case such may happen whether we are again to take possession of the fort should it not be destroyed? [63]

Apparently—as later events were to prove—the company's headquarters did instruct Sinclair to reclaim his post at Walla Walla. After his meeting with Sinclair at the Dalles, MacTavish again wrote the London headquarters on November 7, 1855, as follows:

> Having been informed on the 27th ultimo that the Company's establishment at Walla Walla has been abandoned, I left two days afterwards with the intention of proceeding to the Dalles, but meeting Mr. James Sinclair at the Cascades on the way down, I returned from thence after learning from that gentleman that he considered it proper and necessary to leave everything at Walla Walla in consequence of an imperative order from the Indian Agent, Olney, and accordingly had come to the Dalles with his family, accompanied by Messrs. Wm. Charles and John Ogilvy, Clerk Charles Ogden, and two labouring hands. Mr. Sinclair has acted in this matter with much prudence and discretion, and has evinced sound judgement in the management of the Company's business committed to his charge through a very trying period.[64]

MacTavish also added that:

> Governor Curry of Oregon Territory, being about to despatch some companies of volunteers to Walla Walla to occupy the country, Mr.

> Sinclair together with Mr. Ogilvy, Charles Ogden, and the two men will return with that party from the Dalles with the view of again taking possession of the fort, and remaining there if they can during the present troubles.[65]

Sinclair had now received his orders from his superior officer at Fort Vancouver, Chief Factor MacTavish, who had no alternative but to order Sinclair back to the dangers involved in an effort to reclaim Fort Walla Walla for the Hudson's Bay Company. Sinclair was told to prepare immediately to leave with a party of American volunteers, who were being sent up the Columbia to clear the country of insurgent Indians; in this command he also received his death warrant.

15. DEATH ON THE COLUMBIA

I

It was mid-November, 1855, when the Oregon volunteers and the American troops under the command of Lieutenant-Colonel J. K. Kelly, to which group Sinclair had been assigned by the company officers at Fort Vancouver, were sent up the Columbia River to wage a campaign against the insurgent Indians in the region about Fort Walla Walla. Scouts had returned with word that Chief Peu-peu-mox-mox and his followers had taken possession of the fort, and it was realized that a long guerilla campaign might be required to regain it. The post had been robbed by the Indians and the stores distributed among neighboring tribes to induce them to join battle against the whites.

On November 17, 1855, Sinclair and his fellow soldiers reached Wells Springs on the Umatilla River, where a base camp was set up to prepare to retake Walla Walla, some forty miles distant. The officer commanding this group was a Major Chinn, who kept in close touch with Lieutenant-Colonel Kelly by trusted scouts. Through this means of communication Sinclair was able to get word back regularly to Chief Factor Dugald MacTavish with news of the campaign, especially where it concerned Hudson's Bay Company interests. Sinclair's first letter to MacTavish from the field of action reads:

> We arrived here to find the buildings of Olney's Agency in ashes. Early the next morning all hands were set to work to fortify our position so that we are now stockaded in with two bastions sufficiently strong to keep off any body of Indians. I shall, of course, remain along with the command to watch events.[1]

On November 21, Sinclair again wrote MacTavish:

> The Yellow Serpent—*Peu-peu-mox-mox*—is encamped within a mile of Fort Walla Walla with eight hundred to one thousand men. He commands the approaches to the fort, and if driven in intends to retire into the fort. Our force is not strong enough to drive them away. Major Chinn talks of moving to Umatilla tomorrow and there fortify ourselves until reinforcements come up from the Dalles. We are in a tight place. God knows when we are to get out of it if the Cayuses join Stock Whitley.[2] The Deschutes Chief is up there with about two hundred men stirring up those Indians who would have remained friendly. Nothing is known of the forces on the north side of the Columbia.[3]

Several fierce skirmishes took place between the volunteers and Indians—some running battles—before the decisive encounter took shape ten miles from Walla Walla. On December 5 the Yellow Serpent was taken prisoner by Chinn's men and was killed in a desperate effort to escape. Sinclair wrote the details of the fight to his son-in-law, Dr. Cowan:

> In my last letter I mentioned that I was now on the eve of starting for Walla Walla along with one hundred and fifty mounted volunteers who were to occupy the fort. On the way I met an express—a messenger—proceeding with official information, with the intelligence that a few days after I left the fort a large body of hostile Indians about one thousand strong had plundered it and were then in possession of it. Deeming our force inadequate to retake it, we were compelled to make a halt twenty-five miles from it to wait for reinforcements. In the meantime we fortified our position and soon built a stockaded fort. Here we were cooped up for fifteen days surrounded by a large body of Indians. After receiving reinforcements, we made a night march to the fort which was found deserted and a mass of ruins. I enclose you a piece cut from the paper of the day. We had a pretty hard fight for four days. We, however, drove the Indians from their position, and

drove them before us for forty miles. I was with the party who made the first charge. I had no idea of getting into the fight but the excitement was such there was no keeping out of it.

I am anxious to communicate with Colvile and Fort Hall to acquaint them with the state of affairs, but the country was in that state where there was no moving with safety a few miles from our camp. After waiting for better than a month, I got a chance of writing to Colvile by the return of one hundred and fifty friendly Nez Percés who had escorted Governor Stevens to our camp. Our victory saved him and his party. I have sent instructions to McDonald in charge of Colvile to stop the trade in arms and ammunition. This will bring the Indians down on him, but of the two evils it is better to have the Yankees as friends. Our position is a delicate one to avoid coming in conflict with either party. I am glad to say that the hostile feeling formerly entertained by the Yankee population against the Company is fast giving way, and that they now give us credit when we deserve it. There are, however, a few who would wish to saddle the Company with being the authors of the present Indian difficulties, but the fact that we were obliged to abandon our property to the mercies of the Indians has tended to remove the old feeling against the Company. . . . I was within a yard or two from the great Walla Walla chief, Peu-peu-mox-mox, when he was shot. The whole scalp was taken from his head and cut into twenty pieces. His skull was divided equally for buttons. His ears preserved in a bottle of spirits, and large strips of his skin cut off along his back to be made into razor strops. Such is Indian warfare! But enough of this! [4]

Indian attack upon white settlers became increasingly vicious throughout the Oregon. It had been thought that with the killing of the powerful Yellow Serpent they might decrease in the face of growing American resistance, but such was not the case. By the spring of 1856, most terrible murders and atrocities were committed in various places along the Columbia. The Klickitats were particularly vicious. The American volunteers and troops did all in their power to prevent the terrifying attacks, but more often than not their aid to isolated settlements came too late—with bodies of men, women, and girls left mutilated almost beyond recognition. In view of this, Sinclair was filled with grave concern for the safety of his own family, who were still at the Dalles—some distance from Walla Walla but too uncomfortably close to the source of trouble—living with Mary Sinclair's sister, Mrs. Moar. A body of American soldiers was garrisoned at this place, but not in sufficient numbers to assure complete security.

II

When the campaign about Walla Walla subsided a little, Sinclair, having viewed with dismay the devastation there, returned as quickly as possible to Fort Vancouver to report the facts and submit an estimate of the company's possible loss to Chief Factor MacTavish, scarcely daring to consider his own wrecked fortune. MacTavish appears to have accepted Sinclair's statements as reliable, discouraging as they were, and immediately prepared a special report for the company's London headquarters,[5] placing Sinclair in a completely fair light.

While at Fort Vancouver, Sinclair also wrote Cowan in this fashion:

> Dear Doctor: Maria [6] is still at the Dalles. She still complains. I fear her lungs are seriously affected. Her medical advisor, the United States Military doctor there, has recommended her to take cod liver oil from which she feels considerable relief, but the least damp or rainy weather throws her back so that I am afraid to bring her down here to Fort Vancouver. For the moment Margaret Campbell [7] is with her. Dr. Hemming of the United States Army attends her. Major Haller's lady is very kind to her. They pass a good deal of their time with her. Major Haller is the Commanding Officer at the Dalles. Jessie [8] is here at Fort Vancouver. She is quite a belle, and has brushed up a good deal. Since the arrival here of the 9th Regiment there are whole hosts of ladies, and there are parties and balls once or twice a week to which Mrs. Sinclair and Jessie are always invited. Mr. MacTavish is very kind to them, and we get on very well together. In all my arrangements in the interior in these troublesome times I have had his entire approval and support.
>
> I am preparing the necessary documents regarding our loss from Indian depredations. Out of more than two hundred cows, I recovered only twelve head. All my horses are gone. Out of the Company's horses I managed to collect forty-five out of one hundred and twenty. I had seventy cows and thirty-six yearlings at Thompson's River which my men were compelled to leave there. The dread of the Indians about Okanagan is such that they were afraid to pass there. I only regret that they are not with the rest of my herd so that Uncle Sam could pay for the whole concern.
>
> We have heard the most absurd reports being in circulation at Red River regarding some of those who came with me. One was that John

Moar[9] was insane. Poor John has never been unwell and has no tendency that way. Roderick Sutherland is, I hear, doing very little. Emily[10] was here about six weeks ago to visit Mrs. Sinclair. I have not seen her since January, 1855. Present my compliments to Mr. McDermot. I will write him next mail. I shall go below to Oregon City to see Lane about sending his children to Red River.[11] Sir George Simpson wrote me to co-operate with Mr. MacTavish in this affair. Lane never calls here. He has taken his children from Mrs. Covington and Mrs. Pambrum. I am satisfied the poor children are not so well attended to now. Mrs. Covington was very kind to the boy, and the girl was going to school then with Mrs. Pambrum. Both are very fine children. The girl in particular. I shall do my best to prevail on Lane to part with them. Thomas Bird is doing nothing.

Lord only knows when these Indian troubles will end. In a few weeks three thousand Volunteers and two thousand Regulars will be in the field. A few days ago the Indians attacked the town of Seattle on the Puget Sound in open day, and would have destroyed it but the "Decatur," a sloop of war, got her broadside on, and with shot and shell drove off the Indians. Here at Fort Vancouver the sound of the bugle is to be heard all day. The troops out on drill on the Shanghai tactics; all their movements are made on the trot. Wherever I go I see some preparations for carrying on the war. For my part, for the last four months I have had as much as I want of such military life. Those Indians who are friendly are collected together in certain localities. The whole country is in an uproar from the California frontier to the British. Is Inkster alive? I have not heard from him since I left. My love to Harriet and to my sister Mary. Mrs. Sinclair desires her love to you all and to her mother and sisters. John Campbell is at Colvile. I shall try to get him into the service here. He is disposed to be steady and does not drink. He is obedient and has turned out better than I expected. My sheet is full. I remain, Yours sincere,

JAMES SINCLAIR

P.S. I only arrived here four days ago. My nephew, William, is married to Jemima Kittson, a niece of Mr. Kittson of Pembina. He is at Fort Hall. Compliments to Kittson when you see him. He is now one of our relations! J.S.[12]

III

Sinclair's days of Indian warfare were not yet over. In March, 1856, he once more received orders from Chief Factor MacTavish to return at once to Fort Walla Walla to salvage what company property he could, and to restore the post in preparation for resuming business as soon as the Indian troubles were past. It was March 24 when Sinclair started up the Columbia River from Fort Vancouver. On the way upstream he stopped at the Cascades to await the arrival of the little river steamer to take him on to the Dalles, where he expected to see his ailing daughter, Maria, still there receiving treatment from the American army surgeon.

At such a time as this it seemed almost ludicrous for a steamboat to be traveling the Columbia. The small steamers negotiating the placid reaches of the river between the Cascades and the Dalles had been carried up in pieces by bateaux to be assembled at the Cascades. First the steamer, the *Mary*, had been constructed in this fashion, then in 1855 the *Wasco* put together in the same way. The Indians had been deeply impressed by these boats, calling them the "white man's fire canoes." And so they literally had become during the Indian war, for they were used to transport troops and army supplies up the river.

When Sinclair reached the Cascades on March 24 he found another innovation under way there. A tramway was being constructed around the rapids that had previously caused such difficulty and labor in portaging. The work was progressing quickly, for its completion would greatly facilitate the transport of troops and goods up and down river. To hasten its building a large force of men was at work, and a number of new cabins and warehouses had been constructed along the riverbank to accommodate the workmen and their families. The building of the tramway was no simple engineering feat in view of the peculiar nature of the terrain, with its overhanging cliffs and huge masses of rock. But the difficulties were being overcome with astonishing skill and speed, so that the work was well under way when Sinclair arrived.

As was usual for him when he traveled this way, Sinclair put up at a kind of composite inn and store at the Cascades. It was owned by a man named Bradford, who had constructed it of logs and made it a comfortable enough place to stay. Sinclair spent a good night here, lulled to sleep by the sound of the rushing waters of the great river. He awakened refreshed on the morning of the twenty-fifth and spent the day watching the men at work—some of them hauling timbers into place, others carrying logs to the mill to be sawed into lumber. He also noticed the manner in which the workmen's families had settled into normal life in the small temporary dwellings—women chatting at their washing, and children playing about the doors.

On the morning of March 26 Sinclair was ready to take his departure from the Cascades for the Dalles. The *Mary* was warming up at her dock preparing to shove off when the sharp crack of gunfire suddenly rent the air. For a moment Sinclair could not understand what it meant as he stood near the entrance of Bradford's store. Men started up from their work; women rushed to the doors of their shacks; children raced to their mothers in fear. Then Sinclair realized what had happened. It was Indian attack. Puffs of gun smoke could be seen as rifles cracked, and Indians on horseback raced along the ridges of the cliffs toward the settlement. The Cascade band of Indians who had previously been considered comparatively harmless—holding aloof from the other tribes in their war and pretending to be friendly to the whites—had turned traitor in unison with the more vicious tribes. For a moment, dazed by what had happened, Sinclair stood helpless, watching workmen struggling hopelessly to put up a defense. Then he saw some men and children struck down by the attackers as they came closer in this cleverly prepared raid. Several women and children were running desperately to the store for shelter. Sinclair, fully alert now, tried to help as many as he could get inside, as this was the only place that could withstand even a temporary siege. Those too far away to reach it would be cut down or face the same horrible fate as that of Whitman's people in their flimsy dwellings.

Sinclair helped the last of those who could possibly make it inside the store. Then the doors were slammed shut and barred. Decisions now had to be made quickly, and there seemed no one there but Sinclair capable of rallying those inside to action. A quick survey showed that more than might have been expected had been able to reach the crude shelter. Now, what to do! Sinclair quickly took stock of the store's resources: by chance, but an hour before some volunteers going upriver had left nine government rifles and a quantity of ammunition in the store. Of the forty people in the place only eighteen were capable of putting up any kind of defense in a siege that might go on for days. John MacBain, Sinclair's trusted half-breed interpreter who had come upriver with him to again serve at Walla Walla, now proved of inestimable value.

In the few minutes since the attack began the Indians had taken possession of the bench land above the store, on a height that dominated the building dangerously. To overcome this disadvantage, for the store had only an outdoor stairway leading to the living quarters above that was now useless, Sinclair ordered a hole cut through the ceiling to reach the roof. Several volunteers offered to go to the loft and crawl out on the roof to try to command the river side of the building, sheltering themselves sufficiently to shoot at the Indians on the bluff. Holes were also quickly cut in the four walls of the store, large enough to take a rifle and permit a man to cover each of the four sides of the building.

Just as Sinclair was effectively organizing the defense, one of the workmen's wives, a Mrs. Watkins, was seen running toward the store beside a man named Bush. The Indians' bullets were striking around their feet. One shot brought Bush down just as he and the woman were straining with their last strides to reach the door. Hastening to open the door to let the woman in, Sinclair himself was struck down, dying instantly where he fell.[13]

EPILOGUE: AFTER SINCLAIR'S DEATH

I

The three days after Sinclair's death proved to be a veritable hell for those trapped in Bradford's store at the Cascades of the Columbia River. The only one who could be counted upon to lead in its defense was young John MacBain, who had been Sinclair's almost constant companion from the first day he had come to Walla Walla and replaced Pierre Pambrum in the lad's devotion.

MacBain was not yet twenty years of age, but the responsibilities of a much older man had rested on his shoulders since his father's death some time before. He realized now what was expected of him to replace his master in aiding these bewildered, half-crazed people in this pathetically inadequate stronghold. Watchful every second, MacBain commanded the situation intelligently, calmly, and tirelessly, trying to determine the Indians' plan. Day and night, without rest or relief, MacBain never lost control. He saw that immediately after Sinclair was shot down the steamboat for the Dalles had become a special object for the Indians' attack. They obviously intended to seize and fire it. It was also apparent some of the boat's crew were still aboard. In the face of intense Indian fire from the overhanging cliffs, they were endeavoring to get the boat away from the shore and into midstream,[1] stoking furiously to get up steam, with the hope of getting upriver to the Dalles to secure troops and ultimately relieve the siege at the store. Moving slowly away from the riverbank, then faster and faster pushing into midstream, the little steamer finally disappeared from sight of the store.

MacBain knew that after dark the Indians would turn their fire on the store. Already some of the natives on the cliffs above were hurling rocks on the roof as well as burning balls of dried moss. Several of the rough-hewn shingles caught fire, and the gravest danger in the place was the lack of water.[2] There was very little from the outset, and almost all of it had been drunk by the terrified victims heedless of future need. Now there was only some liquid in a pork barrel left to pour on the blazing roof when a firebrand hit its mark. Carefully estimating his next move, MacBain determined to try to reach the river under cover of darkness to replenish the water casks. He also intended to drag Sinclair's body outside the store and hide it for later burial. The first need was water for drinking and for defense against fire. He knew it would be difficult to get to the river, for he saw that it was the Indians' intent to set the store ablaze after they had fired the workmen's buildings, thus forming a mammoth torch and making the whole scene as light as day to prevent any of the inmates of the store from escaping after dark. This was how the Columbia River Indians waged war. They were cunning and clever and wily as foxes, and MacBain knew their game well enough to try to outwit them.

As darkness fell and before the Indians could get the larger buildings aflame, MacBain stripped and crawled naked down the slide used for the boat landing, stealthily reaching the water's edge. He was able to return with several buckets of water before the intensity of the Indians' fire stopped him, and he dared not make a further attempt for the time being. Indeed, he was not able to make another attempt for another two days, and was compelled to ration severely what water he had brought back to those in greatest need of it.

As dawn was breaking on the morning of March 28 the Indians' fire ceased temporarily. Apparently they had run short of ammunition, but this brought the terrifying realization that this was also the situation within the store. Once more MacBain took advantage of the lull in fire to slip out of the fort; in several swift trips to the river he was able to bring back enough water to fill two barrels. Then he dragged Sinclair's body to the water's edge and, under cover of darkness again, placed it in the water of a deep pool near the bank, securing it firmly so it would not be carried downstream.

With dawn, fire broke out with renewed fury, the Indians having replenished their store of ammunition in some way. With conditions at the store now almost impossible for much longer defense, MacBain called a meeting to decide what should be done when their ammunition was spent. Remembering the fate of the members of Whitman's mission some years before, the inmates agreed that when only four rounds of ammunition remained it should be used to cover their retreat to the river, where an old, large, flat-bottomed boat was pulled up on shore, still untouched by the Indians. By common consent it was decided that all should enter the boat and push off into the stream, going to their death together over the Columbia Cascades rather than fall into the Indians' hands.[3]

When this moment of utter despair was almost reached relief came to the inmates of Bradford's store from an unexpected quarter. The watchful MacBain saw a body of soldiers approaching from the opposite direction from which aid was expected. A group of American cavalry was preparing to move upstream from Fort Vancouver to the Dalles when their officer, Major Philip Sheridan,[4] had been informed of the siege at the Cascades. A desperate Cascade settler had miraculously managed to escape the Indian trap, and had raced downriver to Vancouver with word of the disaster, meeting the soldiers on their way upstream. Only this chance meeting saved the people at Bradford's store, for they could not have withstood long enough for the little steamboat to return with help from the Dalles. It was days later that the little ship, the *Mary*, had been able to complete her mission, reach the Dalles, rally the troops, and return to the Cascades with her sister ship, the *Wasco*, bringing 250 soldiers to raise the siege.

II

Chief Factor Dugald MacTavish was deeply shocked when he learned of Sinclair's death in defense of Bradford's store at the Cascades. He at once sent Sinclair's nephew, William, then employed by the company at Fort Vancouver, to receive his uncle's body and bring it back to Vancouver for full Masonic funeral —Sinclair having been made a charter member of the first lodge formed at St. Paul, Minnesota, some years before. Of Sinclair's death, MacTavish wrote the company's London headquarters on April 5, 1856:

> I advised Sir George Simpson on March 26 of a report current here that a party of hostile Indians had that day surprised the settlement on the Cascades Portage about forty miles from this place, and further that I was anxious about the safety of Mr. James Sinclair who went there on the 24th to proceed to the Dalles to arrange some business matters in connection with the agency there. On the 28th March I again wrote Sir George confirming the report and stated that Mr. Sinclair had passed the Cascades the day previous to the outbreak. I now regret to say that the information I received regarding Mr. Sinclair was incorrect and the painful duty is imposed on me to communicate to you that the gentleman was killed, together with eighteen other citizens, men, women and children, on the morning of the 26th ultimo by the Indians at the Cascades.
>
> Mr. Sinclair's service since he has been attached to this department has been of great importance and value to the business, and he underwent many hardships and privations in the volunteer camp this winter in his endeavour to get possession again of the Company's establishment at Walla Walla. He leaves a widow and several children to mourn his loss, and I am unable to say what provision he has made for them, as we have not succeeded in finding a Will among his papers. I deem it proper to mention that the communication between this place and the Dalles during the present troubles has been interrupted

and considered unsafe. The late attack by the Indians was caused by the military authorities having omitted to station a proper force for the protection of life and property at the Cascades. The portage is from six to eight miles in length, and on the day of the massacre seven soldiers was the strength of the guard there.[5]

When MacTavish's letter reached Governor Simpson he is reported to have said regretfully, "We have lost a good man!"

III

MacTavish's efforts on Sinclair's behalf continued after his death in providing aid to his family. During the summer of 1856 he learned that Sinclair's wife and children were in dire straits. They were living at the Dalles with Mrs. Sinclair's sister, Mrs. Moar, and a child had been born to Sinclair posthumously. Mary Sinclair was asked to go to Fort Vancouver so her case might be considered, and on August 9, 1856, MacTavish wrote to Chief Factor Duncan Finlayson, Simpson's aid:

> We did not find a Will of any kind among Mr. Sinclair's papers. Mrs. Sinclair has four children by her late husband—three girls and one boy, the latter born since his father's death. Mr. Sinclair's daughter, Maria, by a former wife, died here of disease of the heart sometime in June last.[6]

The unfortunate girl, Maria, had survived her father by three months. MacTavish again wrote Finlayson on September 3, 1856, saying:

> The family of the deceased Mr. Sinclair, consisting of the widow and five children, (four of her own and a boy by Sinclair's first wife) I beg to say are still at Vancouver, and I suppose that they remain here for the present as Mrs. Sinclair has given up the idea of returning to Red River.[7]

MacTavish continued to assist the Sinclair family until word reached him that Mary Sinclair had married the American Indian Agent, Nathan Olney. That something was curiously amiss in this marriage is evident, for they remained as man and wife for but one week. Whatever the cause for their almost immediate separation—perhaps the rumor that Olney had but recently been living with an Indian woman—Mary Sinclair and her children were once more in poverty. Realizing the seriousness of their situation, MacTavish again wrote Chief Factor Finlayson on their behalf on June 6, 1857, a little more than a year after Sinclair's death:

> With regard to Mrs. Sinclair, I am uncertain how to act. I have already advised you that on April 1st last—a year after Sinclair's death—she married at the Dalles a man by the name of Olney. On the 19th ultimo, John Moar, Mrs. Sinclair's brother-in-law, wrote me that Mrs. Sinclair had left Olney for reasons unknown, and was residing with her sister, Mrs. Moar.[8]

Vainly Mary Sinclair appears to have appealed for compensation for the loss of her husband's personal property resulting from the Indian war at Walla Walla, persistently claiming that Sinclair had become an American citizen before he had come to reside in the Oregon. Another year passed before she could obtain a legal divorce from Olney, and during this time she appears to have received no support from him. By this time MacTavish had turned the matter over to another Hudson's Bay Company official, James Graham, who, on September 4, 1858, wrote to the company's London headquarters:

> I have addressed Mrs. Sinclair in reference to the course she must pursue to draw her funds from the hands of the Company. The poor lady is in narrow circumstances. Her husband's estate has been finally settled in the Probate Courts of the country, and the probability of any counter claimant springing up is unlikely.[9]

However, it was finally as a dependent of a deceased American citizen, who had suffered loss at the hands of the Indians in the Territory of Washington, that Mary Sinclair got some compensation for the thirty thousand dollars' worth of cattle and other possessions her husband had lost in the destruction of Fort Walla Walla. It was actually not until some thirteen years after Sinclair's death that his old friend, Ulysses S. Grant—then president of the United States—by a special act of Congress "at the prayer of Sinclair's widow granted her a land claim of 640 acres in the Walla Walla valley."[10]

NOTES

PROLOGUE

1. No exact date for James Sinclair's birth has been found. It is believed to be between 1804 and 1806. John V. Campbell, Sinclair's brother-in-law, who accompanied him on the 1854 trek, speaks of Sinclair as being a man of about fifty at that time.

2. Hudson's Bay Co. Archives, London, England (hereafter cited, H.B.C. Arch., Lond.), file B.239/x/42-f-807. Documents relative to William Sinclair, father of James Sinclair, referred to as William Sinclair (I), or William Sinclair, the elder, to avoid confusion with his son William Sinclair (II), who also became a chief factor in the Hudson's Bay Co.

3. *Ibid.*

4. *Ibid.* "William Sinclair (I), father. Native of Harra in the Orkneys, b. 1766. Joined service in 1792. Proceeded to York Factory as 'writer.' From about 1794 employed as 'inland trader' at York Factory. Winter 1794–95 established a post at Nestooyan, which became known as York House, not to be confused with York Factory. In 1795–96 established and wintered at Wegg's House. 1796–97: in 1796 undertook expedition to Nelson River and built Hulse House, which he maintained during the winter. In 1798 built Oxford House where he remained until 1812. Winnipeg, 1811–12.

Jack River (Norway House), 1812–14. Knee Lake, 1815–16. In 1810 William Sinclair had been appointed Chief Factor to 'Winnipeg Factory and its Dependencies,' which included Cumberland House, Swan River, Fort Dauphin, and Brandon House. May 19, 1815, appointed a 'Councillor of Robert Semple, Governor-in-Chief of Rupert's Land.' 1815–18 demoted to 'trader inland' from York Factory. 1818, April 20, died of dropsy. Buried at Schooner Creek on Hayes River near York Factory."

5. *Ibid.* Nothing is known of Nahovway's father. No reference to a man named "Holden" can be found. It is not unlikely that he was an officer, perhaps military, during the construction of Fort Prince of Wales, who assumed the name Holden to disguise his relationship with a Cree woman. It was known that Nahovway's mother was Cree, name unknown. Her grandfather was a chief of the "Company Indians" in that region, this band of Swampy Crees remaining loyal to the Hudson's Bay Co. and resisting the blandishments of the North West Co. traders. William Sinclair (I) met Nahovway at the camp of her grandfather during the period he was establishing inland posts for the Hudson's Bay Co.

6. *Ibid.*

7. *Ibid.*

8. E. E. Rich (ed.), *Journal of Occurrences in the Athabasca Department by George Simpson, 1820 and 1821, and Report,* with introduction by Chester Martin (London: Hudson's Bay Records Soc. [hereafter cited, H.B. Rec. Soc.], I, 1938), p. xx.

9. Arthur S. Morton, *Sir George Simpson* (Toronto: J. M. Dent and Sons, 1944).

10. E. E. Rich (ed.), *Colin Robertson's Correspondence Book, September 1817 to September 1822,* with introduction by E. E. Rich and R. Harvey Fleming (London: H.B. Rec. Soc., II, 1939), p. i.

11. Arthur S. Morton, *A History of the Canadian West to 1870–71* (London: Thomas Nelson and Sons, 1939), p. 543.

12. William Douglas, Fort Garry and the Forks (Manitoba Public Archives [hereafter cited, Man. Pub. Arch.]), pp. 7, 8.

13. Morton, *A History of the Canadian West to 1870–71,* p. 556.

14. H.B.C. Arch., file B.239/x/4a-f-807.

15. *Ibid.*

16. *Ibid.*

17. *Ibid.*

18. Rich (ed.), *Journal of Occurrences,* p. lxxvii.

19. Rich (ed.), *Colin Robertson's Correspondence Book.*

20. H.B.C. Arch., file B. 239/x/4a-f-807.
21. *Ibid.*
22. *Ibid.*
23. *Ibid.*
24. Alberta Provincial Archives, William Sinclair (I) MSS.
25. H.B.C. Arch., Peter Fidler MSS, Brandon House Journal, December 30, 1817.
26. *Ibid.*
27. Isaac Cowie, *The Company of Adventurers on the Great Buffalo Plains, 1867–74* (Toronto: William Briggs, 1913).
28. Man. Pub. Arch., William Sinclair (I) MSS.

CHAPTER 1

1. Man. Pub. Arch., William Sinclair (I), Will.
2. R. Harvey Fleming (ed.), *Minutes of Council, Northern Department of Rupert Land, 1821–31,* with introduction by H. A. Innis (London: H.B. Rec. Soc., III, 1940), p. 60.
3. Man. Pub. Arch., Genealogical Cards: Children of William Sinclair (I) and Nahovway Holden Sinclair. (1) William (II), b. 1794, m. Mary Wadin Mackay, daughter of Madam McLoughlin, wife of Dr. John McLoughlin, Chief Factor of Fort Vancouver. (2) Anne, m. ——— Spencer, d. Goderich, Ontario, 1861. (3) Jane, m. James Kirkness, d. Scotland. (4) Catherine, m. Josiah Cook, d. Orkneys, 1881. (5) Elizabeth (Betsy), m. Robert Seaborn Miles. (6) Phoebe, m. Thomas Bunn as 3rd wife, d. 1848. (7) James, b. 1806 (?), m. 1st Elizabeth Bird, 2nd Mary Campbell, d. Cascades of the Columbia River, 1856. (8) John (no record of later life). (9) Thomas, m. 1st Hannah Cummings, 2nd Caroline Pruden. (10) Mary, m. John Inkster. (11) Colin, b. 1818, d. Red River Settlement.
4. E. E. Rich (ed.), *Journal of Occurrences in the Athabasca Department by George Simpson, 1820 and 1831, and Report* (London: H.B. Rec. Soc., I, 1938), p. 431. See also Fleming, *Minutes of Council,* p. 60.
5. H.B.C. Arch., Lond., file B.239/f/11. "William Sinclair (II) entered the Company as an apprentice in 1810. Three years in Winnipeg River District. 1814–15, assistant at Oxford House. He was of dark complexion, five feet five inches in height. 1816–17 at Jack River (Norway House). 1816–17 under John Lee Lewes at Lesser Slave Lake as clerk. 1818, William Sinclair (II) went to Europe from York Factory on board the *Prince of Wales* (Captain John Davison). Returned same year. 1819–20 at Oxford House. 1820–31 at Island Lake District. 1822–23 went to South Saskatche-

wan River with Chief Factor Donald McKenzie's Bow River Expedition (an expedition of trade and discovery). Bow River Post built by this expedition about four miles below. From 1822–23 served at various posts; was for a time serving under Dr. John McLoughlin in Rainy River District. William Sinclair (II) married Mary Wadin Mackay, daughter of Madam McLoughlin by an earlier marriage, on June 21, 1823, at Norway House, by Rev. John West; see: *Red River Register of Births, Deaths, and Marriages*, No. 63, H.B.C. Arch., Lond. William Sinclair (II) was made Chief Trader in 1844, Chief Factor in 1850. Retired to Brockville, Ontario, in 1863. Died in 1868. Children: Catherine, m. Francis Ermatinger," famous Columbia River trader. "Margaret, m. General Darling," who was for a time posted with the British troops in Red River. The Hudson's Bay Company records state that William Sinclair (II) was "active and steady, but deficient in education." He appears but little in the life of James Sinclair, and was entirely a company man, his life devoted to its service.

6. Rich, *Journal of Occurrences*, p. 431.

7. H.B.C. Arch., Ships' Records.

8. Man. Pub. Arch., Sinclair (I), Will.

9. H.B.C. Arch., file B.239/11.

10. Sinclair (I), Will.

11. *Ibid.*

12. Barbara Johnstone, "Sinclair Homestead," *Winnipeg Tribune*, April 12, 1952.

13. Man. Pub. Arch., Mrs. Copley MSS, Career of James Sinclair. See also B.C. Prov. Arch., Mrs. A. M. Cowan MSS, James Sinclair.

CHAPTER 2

1. H.B.C. Arch., Lond., file C.1/228; file B.135/a/129.

2. *Ibid.*

3. *Ibid.*

4. *Ibid.*

5. H.B.C. Arch., file B.3/c/131; file B.3/a/132.

6. *Ibid.*

7. H.B.C. Arch., file 115/a/39. For a contemporary picture of the country traversed by Sinclair from Albany Post to Red River, see Paul Kane, *Wanderings of an Artist* (Toronto: Radisson Soc., 1925).

8. W. J. Healey, *Women of the Red River* (Winnipeg: Women's Canadian Club, 1923), p. 166.

9. *Ibid.*, pp. 163–65.

10. E. E. Rich (ed.), *Journal of Occurrences in the Athabasca Department by George Simpson, 1820 and 1821, and Report* (London: H.B. Rec. Soc., I, 1938), p. 431.

11. R. Harvey Fleming (ed.), *Minutes of Council, Northern Department of Rupert Land* (London: H.B. Rec. Soc., III, 1940), p. lix.

12. *Ibid.*, p. 316.

13. Margaret A. Macleod (ed.), *The Letters of Letitia Hargrave* (Toronto: Champlain Soc., 1947).

14. Arthur S. Morton, *Sir George Simpson* (Toronto: J. M. Dent and Sons, 1944), p. 159.

CHAPTER 3

1. For an appraisal of Andrew McDermot, see Alexander Ross, *The Red River Settlement* (London: Smith-Elder, 1856); also William Douglas, Fort Garry and the Forks (Man. Pub. Arch.); George Bryce, *Worthies of Old Red River* (Man. Hist. and Scient. Soc. Reports, No. 48, 1896); W. J. Healey, *Women of the Red River* (Winnipeg: Women's Canadian Club, 1923).

2. *Ibid;* also J. Wesley Bond, *Notes on a Trip from St. Paul to Pembina and Selkirk* (New York: Harpers, 1853).

3. H.B.C. Arch., Lond., file B.239/d/238, Accounts; Settlers' Ledger 1821–29, p. 262.

4. St. John's Parish Register, Winnipeg, Manitoba.

5. R. Harvey Fleming (ed.), *Minutes of Council, Northern Department of Rupert Land* (London: H.B. Rec. Soc., III, 1940), p. 316.

CHAPTER 4

1. St. John's Parish Register, Winnipeg, Manitoba.

2. *Ibid.*

CHAPTER 5

1. For a comprehensive picture of the entire free-trade problem in Red River, the half-breed situation, and the part played by James Sinclair in both, see W. L. Morton's Introduction to E. E. Rich (ed.), *London Correspondence Inward from Eden Colvile, 1849–52* (H.B. Rec. Soc., XIX, 1956). For further study in relation to the early half-breed unrest and later uprising, see George F. G. Stanley, *The Birth of Western Canada* (Toronto: Longmans, Green and Co., 1936), and M. Giraud, *Le Métis canadien* (Paris: Institute d'Ethnologie, 1945).

2. B.C. Prov. Arch., Donald Ross Papers, Alexander Christie Correspondence.

3. See John Perry Pritchett, *The Red River Valley, 1811–49* (New Haven: Yale University Press, 1942); E. H. Oliver (ed.), *The Canadian North-West, Its Early Development and Legislative Records* (2 vols.; Ottawa: Government Printing Bureau, 1914, Canadian Archives, No. 9); H. G. Gunn, *Fight for Free Trade in Rupert's Land* (Proceedings IV, Mississippi Valley Hist. Assoc., 1910–11); Alexander Begg, *History of the North-West* (3 vols.; Toronto: Hunter, Rose, 1894); W. L. Morton (introd.), *London Correspondence Inward from Eden Colvile.*

4. H.B.C. Arch., Lond., Hargrave Correspondence: Duncan Finlayson to James Hargrave, April, 1842.

5. Hargrave Correspondence: John Charles to James Hargrave, December, 1834.

6. Quoted in W. Kaye Lamb, Introduction to E. E. Rich (ed.), *The Letters of John McLoughlin from Fort Vancouver to the Governor and Committee, Third Series, 1844–46* (London: H.B. Rec. Soc., VII, 1944).

7. H.B.C. Arch., file A./6/25/fo/28, pp. 137–88.

8. H.B.C. Arch., file A./6/25/fo/51d.

9. H.B.C. Arch., file B./223/b/28. fos. 58–65.

10. H.B.C., P.A.S.C. Deeds and Agreements, 1841.

CHAPTER 6

1. H.B.C. Arch., Lond., P.A.S.C. Miscellaneous Papers, 1841. Also E. E. Rich (ed.), *The Letters of John McLoughlin from Fort Vancouver to the Governor and Committee, Second Series, 1839–44* (London: H.B. Rec. Soc., VI, 1943), pp. 77 n, 78 n, 79 n.

2. G. P. de T. Glazebrook (ed.), *The Hargrave Correspondence, 1821–1842* (Toronto: Champlain Soc., 1938): Letter George Gladman to James Hargrave, March 27, 1841.

3. H.B.C. Arch., Simpson Inward Correspondence: Duncan Finlayson to Simpson, May 1, 1841.

4. H.B.C. Arch., file D.4/109, p. 28.

5. Picture in B.C. Prov. Arch. stated to be that of James Sinclair, after the style of Paul Kane, outstanding Canadian artist of this era.

6. E. E. Rich (ed.), *Simpson's 1828 Journey to the Columbia; Part of Dispatch from George Simpson, Esq., Governor of Rupert's Land, to the Governor and Committee of the Hudson's Bay Com-*

pany (H.B. Rec. Soc., X, 1947), p. 248; H.B.C. Arch., file D.4/591, p. 12.

7. H.B.C. Arch., file D.4/591. Letter from Simpson to Sinclair, July 26, 1841.

8. Alberta Prov. Arch., Rev. R. T. Rundle Journal.

9. Now known as Lake Minnewanka, a misspelling of the Indian word Minnee-wah-kah, near the present site of Banff, Alberta.

10. Governor Simpson claimed to be the first white man to travel through the Devil's Gap. J. N. Wallace, in his paper, Passes of the Rocky Mountains along the Alberta Boundary (Alberta Prov. Arch.), says: "It has been claimed that Rundle, the missionary, was the first white man to reach the site of Banff, and that he camped at the foot of Cascade Mountain in August, 1841. If the claim rests on that date, it cannot be sustained that Simpson would appear to have been there before him."

11. Lake Minnewanka, nine miles from Banff, was named Lake Peechee, a few weeks earlier than Sinclair's arrival, in honor of Simpson's guide.

12. The peaks Sinclair probably saw were Mount Costigan, Mount Aylmer, Mount Inglismaldie, Mount Girouard, and Mount Peechee. For further description of this country see M. B. Williams, *Through the Heart of the Rockies and Selkirks* (Ottawa: Minister of the Interior, 1921), pp. 31–33: also, A. O. Wheeler, F.R.G.S., *The Selkirk Range* (2 vols.; Ottawa: Government Printing Bureau, 1905), pp. 128–31.

13. Mackipictoon took the Sinclair party along what is believed to have been Carrot Creek, emerging into the Bow River Valley and crossing this river near the present town of Canmore, Alberta. The pass up which the Indian then led them is called today Whiteman Pass, possibly named after the several white men who had joined Sinclair's party at the last moment at Fort Garry and had come from the maritime provinces. The remainder of Sinclair's party were *Métis*. J. N. Wallace intimates that Mackipictoon's trail took the party some twenty-five miles, if measured as the crow flies, to the southeast of Simpson Pass. Whiteman Pass is at the head of a branch of the Spray River and is some 7,112 feet high at the summit, approximately two hundred feet higher than Simpson Pass.

14. Now familiar to tourists as the beautiful "Three Sisters," seen from the Calgary-Banff highway and the main line of the Canadian Pacific Railway.

15. The Upper and Lower Spray lakes.

16. These peaks would probably be Mounts Nestor, Buller, Engadine, Fortune, and Turner.

17. The party is thought to have followed the present Whiteman Creek, crossing the height-of-land between Mount Currie and Mounts Warre and Vavasour. See Canadian Pacific Railway Co. map, "The Canadian Rockies," compiled and drawn under the supervision of Arthur O. Wheeler, F.R.G.S., December, 1930.

18. This beautiful mountain is Mount Assiniboine, 11,860 feet high, the loftiest peak in the Banff park. There is a point of dispute regarding the possibility of the Sinclair party's glimpsing this mountain from the summit of Whiteman Pass. M. B. Williams, in *Through the Heart of the Rockies and Selkirks*, p. 43, confirms the likelihood of them seeing it, in this statement: "It was named after the Assiniboine tribe of Indians by Dr. Dawson, the distinguished Canadian geologist, who first saw its glistening cone in 1885 from White Man Pass. (The name Assiniboine in Indian signified 'stone boiler' from the practice of the tribe of cooking by means of hot stones dropped into a vessel of water.)" The engineers of Calgary Power Ltd., who have gained wide knowledge of this region through the developments of Calgary Power Ltd. along the Spray and Kananaskis rivers and lakes, have submitted the information that it is unlikely the members of the Sinclair party could see Mount Assiniboine from the summit of Whiteman Pass, differing in this opinion from that of Dr. Dawson, who was also a most careful observer and scientist. Calgary Power Ltd. also states that it is quite possible that the Sinclair party may have glimpsed the mountain in their descent from the pass as they followed the course of the Cross River toward the Kootenay River Valley.

19. Now known as the Selkirk Range.

20. Whiteman Pass.

21. They appear to have followed up Swede Creek toward the summit.

22. Now known as Lake Olive.

23. Now known as Sinclair Canyon.

24. Now known as Sinclair River.

25. Now known as Sinclair Hot Springs or Radium Hot Springs.

26. Where the present Banff-Windermere highway emerges into the Columbia River Valley and follows it down some distance above Lake Windermere.

27. A. O. Wheeler, F.R.G.S., *The Selkirk Range*, p. 207n, defines these lakes in this manner: the second lake, "Columbia lake; the first or northerly one is now known as Lake Windermere."

28. Now known as Mount Nelson, about 10,000 feet high.
29. Canal Flats.
30. Now known as Moyie Lake.
31. H.B.C. Arch., file D.4/591.
32. The Dalles of the Columbia River.
33. Now Mount Baker.
34. Now Mount Rainier.
35. Now Mount Hood.
36. H.B.C. Arch., file D.4/111, D.47.
37. H. O. Lang (ed.), *History of the Willamette Valley, Together with Personal Reminiscences of Its Early Pioneers* (Portland, Ore., 1885), Henry Buxton and Dr. Robert Newell report, pp. 246–47, 606–7; also Rich, *The Letters of John McLoughlin*, Series II, pp. 77n, 78n, 79n.

CHAPTER 7

1. H.B.C. Arch., Lond., file A.6/26-fo-14-14d, letter from the Governor and Committee to Duncan Finlayson, June 1, 1842.
2. E. E. Rich (ed.), *The Letters of John McLoughlin from Fort Vancouver to the Governor and Committee, Second Series, 1839–44* (London: H.B. Rec. Soc., 1943), pp. 77, 78, 79.
3. H.B.C. Arch., file Cf. B.223/b/41-fo-78-78d, P.S.A.S. Inward Correspondence: McLoughlin–Governor and Committee.
4. *Ibid.*
5. "Story of Harriet Sinclair Cowan," in W. J. Healey, *Women of the Red River* (Winnipeg: Women's Canadian Club, 1923), pp. 15–52.
6. *Ibid.*
7. *Ibid.*
8. *Ibid.*
9. *Ibid.*
10. *Ibid.*
11. St. John's Parish Register, Winnipeg, Manitoba; and H.B.C. Arch., file 236.
12. *Ibid.*

CHAPTER 8

1. St. John's Parish Register, Winnipeg, Manitoba. There is reference to the death of an Elizabeth Bird some time in April, 1845. This may well have been Sinclair's wife, since there appears to be no other record of an Elizabeth Bird Sinclair's death at this time.
2. A child was born to Elizabeth and James Sinclair for whom

there is a baptism record, February 6, 1845, by Reverend J. McCallum, in the St. John's Parish Register, Winnipeg, Manitoba.

3. H.B.C. Arch., file D.4/67, letter from Governor Simpson to the London Committee, May 4, 1845.

4. *Ibid.*

5. *Ibid.*

6. Alexander Begg, *The History of the North-West* (Toronto: Hunter, Rose, 1894), pp. 261–64.

7. *Ibid.*

8. *Ibid.*

9. *Ibid.*

10. *Ibid.*

11. H.B.C. Arch., file D.4/67, a letter from Governor Simpson to Rt. Hon. Lord Metcalfe, Lachine, November 6, 1845.

12. B.C. Prov. Arch., letter from Andrew McDermot to Governor Alexander Christie, November 13, 1845.

13. B.C. Prov. Arch., a letter from Governor Alexander Christie to Andrew McDermot, November 18, 1845.

14. B.C. Prov. Arch., November 30, 1845.

15. B.C. Prov. Arch., December 9, 1845.

16. B.C. Prov. Arch., January 9, 1846.

17. B.C. Prov. Arch., January 9, 1846.

18. B.C. Prov. Arch., January 11, 1846.

19. H.B.C. Arch., Simpson Inward Correspondence: James Sinclair to Governor Simpson, Red River Settlement, June 4, 1846.

20. H.B.C. Arch., file D.4/68, a letter from Governor Simpson to James Sinclair, Fort Garry, June 8, 1846.

CHAPTER 9

1. Margaret A. Macleod (ed.), *The Letters of Letitia Hargrave* (Toronto: Champlain Society, 1947).

2. Kenneth Wiggins Porter, *John Jacob Astor* (2 vols.; Cambridge, Mass.: Harvard University Press, 1931).

3. B.C. Prov. Arch., letter from James Sinclair to Chief Factor Donald Ross, February 6, 1848.

4. *Ibid.*

5. B.C. Prov. Arch., letter from Chief Factor Donald Ross to James Sinclair, February 18, 1848.

6. E. E. Rich (ed.), *Journal of Occurrences in the Athabasca Department by George Simpson, 1820 and 1821, and Report* (London: H.B. Rec. Soc., I, 1938), p. 432.

7. Alberta Prov. Arch., Chief Trader Colin Campbell MSS, Fort Dunvegan Journal.

8. St. John's Parish Register, Winnipeg, Manitoba; and H.B.C. Arch., Lond., Red River Register 412, No. 2: "James Sinclair, widower of Red River and Mary Campbell, spinster, of the same place, were married by Special Licence at Mr. Sinclair's establishment by William Cockran, Chaplain to the Hudson's Bay Company, on April 20, 1848."

9. "Story of Harriet Sinclair Cowan," in W. J. Healey, *Women of the Red River* (Winnipeg: Women's Canadian Club, 1923).

10. B.C. Prov. Arch., letter from John Inkster to B.C. Prov. Arch. re: Mary Campbell Sinclair.

11. "Story of Harriet Sinclair Cowan," in Healey, *Women of the Red River.*

12. *Ibid.;* and B.C. Prov. Arch., Cowan MSS.

13. *Ibid.*

14. "Story of Harriet Sinclair Cowan," in Healey, *Women of the Red River.*

15. *Ibid.;* see also Lloyd Lewis, *Captain Sam Grant* (Boston: Little, Brown and Co., 1950).

16. *Ibid.*

17. *Ibid.*

CHAPTER 10

1. H.B.C. Arch., Lond., Red River Register 156 N.: "Mary, illegitimate daughter of James Sinclair and Jane Whitford, baptized by Robert James, Missionary."

2. A. K. Isbister, *A Few Words on the Hudson's Bay Company, with a Statement of the Grievances of the Natives and the Half-Caste Indians, Addressed to the British Government through their Delegates Now in London*, presented by A. K. Isbister (London, 1847); H.B.C. Arch., Lond., file 113; letter from B. Hawes to A. K. Isbister, January 23, 1849; *Report Ordered by the House of Commons: Hudson's Bay Company (Red River Settlement)*, (London, 1849); E. H. Oliver (ed.), *The Canadian North West, Its Early Development and Legislative Records* (2 vols.; Ottawa: Government Printing Bureau, 1914, Canadian Arch., No. 9); W. L. Morton, Introduction to E. E. Rich (ed.), *London Correspondence Inward from Eden Colvile 1849–52* (H.B. Rec. Soc., XIX, 1956), pp. lxvii–lxxviii; *Report from the Select Committee on the Hudson's Bay Company, Ordered by the House of Commons* (London, 1857);

John Perry Pritchett, *The Red River Valley, 1811–49* (New Haven: Yale University Press, 1942).

3. *Ibid.*

4. Chief Justice E. K. Williams, Early Red River Trials (Man. Pub. Arch.); see also Morton, *London Correspondence Inward from Eden Colvile.*

5. B.C. Prov. Arch., Alexander Ross MSS.

6. Imperial Blue Book on Affairs Relating to Canada, No. 41.

7. *New Monthly Magazine* (New York), Vol. XXI (August, 1860), Vol. XXII (February, 1861).

CHAPTER 11

1. H.B.C. Arch., Lond., Red River Land Register B.

2. Man. Pub. Arch., Harriet Sinclair MSS.

3. *Ibid.*

4. Earl of Southesk, *Saskatchewan and the Rocky Mountains* (Toronto: Campbell, 1875), pp. 8, 9.

5. *Ibid.*

6. Man. Pub. Arch., Mrs. Copley MSS, Career of James Sinclair; B.C. Prov. Arch., Mrs. A. M. Cowan MSS, James Sinclair.

7. Man. Pub. Arch., Colin Sinclair MSS.

8. *Ibid.*

9. Mary Lane, Andrew McDermot's daughter.

10. McLaughlin, the Red River free trader, who was Andrew McDermot's relation.

11. Chief Factor Peter Skene Ogden of Fort Vancouver.

12. A controversial legal case prosecuted by Recorder Adam Thom at Fort Garry.

13. Chief Factor John Ballenden of Fort Garry, involved in a legal suit brought by Recorder Adam Thom.

14. Chief Trader John Black of Fort Garry.

15. Andrew McDermot's country place in Red River.

16. Cuthbert Grant, leader of the *Métis.*

17. Sheriff Alexander Ross.

18. A well-known Red River settler.

19. James Sinclair's second wife, Mary Campbell Sinclair.

20. B.C. Prov. Arch., Sinclair Collection.

21. Man. Pub. Arch., Harriet Sinclair Cowan MSS.

22. Man. Pub. Arch., Bishop David Anderson MSS, The Red River Flood, 1852; Public Archives of Canada, Ottawa, Dr. William Cowan MSS.

23. St. John's Parish Register, Winnipeg, Manitoba; and W. J.

Healey, *Women of the Red River* (Winnipeg: Women's Canadian Club, 1923).

CHAPTER 12

1. H.B.C. Arch., Lond., file D.4/43. Inward Correspondence: James Sinclair to Governor Simpson, August 28, 1853.
2. *Ibid.*
3. H.B.C. Arch., Lond., file D./4/74, letter from Simpson to James Sinclair, October 8, 1853.
4. H.B.C. Arch., file D.5/48/4, James Sinclair to Governor Simpson, November 1, 1853.
5. Some of the letters referred to by date in this quotation have not been found.
6. H.B.C. Arch., file D./4/74, letter from Governor Simpson to Sinclair, Lachine, Quebec, December 22, 1853.
7. Sinclair's father-in-law, Chief Trader Colin Campbell.
8. Isaac Ingall Stevens, Governor of Washington Territory.
9. H.B.C. Arch., file D.82/f/36, letter from Governor Simpson to Sinclair, February, 1854.
10. The Colt revolver, made by the Colt Firearms Co., widely advertised in 1853.
11. H.B.C. Arch., file B.233/o/2, letter from Governor Simpson to the Board of Management, Oregon Department, Lachine, Quebec, September 7, 1854.
12. "John V. Campbell's Narrative," *Washington State Historical Quarterly*, Vol. VIII (January, 1916).
13. *Ibid.*
14. Pub. Arch. of Canada, Ottawa, Dr. William Cowan Diaries MSS; also H.B.C. Arch., file B.223/o/2, letter from Governor Simpson to the Board of Management, Oregon Department, Lachine, Quebec, September 7, 1854.
15. Dr. William Cowan Diaries MSS.

CHAPTER 13

1. Pub. Arch. of Canada, Ottawa, Dr. William Cowan Diaries MSS.
2. *Ibid.*
3. "John V. Campbell's Narrative," *Washington State Historical Quarterly*, Vol. VIII (January, 1916).
4. Dr. William Cowan Diaries MSS.
5. *Ibid.*

6. Chief Factor William Sinclair (II), James Sinclair's oldest brother.
7. James Sinclair's hired man.
8. B.C. Prov. Arch., James Sinclair's letter, Cowan Collection.
9. "John V. Campbell's Narrative."
10. *Ibid.*
11. *Ibid.*
12. *Ibid.*
13. *Ibid.*
14. *Ibid.*
15. *Ibid.*
16. *Ibid.*
17. *Ibid.*
18. *Ibid.*
19. *Ibid.;* also B.C. Prov. Arch., Mrs. Copley MSS, Career of James Sinclair; and Man. Pub. Arch., Mrs. A. M. Cowan MSS, James Sinclair.
20. *Ibid.*
21. *Ibid.*
22. Henry J. Moberly, *When Fur Was King* (New York: E. P. Dutton and Co., 1929).

CHAPTER 14

1. "John V. Campbell's Narrative," *Washington State Historical Quarterly*, Vol. VIII (January, 1916).
2. North of the present town of Innisfail, Alberta.
3. Three miles east of the present town of Olds, Alberta.
4. North of the present town of Cochrane, Alberta.
5. Between the present towns of Cochrane and Morley, Alberta; Morley is the site of the Stony Indian Reserve.
6. "John V. Campbell's Narrative"; also B.C. Prov. Arch., Mrs. Copley MSS, Career of James Sinclair; Man. Pub. Arch., Mrs. A. M. Cowan MSS, James Sinclair.
7. "John V. Campbell's Narrative."
8. *Ibid.*
9. Kananaskis River.
10. Piegan Post, also known as Old Bow Fort. See H.B.C. Arch., Winnipeg, Douglas Mackay MSS, on history of Old Bow Fort; also J. E. A. MacLeod, Q.C., *Notes on Old Bow Fort* (Toronto: Canadian Historical Review, 1931), and *Piegan Post and the Blackfoot Trade* (Toronto: Canadian Historical Review, 1943).
11. There are two passes at Kananaskis, Upper Pass and Lower

Pass; one of these was discovered by James Sinclair, and one in 1858 by Captain John Palliser, to whom is attributed the discovery of Kananaskis Pass as a whole.

12. Mention is made of this region in Captain John Palliser, *The Journals, Detailed Reports, and Observations Relative to the Exploration by Captain Palliser of That Portion of British North America . . . between the Western Shores of Lake Superior and the Pacific Ocean during the Years 1857, 1858, 1859, and 1860* (London: Parliamentary Blue Book, 1863).

13. "John V. Campbell's Narrative." A small grave of a child, probably that of the Flett baby, is said to have been found in this region.

14. *Ibid.* See also Palliser, *Journals, Detailed Reports and Observations;* and Captain Thomas Blakiston, *Report on the Exploration of the Kootanie and Boundary Passes of the Rocky Mountains in 1858* (Woolwich: Occasional Papers of the Royal Artillery Institution, 1860). Blakiston, who had accompanied Palliser across the Rockies in 1858, writes that at this point he saw "the remains of wooden carts which had been abandoned by a party of emigrants under James Sinclair on the way to the Columbia in 1854, near the confluence of the Kananaskis River and the Bow."

15. "John V. Campbell's Narrative."

16. *Ibid.*

17. *Ibid.*

18. *Ibid.*

19. *Ibid.*

20. It is believed that the Sinclair party in 1854 took the South Kananaskis Pass, since they are said to have walked across the height-of-land. However, this is an open question. It is almost impossible to know, from extant information exactly which of the two Kananaskis passes was traversed by Sinclair in 1854. It is presumed it was the more difficult South Kananaskis Pass because of the hardships endured by the party in crossing as described by John Campbell, with the people leading the stock. Even a modern survey of the possible route could not determine what conditions were a century ago, with changes of erosion, rock fall, etc. Palliser's party in 1858 went across on horseback, only possible by the North Kananaskis Pass. See J. N. Wallace, Passes of the Rocky Mountains along the Alberta Boundary (Alberta Prov. Arch.).

21. *Ibid.*

22. "John V. Campbell's Narrative."

23. This creek, leading from the South Kananaskis Pass and tak-

ing the party down to the Palliser River, is now known as Beatty Creek.

24. Now known as the Palliser River.

25. The valley of the Kootenay River.

26. Now known as Mounts Craddock, McHaig, Defender, Prince Henry, Prince Edward, Prince Albert, Prince George, Princess Mary, etc.

27. Now known as Fenwick Creek.

28. Sinclair's infant daughter.

29. Mrs. Sinclair's single sister, Margaret Campbell.

30. Mrs. Colin Campbell of the Red River Settlement.

31. Son of Chief Factor James Curtis Bird.

32. B.C. Prov. Arch., Cowan Collection: letter from James Sinclair to Dr. William Cowan.

33. "John V. Campbell's Narrative."

34. *Ibid.*

35. *Ibid.*

36. *Ibid.*

37. *Ibid.*

38. *Ibid.*

39. Some of the letters referred to here are missing from the H.B.C. Arch., Lond.

40. H.B.C. Arch., file D.75, letter from Governor Simpson to James Sinclair, September 12, 1854.

41. H.B.C. Arch., file D.235/e-2, letter from Governor Simpson to Board of Management, Oregon, September 7, 1854.

42. Bill passed to encourage United States settlers with grants of land in the Oregon and Washington territories.

43. B.C. Prov. Arch., letter from James Sinclair to Dr. William Cowan, January 3, 1855.

44. Andrew McDermot's son-in-law.

45. Andrew McDermot's grandchildren.

46. Wife of the settler whose sheep had been killed by the sleigh dogs at Fort Pitt.

47. H.B.C. Arch., file B.223/b/41, letter from Governor Simpson to Dugald MacTavish, June 20, 1855.

48. "John V. Campbell's Narrative."

49. This is considered to have been one of the greatest treaty conclaves ever held with the Indians in the United States.

50. A parley among the Indians themselves.

51. Sinclair's delicate daughter by his first marriage.

52. Chief Factor James Douglas, Fort Victoria.

53. This would appear to refer to the Haida Indian raids on Victoria.

54. Sinclair's young children.

55. Andrew McDermot's granddaughter. These children were sent back ultimately to Andrew McDermot's home in Red River.

56. B.C. Prov. Arch., Cowan Collection.

57. Pearson made a most remarkable trip across the Rockies to warn Governor Stevens, escaping the pursuing Indians by adroit maneuvering and endurance.

58. H.B.C. Arch., file B.223/b/41, letter from James Sinclair to Dugald MacTavish, October 23, 1855.

59. Letter from Nathan Olney to James Sinclair enclosed in Sinclair's letter to MacTavish.

60. "Reminiscences of Leila McKay," *Oregon Historical Society Quarterly*, March, 1935.

61. Letter from Nathan Olney to James Sinclair mentioned above.

62. Man. Pub. Arch., Mrs. Copley MSS, Life of James Sinclair.

63. H.B.C. Arch., file B.223/b/41.

64. *Ibid.*

65. *Ibid.*

CHAPTER 15

1. H.B.C. Arch., file B.223/b/41, letter from James Sinclair to Dugald MacTavish, November 17, 1855.

2. A disgruntled half-breed troublemaker.

3. H.B.C. Arch., file B.223/b/41, letter from James Sinclair to Dugald MacTavish, November 21, 1855.

4. B.C. Prov. Arch., letter from James Sinclair to Dr. William Cowan.

5. H.B.C. Arch., file B.223/b/41, letter from Dugald MacTavish to the Hudson's Bay Co., London, January 11, 1856.

6. Sinclair's delicate daughter.

7. Sinclair's wife's sister.

8. Sinclair's wife's friend.

9. Sinclair's brother-in-law.

10. Wife of the settler whose sheep were killed at Fort Pitt.

11. Andrew McDermot's grandchildren.

12. B.C. Prov. Arch., letter from James Sinclair to Dr. William Cowan, February 10, 1856.

13. For a description of Sinclair's death as witnessed at the scene of the attack, see Hubert H. Bancroft, *History of Washington, Idaho, and Montana, 1845–80* (San Francisco: History Co., 1890),

pp. 144–47. For another account of James Sinclair's death see Captain John Palliser, *The Journals, Detailed Reports, and Observations Relative to the Exploration by Captain Palliser of that Portion of British North America . . . between the Western Shores of Lake Superior and the Pacific Ocean during the Years 1857, 1858, 1859, and 1860* (London: Parliamentary Blue Book, 1863), pp. 46–48.

EPILOGUE

1. Hubert H. Bancroft, *History of Washington, Idaho, and Montana, 1845–80* (San Francisco: History Co., 1890). pp. 144–47.
2. *Ibid.*
3. *Ibid.*
4. Philip Sheridan was later the famous General Sheridan, hero of the American Civil War.
5. H.B.C. Arch., Lond., file B.223/b/41.
6. H.B.C. Arch., file B.223/b/46.
7. *Ibid.*
8. *Ibid.*
9. H.B.C. Arch., file B.26/b/20, letter from James Graham to Thomas Fraser.
10. Bancroft, *History of Washington, Idaho, and Montana*, pp. 144–47.

BIBLIOGRAPHY

PRIMARY SOURCES

Unpublished

Alberta Provincial Archives

Colin Campbell, Fort Dunvegan Journal.
Father Lacombe Diary.
J. N. Wallace, The Passes of the Rocky Mountains along the Alberta Boundary; Early Explorations along the Bow and Saskatchewan Rivers; papers read before the Calgary Historical Society.
Reverend R. T. Rundle Journal.
William Sinclair (I), York Factory to Oxford House Journal.
William Sinclair (II), Collection.

British Columbia Provincial Archives

Andrew McDermot letters.
Donald Ross Collection.
Dr. William Cowan Letters.
Governor Alexander Christie Letters.
Mrs. A. M. Cowan MSS.
Sheriff Alexander Ross Report of Sayer Trial.

Hudson's Bay Company Archives, London

Dr. John McLoughlin Correspondence.

Dugald MacTavish Letters.
Hargrave Correspondence.
James Sinclair file.
Peter Fidler MSS, Brandon House Journal.
Red River Register of Births, Deaths, and Marriages.
Settlers' Ledger.
Sir George Simpson Inward and Outward Correspondence.
William Sinclair (I) file.
William Sinclair (II) file.

Hudson's Bay Company Archives, Winnipeg

Douglas Mackay MSS, Old Bow Fort.

John Jacob Astor Hotel, Mackinaw Island, Michigan

American Fur Company Letter Books.

Manitoba Public Archives

Bishop David Anderson MSS.
Chief Justice E. K. Williams, Early Red River Trials.
Colin Sinclair MSS.
Garrioch Journals.
Genealogical Cards.
Mrs. Copley MSS.
William Douglas, Fort Garry and the Forks; Early History of Winnipeg; papers read before the Manitoba Historical and Scientific Society.
William Sinclair (I) Will.
St. John's Parish Registry.

McGill University Library, Montreal

Masson Papers.
Roderick Mackenzie Reminiscences.

Minnesota Historical Society

Sibley Papers.

Ontario Public Archives

David Thompson Journals and Maps.

Public Archives of Canada, Ottawa

Bulger Papers.
Dr. William Cowan Diaries.

Ermatinger Papers; transcript in B.C. Archives.
Selkirk Transcripts and Correspondence.

Published

Blakiston, Captain Thomas. *Report on the Exploration of the Kootanie and Boundary Passes of the Rocky Mountains in 1858.* Woolwich: Occasional Papers of the Royal Artillery Institution, 1860.

Bryce, George. *Worthies of Old River.* Manitoba Historical and Scientific Society Reports, No. 48, 1896.

Douglas, William. *New Light on the Old Forts of Winnipeg.* Series 3, No. 11. Winnipeg: Manitoba Historical and Scientific Society, 1956.

———. *The "Forks" Becomes a City.* Winnipeg: Manitoba Historical and Scientific Society, 1945–46.

Fleming, R. Harvey (ed.). *Minutes of Council, Northern Department of Rupert Land, 1821–31,* with introduction by H. A. Innis. London: Hudson's Bay Record Society, III, 1940.

Glazebrook, G. P. de T. (ed.). *The Hargrave Correspondence, 1821–1842.* Toronto: Champlain Society, 1938.

Great Britain. *Correspondence Relative to the Complaints of the Inhabitants of the Red River Settlement.* London, 1849.

———. *Papers Relating to the Red River Settlement.* London, 1819.

———. *Papers Relating to the Hudson's Bay Company.* London, 1849.

———. *Papers Relating to the Legality of the Powers in Respect to Trade, Taxation and Government.* London, 1850.

———. *Report from the Committee Appointed to Enquire into the State and Condition of the Countries Adjoining to Hudson's Bay and of The Trade Carried on There.* London, 1849.

———. *Report Ordered by the House of Commons: Hudson's Bay Company; (Red River Settlement).* London, 1849.

———. *Report from the Select Committee on the Hudson's Bay Company, Ordered by the House of Commons.* London, 1857.

Gunn, H. G. *Fight for Free Trade in Rupert's Land.* Proceedings IV, Mississippi Valley Historical Association, 1910–11.

Isbister, A. K. *A Few Words on the Hudson's Bay Company, with a Statement of the Grievances of the Natives and the Half-Caste Indians; Presented by A. K. Isbister, and Addressed to the British Government through Their Delegates Now in London.* London, 1847.

"John V. Campbell's Narrative," *Washington State Historical Quarterly*, Vol. VIII (January, 1916).

Oregon Historical Quarterly, *Vols.* I, II, X, XI, XII, XIII, XIV, and XXIX.

Palliser, Captain John. *The Journals, Detailed Reports, and Observations Relative to the Exploration By Captain Palliser of That Portion of British North America . . . between the Western Shore of Lake Superior and the Pacific Ocean during the Years 1857, 1858, 1859, and 1860.* London, Parliamentary Blue Book, 1863.

"Reminiscences of Leila McKay," *Oregon Historical Quarterly*, March, 1935.

Rich, E. E. *The History of the Hudson's Bay Company, 1670–1870.* 2 vols. London: Hudson's Bay Record Society, 1958–59.

Rich, E. E. (ed.). *Journal of Occurrences in the Athabasca Department by George Simpson, 1820 and 1821, and Report,* with introduction by Chester Martin. London: Hudson's Bay Record Society, I, 1938.

———. *Colin Robertson's Correspondence Book, September 1817 to September 1822,* with introduction by E. E. Rich and R. Harvey Fleming. London: Hudson's Bay Record Society, II, 1939.

———. *The Letters of John McLoughlin from Fort Vancouver to the Governor and Committee, First Series, 1825–38,* with introduction by W. Kaye Lamb. London: Hudson's Bay Record Society, IV, 1941.

———. *The Letters of John McLoughlin from Fort Vancouver to the Governor and Committee, Second Series, 1839–44,* with introduction by W. Kaye Lamb. London: Hudson's Bay Record Society, VI, 1943.

———. *The Letters of John McLoughlin from Fort Vancouver to the Governor and Committee, Third Series, 1844–46,* with introduction by W. Kaye Lamb. London: Hudson's Bay Record Society, VII, 1944.

———. *Simpson's 1828 Journey to the Columbia; Part of Dispatch from George Simpson, Esq., Governor of Rupert's Land, to the Governor and Committee of the Hudson's Bay Company,* with introduction by W. Stewart Wallace. London: Hudson's Bay Record Society, X, 1947.

Rich, E. E. (ed.). with A. M. Johnson (assist. ed.). *Peter Skene Ogden's Snake River Journals, 1824–25, and 1825–26,* with introduction by Burt Brown Barker. London: Hudson's Bay Record Society, XIII, 1950.

———. *London Correspondence Inward from Eden Colvile, 1849–52*, with introduction by W. L. Morton. London: Hudson's Bay Record Society, XIX, 1956.

Williams, Chief Justice E. K. *Aspects of the Legal History of Manitoba.* Series III, No. 4. Winnipeg: Manitoba Historical and Scientific Society, 1947–48.

SECONDARY SOURCES

Adam, Graeme Mercer. *The Canadian Northwest.* Toronto: Hunter, Rose, 1885.

Amos, Andrew. *Report of the Trials in the Courts of Canada Relative to the Destruction of the Earl of Selkirk's Settlement on the Red River.* London: John Murray, 1820.

Anderson, David. *Notes of the Flood at the Red River.* London: Hatchards, 1852.

Baillie-Groham, W. "Sports and Life in the Hunting Grounds of Western Canada," *Field Magazine* (London), May 11, 1889.

Ballantyne, R. M. *Hudson's Bay, or Everyday Life in the Wilds of North America during Six Years Residence in the Territories of the Honourable Hudson's Bay Company.* Edinburgh: Wm. Blackwood and Sons, 1848.

Bancroft, Hubert H. *History of Oregon.* San Francisco: History Co., 1886–88.

———. *History of the Northwest Coast.* San Francisco: History Co., 1890.

———. *History of Washington, Idaho, and Montana, 1845–80.* San Francisco: History Co., 1890.

Baring, G. *History of the Orkney Islands.* Edinburgh: Privately printed, 1865.

Barrow, John. *The Geography of Hudson Bay.* London: Hakluyt Society, 1852.

Begg, Alexander. *The Creation of Manitoba.* Toronto: Hunter, Rose, 1871.

———. *The Great Canadian North-West.* Montreal: Lovell, 1881.

———. *The History of the North-West.* Toronto: Hunter, Rose, 1894.

Bell, Charles Napier. *The Earliest Fur Traders on the Upper Red River and Red Lake, 1783–1810.* Winnipeg: Manitoba Historical and Scientific Society, 1926.

———. *The Selkirk Settlement and the Settlers.* Winnipeg: Commercial Press, 1887.

Billington, Ray Allen. *Westward Expansion.* New York: Macmillan Co., 1950.

Bond, J. Wesley. *Minnesota and Its Resources* and *Campfire Sketches.* New York: Redfield, 1853.

Bryce, George. *A History of Manitoba: Its Resources and People.* Toronto: Canadian History Co., 1906.

———. *Mackenzie, Selkirk, Simpson.* Toronto: Morang, 1905.

———. *The Remarkable History of the Hudson's Bay Company.* Toronto: William Briggs, 1900.

———. *Scotsmen in Canada.* London: Sampson Low, 1911.

———. *Life of Simpson.* Toronto: Oxford University Press, 1927.

———. *Late A. K. Isbister.* Winnipeg: Manitoba Historical and Scientific Society, 1883.

———. *First Recorder of Rupert's Land.* Winnipeg: Manitoba Historical Society, 1890.

Burpee, Lawrence. *The Search for the Western Sea.* Toronto: Macmillan Co., 1935.

———. *The Old Athabaska Trail.* Toronto: Ryerson Press, 1926.

Butler, William Francis. *The Wild North Land.* New York: Amsterdam Book Co., 1903.

———. *The Great North Land.* London: Sampson Low, 1874.

Buxton, George Frederick. *Life in the Far West.* Norman: University of Oklahoma Press, 1950.

Campbell, Marjorie Wilkins. *The Saskatchewan.* New York: Rinehart and Co., 1950.

———. *The North West Company.* New York: Rinehart and Co., 1957.

Campbell, Roderick. *Father of St. Kilda.* London: Peter Russell, 1901.

Carey, C. H. *History of Oregon.* Chicago: Pioneer Historical Publishing Co., 1922.

———. *A General History of Oregon prior to 1861.* 2 vols. Portland, Ore.: Metropolitan Press, 1935.

Carter, Herbert Hyson. *Sea of Destiny, the Story of Hudson Bay.* Toronto: George J. McLeod, 1940.

Chappell, Edward. *A Narrative of a Voyage to Hudson Bay.* London, 1817.

Chittenden, Hiram M. *The American Fur Trade of the Far West.* 2 vols. New York: F. P. Harper, 1902.

———. *Life and Letters of Father de Smet.* 4 vols. New York: F. P. Harper, 1905.

Cleland, Robert Glass. *The Reckless Breed of Men.* New York: Alfred A. Knopf, 1940.

Coués, Elliot. *New Light on the Early History of the Great Northwest: The Manuscript Journals of Alexander Henry and David Thompson, 1799–1814.* 2 vols. New York: F. P. Harper, 1897.

———. *Forty Years as a Fur Trader in the Upper Missouri.* New York: F. P. Harper, 1897.

Cowie, Isaac. *The Company of Adventurers on the Great Buffalo Plains, 1867–74.* Toronto: William Briggs, 1913.

Cox, Ross. *Adventures on the Columbia River.* London, 1832. (The American Exploration and Travel Series, No. 24.) Norman: University of Oklahoma Press, 1957.

Davidson, Gorgon Charles. *The North West Company.* Berkeley: University of California Press, 1918.

Dennison, Walter Trail. *Orcadian Sketch Book.* Kirkwall, Scotland: Privately printed, 1880.

De Voto, Bernard. *The Year of Decision.* New York: Houghton-Mifflin and Co., 1943.

———. *Across the Wide Missouri.* New York: Houghton-Mifflin and Co., 1947.

Dugas, George. *The Canadian West: Its Discovery, Its Development.* Montreal: Librarie Beauchemin, 1905.

———. *Le mouvement de Métis.* Montreal: Bibliothèque religieuse et nationale, 1945.

Duncan, D. M. *A History of Manitoba and the Northwest Territories.* Toronto: W. J. Gage and Co., 1902.

Dunn, John. *History of the Oregon Territory and British North American Fur Trade.* London: Edwards and Hughes, 1846.

Ellice, Edward. *A Narrative of Occurrences in the Indian Countries of North America.* London, 1817.

Fitzgerald, James Edward. *Examination of the Charter and Proceedings of the Hudson's Bay Company, 1819–22.* 2 vols. London: W. B. Saunders Co., 1849.

Frémont, John C. *Report of the Exploring Expedition in the Rocky Mountains in the Year 1842, and to Oregon and North California in the Years 1843–44.* Washington: Gales and Seaton, 1845.

Galbraith, Kenneth. *The Hudson's Bay Company as an Imperial Factor, 1821–59.* Berkeley: University of California Press, 1957.

Garrioch, A. C. *First Furrows: A History of the Early Settlement of the Red River Country.* Winnipeg: Stovel, 1923.

Gates, C. M. *Five Fur Traders of the Northwest.* St. Paul: University of Minnesota Press, 1933.

Ghent, W. J. *The Road to Oregon.* New York: Longmans, Green and Co., 1929.

Gibbon, John Murray. *Romance of the Canadian Canoe.* Toronto: Ryerson Press, 1951.

———. *Orkneymen in Canada.* Series 50. Toronto: Royal Society of Canada, 1950.

Giraud, Marcel. *Le Métis canadien.* Paris: Institute d'Ethnologie, 1945.

Graham, Clara. *Fur and Gold in the Kootenays.* Vancouver: Privately printed, 1928.

Grant, George M. *Ocean to Ocean: Sandford Fleming's Expedition through Canada in 1872.* Toronto: Radisson Society, 1925.

Gray, William H. *A History of Oregon, 1782–1849.* Portland, Ore.: Hams and Homan, 1870.

Greenbie, Sydney. *Frontiers of the Fur Trade.* New York: John Day Co., 1929.

Gunn, Donald, and Charles R. Tuttle. *History of Manitoba from the Earliest Settlement to 1835.* Ottawa: Maclean, 1880.

Hargrave, Joseph James. *Red River.* Montreal: Lovell, 1871.

Harmon, Daniel William. *A Journal of Voyages and Travels in the Interior of North America, 1811–19.* Toronto: Morang, 1904.

Healey, W. J. *Women of the Red River.* Winnipeg: Women's Canadian Club, 1923.

Heeney, William Bertel. *John West and His Red River Mission.* Toronto: Musson Book Co., 1920.

Hill, Robert B. *Manitoba: History of Its Early Settlement, Development, and Resources.* Toronto: William Briggs, 1890.

Hind, Henry Y. *Narrative of the Canadian Red River Exploring Expedition in 1857 and of the Assiniboine and Saskatchewan Exploring Expedition of 1858.* 2 vols. London: Longmans, Green and Co., 1860.

Holbrook, Stewart J. *The Columbia.* New York: Rinehart and Co., 1955.

Hope-Moncrieff, A. R. *The Highlands and Islands of Scotland.* London: A. and C. Black, 1907.

Howard, Joseph Kinsey. *Montana, High, Wide, and Handsome.* New Haven: Yale University Press, 1938.

Howay, F. W., W. N. Sage, and H. F. Angus. *British Columbia and the United States.* Toronto: Ryerson Press, 1942.

Innis, Harold A. *Fur Trade in Canada.* New Haven: Yale University Press, 1930.

Jenness, Diamond. *The Indians of Canada.* Ottawa: King's Printer, 1932.

Kane, Paul. *Wanderings of an Artist among the Indians of North*

America. London: Longmans, Green and Co., 1859; Toronto: Radisson Society, 1925.

Kavanag, Martin. *The Assiniboine Basin.* Winnipeg: Public Press, 1946.

Keating, W. H. *Narrative of the Expedition to the Sources of the St. Peter's River, Lake Winnipeg, and Lake of the Woods, 1822–23.* Philadelphia: University of Pennsylvania, 1825.

Knox, Olive. "The Red River Cart," *Beaver Magazine* (Winnipeg), 1944.

Lambert, John. *Travels through Canada and the United States of North America in Years 1806, 1807, and 1808.* 2 vols. London: Printed for Baldwin, Cradock, and Jay, 1816.

Laut, Agnes C. *Conquest of the Great North West, Being the Story of the Hudson's Bay Company.* Toronto: Musson Book Co., 1914.

Lingard, Charles Cecil. *Territorial Government in Canada.* Toronto: University of Toronto Press, 1946.

Lewis, Lloyd. *Captain Sam Grant.* Boston: Little, Brown and Co., 1950.

Lower, A. R. M. *Colony to Nation.* Toronto: Longmans, Green and Co., 1946.

Lyman, Horace S. *History of Oregon.* 4 vols. New York: North Pacific Publishing Society, 1903.

MacBeth, Roderick George. *The Making of the Canadian West.* Toronto: William Briggs, 1898.

———. *The Romance of Western Canada.* Toronto: William Briggs, 1898.

———. *The Selkirk Settlers in Real Life.* Toronto: William Briggs, 1897.

MacDiarmid, Hugh. *The Islands of Scotland.* London: B. T. Batsford, 1939.

Mackay, Douglas. *The Honourable Company.* Toronto: McClelland and Stewart, 1936.

Mackenzie, Alexander. *Voyages from Montreal on the River St. Laurence through the Continent of North America to the Frozen and Pacific Oceans in the Years 1789–93.* London: Cadell, 1801.

Mackenzie, Cecil. *Donald Mackenzie, King of the Northwest.* Los Angeles: Ivan Deach, Jr., 1937.

Macleod, Margaret A. "Cuthbert Grant of Grantown," *Canadian Historical Review,* Vol. XXI (March, 1940).

Macoun, John. *Manitoba and the Great North West.* Guelph, Ont.: World Publishing Co., 1882.

MacWilliams, Margaret. *Manitoba Milestones.* Toronto: J. M. Dent and Sons, 1928.
Manton, Marble. "To the Red River and Beyond," *Harper's New Monthly Magazine,* August, 1860.
Martin, Archer. *The Hudson's Bay Company's Land Tenures, and Assiniboia by Lord Selkirk's Settlers.* London: William Clowes and Sons, 1898.
Martin, Chester. *Lord Selkirk's Work in Canada.* Toronto: Oxford University Press, 1916.
———. *Red River Settlement.* Ottawa: Archives Branch, 1910.
Masson, L. F. *Les bourgeois de la companie du nord'ouest.* 2 vols. Quebec: Côté, 1889.
Merk, Frederick. *Fur Trade and Empire.* Cambridge, Mass.: Harvard University Press, 1931.
Milton, William Fitzwilliam, and W. B. Cheadle. *The North-West Passage by Land.* London: Cassell and Co., 1865.
Moberly, Henry J. *When Fur Was King.* New York: E. P. Dutton, 1929.
Montgomery, Richard G. *The White-headed Eagle.* New York: Macmillan Co., 1934.
Morice, Adrien Gabriel. *La race métisse: Étude en marge d'un livre recent.* Winnipeg: Privately printed, 1938.
Morris, Alexander. *Treaties of Canada with Indians of Manitoba and the North West Territories.* Toronto: Belfords, 1880.
Morrison, L. A. *The History of the Sinclair Family in Europe and America for Eleven Hundred Years.* Boston: Privately printed, 1898.
Morton, Arthur S. *A History of the Canadian West to 1870–71.* London: Thomas Nelson and Sons, 1939.
———. *Sir George Simpson.* Toronto: J. M. Dent and Sons, 1944.
———. *Under Western Skies.* Toronto: Thomas Nelson and Sons, 1937.
Morton, W. L. "The Canadian Métis," *Beaver Magazine* (Winnipeg), September, 1950.
———. *Manitoba.* Toronto: University of Toronto Press, 1957.
Mountain, G. J. *The Rainbow of the North: The Journal of the Bishop of Montreal.* London: Seeley, Service and Co., 1845.
Nevins, Allan. *Frémont, Pathmaker of the West.* Toronto: Longmans, Green and Co., 1957.
Nute, Grace Lee. *Caesars of the Wilderness.* New York: Appleton-Century-Crofts Inc., 1923.
———. *The Voyageurs.* New York: Appleton-Century-Crofts Inc., 1931.

Olcott, Charles S. "The Orkneys and Shetlands," *National Geographical Magazine*, 1921.

Oliver, E. H. (ed.). *The Canadian North West, Its Early Development and Legislative Records*. 2 vols. Ottawa: Government Printing Bureau, 1914, Canadian Archives, No. 9.

Patterson, H. S., Q.C. "On the Trail of Palliser," *Beaver Magazine* (Winnipeg), March, 1937.

Porter, Kenneth Wiggins. *John Jacob Astor*. 2 vols. Cambridge, Mass.: Harvard University Press, 1931.

Pritchett, John Perry. *The Red River Valley, 1811–49*. New Haven: Yale University Press, 1942.

Rife, C. W. "Norman W. Kittson, Fur Trader at Pembina," *Minnesota History*, Vol. VI (1923).

Robinson, H. M. *The Great Fur Land, or Sketches of Life in the Hudson's Bay Territory*. London: Sampson Low, 1879.

Roe, F. G. *The North American Buffalo*. Toronto: University of Toronto Press, 1951.

Ross, Alexander. *The Red River Settlement, Its Rise, Progress, and Present State*. London: Smith-Elder, 1856.

———. *Fur Hunters of the Far West*. 2 vols. London: Smith-Elder, 1855.

Russell, Alexander J. *Red River Country: Hudson Bay and Northwest Territories Considered in Relation to Canada*. Montreal: Desbarats, 1870.

Ryerson, John. *Hudson's Bay or a Missionary Tour*. Toronto: G. R. Sanderson, 1855.

Saint Clair, R. W. *The Saint Clairs of the Isles*. Auckland: Privately printed, 1898.

Sage, Walter N. *Sir James Douglas and British Columbia*. Toronto: University of Toronto Press, 1930.

Schooling, William. *The Governor and Company of Adventurers of England Trading into Hudson's Bay during 250 Years between 1670–1920*. London: Hudson's Bay Co., 1920.

Scott, L. M., and H. W. Scott. *The History of the Oregon Country*. 6 vols. Cambridge, Mass.: Harvard University Press, 1924.

Simpson, George. *Narrative of a Journey round the World during the Years 1841 and 1842*. 2 vols. London: Colburn, 1847.

Smith, Arthur D. Howden. *John Jacob Astor*. Philadelphia: J. B. Lippincott Co., 1929.

Southesk, Earl of. *Saskatchewan and the Rocky Mountains*. Toronto: Campbell, 1875.

Stevens, Wayne Edon. *The Northwest Fur Trade, 1763–1800*. Urbana, Ill.: University of Illinois, 1928.

Stanley, George F. G. *The Birth of Western Canada.* Toronto: Longmans, Green and Co., 1936.

Tremaudan, A. H. de. *The Hudson Bay Road, 1498–1915.* London: J. M. Dent and Sons, 1915.

———. *Histoire de la nation métisse dans l'ouest canadien.* Montreal: Éditions Albert Levesque, 1935.

Upham, Charles Wentworth. *Life and Explorations of John Charles Frémont.* Boston: Privately printed, 1856.

Voorhis, Ernest. *Historical Forts and Trading Posts.* Ottawa: Department of Interior, 1930.

Wade, J. N. *The Overlanders of '62.* Victoria: British Columbia Archives Publication, 1931.

Wallace, J. N. *The Wintering Partners of the Peace River.* Ottawa: Publication of the Archives of Canada, 1906.

Warre, Captain H. *Sketches of North America and the Oregon Territory.* London: Dickinson, 1848.

West, John. *The Substance of a Journal during a Residence at the Red River Colony, 1824.* London: Seeley, Service and Co., 1824.

Wheeler, A. O. *The Selkirk Range.* 2 vols. Ottawa: Government Printing Bureau, 1905.

Williams, M. B. *Through the Heart of the Rockies and Selkirks.* Ottawa: Department of Interior, 1921.

Willson, Beckles. *The Great Company.* Toronto: Copp-Clark Co., 1899.

Winther, Oscar O. *The Old Oregon Country.* Palo Alto, Calif.: Stanford University Press, 1950.

Wood, Kerry. *The Great Chief Mackipictoon.* Toronto: Macmillan Co., 1957.

Wood, Louis Aubrey. *The Red River Colony.* (Chronicles of Canada, Vol. XXI.) Toronto: Glasgow Brook and Co., 1915.

INDEX